The Craft of Christian Songwriting

by Robert Sterling

ROWMAN & LITTLEFIELD PUBLISHERS, INC.

Lanham • Boulder • New York • Toronto • Oxford

Published in 2009 by Rowman & Littlefield
An Imprint of The Rowman & Littlefield Publishing Group
4501 Forbes Boulevard, Suite 200
Lanham, Maryland 20706

Cover photo: istockphoto
Cover design by Stephen Ramirez
Book design by Kristina Rolander

Library of Congress Cataloging-in-Publication Data is available upon request.
ISBN 978-1-4234-6339-9

www.rowman.com

Acknowledgments

This book never would have been conceived, let alone written, if I hadn't first been a part of the Gospel Music Association's Academy of Gospel Music Arts (AGMA). Begun in 1995 by my good friend Frank Breeden, the AGMA conducted seminars that became the laboratory in which much of the philosophy and content of this book was developed. My heartfelt appreciation goes to Frank and the amazing faculty he assembled in those first two years of the AGMA: Reed Arvin, Tom Jackson, Dan Keen, John Mays, and Billy Sprague. Shortly after that, four more very talented thinkers came aboard: Grant Cunningham, Kyle Matthews, Greg McNey, and Steve Siler. All of these guys contributed to the AGMA's curriculum and, more importantly, to its engaging philosophy of raising the standard of Christian music. The influence of every one of these people is woven into the fabric of this book.

Thanks to every songwriter—living or dead—of every song I mention in this book. Their creative legacy of great songs will inspire new writers for generations to come.

From 1991 until 2007, it was my privilege to be signed with Word Music as an exclusive songwriter and arranger. For those 16 years, I worked with a talented staff of editors and marketing folks whose hard work enabled me to write the kinds of songs I believed in and to explore new territory in the field of church music. Particular thanks go to three men who have all moved on to other areas, but without whom my tenure with Word would have been far less gratifying. They are Don Cason, Greg McNey, and Dennis Worley.

Additional thanks go to Word Entertainment and Music Publishing Company of America for their gracious permission to reprint full lyrics for this project. Also, thanks to Lowell Alexander, Claire Cloninger, Chris Machen, and Warren Sellers for allowing me to share their "babies" with you—the reader—in the chapter on song analysis.

My thanks to ASCAP, where I have been a songwriter member and a publishing member for as long as I can recall.

Thanks to Bill Green, Kurt Kaiser, Jim West, Bill Saunders, Elwyn Raymer, and others like them who hired me, provided me opportunities, and shared their wisdom in the early stages of my career. Foremost in this group is Charles F. Brown ("Charlie" to his students), who opened the doors of the music business to me when I left the nest in Waco.

My undying appreciation goes to all the co-writers I have worked with in my career for sharing your creativity with me. They have all taught me much about the craft of songwriting, and what it means to be a Christian songwriter. A few of them must be mentioned by name:

Lowell Alexander, Deborah Craig-Claar, Claire Cloninger, Chris Machen, John Mandeville, Michael W. Smith, Scott Williamson, and Karla Worley.

Thanks to all the artists who have recorded my songs over the years, and to all the choirs and soloists who sing my music in church. You are my voice.

To the brave writers who responded to my Twenty Questions and allowed me to use their insights in this book, I say thanks again and again and again: Lowell, Sue, Deborah, Charlie, Kurt, JP, Claire, Paul, Babbie, Kyle, and Tony. And to my proofreaders: Cindy, Ed, and Deborah—I owe you.

Thanks to my parents, Bob and Sarah Sterling, who are both with the Lord now. Mom was my first writing partner and my biggest fan. Dad, who didn't understand a lick about music, was my biggest supporter. I hope I continue to make you both proud.

Thanks to my sons, Matthew and Aaron, whose very existence pushes me to be a better father, a better writer, and a better person.

The words will never exist to sufficiently thank my beautiful wife, Cindy. I love you forever.

And finally, I thank the Lord God and Savior of my life, Jesus, who in His mercy saved me, and in His grace gave me music. Soli Deo Gloria.

ROBERT STERLING

Table of Contents

3 The Shape of a Song (Thought and Form)

4 Lyrical Odds and Ends (Key Lines, Word Play, and Economy)

5 Poetic Devices (Sound Effects and Figures of Speech)

6 Musical Beginnings (Melody, Harmony, and Rhythm)

7 Writing Is Rewriting (Your Song Isn't Finished Just Yet)

8 Collaboration (The Two-Headed Writing Monster)

Introduction

We must strive to become better than we once were, or shrivel up into less than we once were. There is no neutral condition.

—Harold Best

Beginnings

I am a songwriter. More specifically, I am a Christian who is a songwriter. And because most of the songs I write are explicitly Christian in their message, I am a Christian songwriter—a writer of Christian songs. On my IRS Form 1040, it says I am a "composer/music producer." Perhaps my accountant thinks that sounds more impressive than just "songwriter." I will grant you that "composer/music producer" better describes the gamut of work I have done for the past 30 years than does "songwriter." Since graduating from college in 1977, I can truthfully say that I have never held a real job. Somehow, for three decades, I have been fortunate enough to support my family and myself (much of the time by the skin of my teeth) as an independent composer, arranger, orchestrator, music producer, and songwriter.

I did not set out to be a songwriter. From my senior year in high school and all through college, I dreamed of being a session drummer and arranger. But like most working musicians, my path was forged as much by opportunity as anything else. In other words, I followed the money. I was barely out of college when I started writing radio jingles for a small advertising agency in Waco, Texas. That soon led to a 12-year stint in Dallas, chasing larger ad agencies with better clients and bigger budgets. During that time in Big D, I wrote music to sell tacos, shopping malls, an airline (now defunct), men's clothing, pesticides, frozen cobbler, banks, cars, jewelry, instant rice, the New York Jets, the Texas Rangers (the baseball team—not law enforcement), and the National Power Company of England. I composed scores for multimedia productions in San Francisco, Dallas, Washington DC, and Calgary, Alberta. I scored a documentary on the life of the missionary Annie Armstrong and another for a veteran's chapel in the mountains of New Mexico. I arranged and orchestrated television music for the late Zola Levitt. I wrote "ID" packages for WABC radio in New York City, KSFO radio in San Francisco, and Dick Clark's syndicated radio show *Rock, Roll, and Remember.* Along the way, I was privileged to record jingles featuring the singing talents of the legendary Mel Tormé, pop icon B. J. Thomas, jazz singer Diane Schuur, and rocker Bill Champlin. I did all this to pay the bills, and it was, for the most part, genuinely fun and engaging work.

All the while, I filled my creative downtime writing songs. I began writing songs when I was a teenager, probably to impress some cute girl. While I was still in college, a new vocal group, Spirit of Love, recorded one of my songs on their first (and only) LP, for Word Records. After one playback of that magical vinyl disc, I was forever hooked on the idea of writing songs—real songs recorded by artists and professional musicians. Over the next decade or so, I managed to get a few more cuts on independent records. Some of those early songs still generate income for me today. I also landed my first two major recordings: a No. 1 single on a Sandi Patti record, and a No. 2 single for Steve Archer. As more opportunities came my way in the songwriting world, I grew increasingly frustrated with the radio and TV jingle jungle. After 12 years, there was very little about it I found to be creatively fulfilling. Musically, I wanted to spread my wings beyond the "gone in 60 seconds" border of radio commercials extolling the virtues of burritos. So, in 1990, after nearly two years of prayer and soul-searching, I moved my family to Nashville to focus my career on songwriting and record production. I wrote my last jingle the week before we left Texas.

Nashville

Once in Nashville, the Lord opened doors for me for which I am eternally grateful. I signed as an exclusive songwriter and arranger with Word Music in 1991, a relationship that continued for 16 years. During my first few years in Nashville, I produced records for the Talleys, pianist Kurt Kaiser, and, most notably, Point of Grace. I was nominated for a Grammy (I lost) and for some Dove Awards (I won). Christian artists of every genre from adult contemporary to southern gospel recorded my songs. I made it to the top of the Christian radio charts in just about every genre, too. I was given plaques for No. 1 singles, a really cool jacket from ASCAP that says I'm in their "#1 Club," and a handful of Gold Records for my walls. This was all great fun, not to mention that I also got to work with some terrifically talented people.

All the while, my work as a choral composer and arranger was growing. This provided me additional opportunities as a songwriter. (Choral musicals contain mostly new songs, and somebody's gotta write 'em.) Because I could write songs, arrange and orchestrate them, and produce them in the studio, I was a triple threat for Word Music. After a while, I stopped venturing into the world of artist recordings and focused on the choral music world where the writer is the artist.

Many of the best songs I have written have been composed for choral music. The craft of writing is all the more evident when the music is put on paper. That's because there is often extra scrutiny placed on songs that are put in print for choirs to sing. Choral music editors do not hesitate to question the range of a melody or the theology of lyrics if they think something is amiss. Tiny flaws in a tune or a lyric might fly by on an artist recording, but those flaws sit in plain view on the printed page for every choir member to see and sing time and again in rehearsal. It is humbling and a bit intimidating to know that every Wednesday night and Sunday morning there are real live people singing the songs I write.

The artist records, the No. 1 songs, and the steady stream of choral music all happened because I finally found the courage to leave Texas and move to Music City. Truthfully, the smartest thing I ever did in my life, after marrying my wife, was to move to Nashville. That's where I really became a songwriter.

Teaching Songwriting

In 1995 I received a call to join the Gospel Music Association's newly formed Academy of Gospel Music Arts (AGMA) as a songwriting instructor. To be honest, I had never before given a single moment's thought as to how to write songs. I just wrote them. I didn't know you could learn songwriting by any method other than just doing it. This led me to ask the question: Can songwriting be taught?

So far as I knew at that time, songwriting was a combination of talent and effort. Period. You can't teach talent and you can't teach effort, can you? Wait a minute—maybe you can to a degree. You certainly can unlock someone's talent, even help that talent grow. You certainly can show someone ways to maximize her efforts. You most definitely can open a person's eyes to the tools of the craft. It is not unlike teaching someone to play the piano or play golf. The pupil's natural talent and willingness to work will largely determine how far the pupil progresses. I became convinced that songwriting could indeed be taught.

I knew that if I were to properly teach songwriting, I would need to study the creative process—something that had always been intuitive to me. After reading several books on songwriting (most of which are in this book's bibliography), I was heartened to discover that I was already following the rules of songwriting without even knowing them. I was employing the use of imagery without consciously thinking about it. I was writing melodies that were singable, but I had never been taught that the average human has a range of less than two octaves. But still, it was enlightening to read what others had written about songwriting. More than 25 years after my first recorded song, I was learning there was a genuine craft to writing a song.

I taught songwriting for the AGMA for the next eight years, heading up the writing faculty for five of those years. Combining what I had learned from books and what I already knew from years of experience, I taught hundreds of new Christian songwriters about rhyme scheme and imagery and the basics of melody. I preached about the overuse of "churchy" lyrics and the need for rewriting. I introduced the idea of collaboration, and how important it is, to many of these beginners. I listened to a thousand song demos, offering straightforward criticism as to what might improve the songs. I met wonderful people from all across the United States who all shared a heartfelt desire to express their love of God in song, but who had little specific knowledge as to how to go about doing that.

There were plenty of good books on songwriting for me to recommend to those who attended my AGMA seminars. None of those books, however, addressed the specific and sometimes quirky limitations of Christian songs or the spiritual motivations that drive most novice Christian writers. I became convinced there was a need for a book that explained the basic craft of songwriting to beginning songwriters who were Christians. That conviction became the primary impetus for this book. My experiences with the AGMA are the basis for much of this book's content. Several of the chapters are based directly on my seminar outlines. Ideas and information I gleaned from my fellow faculty members over eight years' time are embedded in every page of this text.

I also had a secondary motivation for writing this text. I believe that the craft of songwriting is largely being ignored in today's Christian music—and that is a shameful thing. There was a time, albeit a very long time ago, when the Church was the major influence on the arts. For centuries, whether in music or painting or sculpture, the Church was responsible for some of the most exquisite art this world has ever known. That is no longer the case. Instead, today Christian music is blindly following the same path as the rest of American pop culture, heading into the downward spiral toward the lowest common denominator.

The Decline and Fall of Pop Music

The text of this book makes occasional references to the "art" of songwriting. I do believe songwriting is an art, but I am not so pretentious as to think it is high art. Let's acknowledge that songwriting is a popular art form, creative and inventive, sometimes elusive, occasionally breathtaking, and for the most part, temporal and fleeting. In the hands of a gifted and skilled writer, songwriting sometimes approaches high art. But for everyday purposes, songwriting is as much a craft as it is an art. Very few of the songs we sing today will stand the acid test of time, which is, perhaps, the best determiner as to what is and is not considered art. Ninety-nine percent of the hit songs on the radio remain in the public consciousness for less than a few weeks, let alone for hundreds of years. Speaking for myself, I would feel as though I had won the Mozart Award for Musical Longevity if even a handful of my songs lasted a single generation beyond my shuffling off this mortal coil.

That said, I believe songwriting reflects the heart of modern culture as transparently as any art form. And to clearly chart the undeniable degeneration of American popular culture, we need look no further than the popular song. In the 1930s, giants such as Cole Porter, George and Ira Gershwin, and Irving Berlin set the standards for craft in songwriting. In the 1960s Paul McCartney, Carole King, and Bob Dylan were all still working within the accepted standards of the craft, even as the vernacular shifted and subject matters broadened. Now jump to today. It is stunning to see how, in only 70 years or so, the quality of American popular songs has plummeted from the high standards of Tin Pan Alley to the often nihilistic and hate-filled lyrics of speed metal and hip-hop. I agree with Hugh Prestwood's assessment of the situation. Prestwood teaches advanced songwriting for the New School in Manhattan and for the Nashville Songwriter's Association International (NSAI). He has written dozens of hit songs and has won just about every songwriting award on the planet. On his Website (hughprestwood.com), he offers this rather frank assessment of why American pop music has declined so far so fast:

> Adult taste has almost nothing whatsoever to do with pop music now. Pop music is being speedily driven to drooling imbecilic hell by teens. As far as the music business

is concerned, the music has become a bit player in an absurd circus. Starring in the circus are sex appeal, charisma, attitude, on-stage theatrics, and shock value. ("MTV, Adolescents, the Church of Hollywood, and the Collapse of Grace," hughprestwood. com, 2007)

Perhaps Prestwood's most stinging observation is that music has become a bit player in its own business. The quality of the music written and recorded for major label releases is no longer the prime concern of the labels. Their prime concern is not even "Will it sell?" No, the prime concern is now "Will it sell a lot, and fast?" American pop culture worships success, so if something is successful, then it is deemed good. This warped equation that "success equals quality" has made it difficult to objectively discuss the true distinction of a song. How can one say a song isn't any good if it was a huge hit? It sold millions of copies so it must be good, right? The "success equals quality" lie is driven deeper into our psyches by the hyperbolic vocabulary of music marketers intent on selling us their label's latest music. Every new artist release is hailed as "cutting edge." Every new song is an "instant classic." Every performance is worthy of a standing ovation. To say something is "good" is an insult, because it's not "fantastic." Give me a break. If all the semicreative pop musicians that the media regularly hail as "genius" really are geniuses, then what word do we use to describe Beethoven?

Christian Copycats

The decline of Christian music may not appear so stark as its pop counterpart's. After all, Christian songs never stoop so low as to be degrading and obscene—an apparent goal of many rap songs. But let's not fool ourselves. Christian music looks and sounds much like pop music these days. The pop music world defines almost every trend in Christian music. (Oh, that it were the other way around.) Christian music is produced and marketed with the same basic goal as pop music—sell more music. If the goal is to have larger sales, it stands to reason the product will be aimed at a broader, and shallower, audience. Everybody can swim in the shallow end of the pool, so let's make the music a little less deep.

While there is an inherent conflict between commerce and the Gospel (Jesus spoke more about the dangers of money than any other single subject), I offer that selling is not, in and of itself, an evil thing. In my years working in the Christian-music business, I have found the men and women who toil in Christian-music companies to be honorable people, who see their job as much as a mission as a career. They believe in the life-affirming qualities of the books, records, and music they promote. Still, their companies must make a profit, or they will go out of business. Selling is necessary. But when selling becomes the driving force of any company, Christian or not, it is tempting, if not inevitable, to make quantity more important than quality. In a purely bottom-line world, accessibility always trumps excellence.

If pop music has sacrificed substance for style, then Christian music has sacrificed substance for the appearance of substance. Today's popular Christian songwriter has learned that if you string together enough spiritual catchphrases and repeat them ad infinitum, you really don't have to say anything at all. I fear future music historians will be far less than kind to the

Christian music being written today. Listen to Christian Hit radio or examine the lyrics of the latest crop of praise-and-worship songs, and you will find significant evidence that creativity and craftsmanship in Christian music are in decline. Christian music, like the rest of American culture, is dumbing down.

The immediate effects of this trend are obvious, and all negative. The first thing to go has been craftsmanship. The use of imagery in many current Christian songs is nonexistent. Rhyme schemes, if the song rhymes at all, are simplistic. The song form may have only one verse and a chorus, which are to be repeated ad nauseam. These songs are incomplete and musically malnourished. (I admit that in an effort to place songs in this marketplace, I have written a couple of these "one-verse-repeat-chorus-forever" songs. Still, whenever I hear them they feel unfinished.) The emphasis in writing praise songs is often placed on "authenticity" and "inspiration," so rewriting is out of the question—the idea being that working on the song after the first draft would somehow diminish its immediacy or its connection to God. That is nonsense, as I hope this book will make plain. But I fear that this is a prevailing myth that influences many sincere but misguided young Christian songwriters.

When the rules of craft and form no longer matter, song structure crumbles and the creative process loses its discipline. Without discipline, standards evaporate, and we are left with songs that lack musical integrity, songs that are lyrically empty, or, worse still, songs that are theologically unsound. That is a sad enough thing to happen in secular pop music, but it is devastating in Christian music. But how are we to avoid this if the craft of writing is ignored? What other result can we expect when structure no longer matters? Whether we are writing songs or building cabinets, if there is no discipline in the craft, the end result will be a shoddy product. We see the results of this debilitating trend in Sunday services where worshippers are led in song after song that say little more than "I love how I love You, Lord." Worship leaders, Christian-music companies, and professional Christian musicians try to sweep the weaknesses of these songs under the carpet of "ministry." Christian radio fills the airwaves with these same tepid tunes, trying to convince us that it is good music. But to say that much of this music is even mediocre is being kind.

If this trend continues unabated, the long-term effect could be more devastating still. There is an undeniable tendency to ascribe value and veracity to the Christian songs we sing in church and hear on CDs and on the radio. The great hymn writers understood the typical churchgoer received as much knowledge of theology from the songs sung in worship as from the sermon or Bible study. Unfortunately, as we absorb many of these new songs, we drink in a theology that is the spiritual equivalent of a Diet Coke—tasty, but empty calories. Please understand that I do not believe the writers of this growing library of songs are purposefully attempting to foist limp theology on the church. I have no doubt that their intentions are pure. But I fear that they too often settle for lyrics that feel good, and never question whether their words are saying anything of any lasting consequence. I even allow for the possibility that the writers sometimes think they said something other than what their lyrics actually say. (Such is the power and importance of the right words in a song.)

Fortunately, from what I gather, young Christians who are the target audience for this music are growing tired of a steady diet of musical pabulum that offers no art and little, if any, theology. This is good news, because if Christian consumers are weary of three-chord wonders that incessantly drone "God is awesome," then perhaps there is hope for a return to Christian songs that are deeper in both music and meaning.

Making a Change

There are signs that a return to deeper Christian music has already begun. I take encouragement from the creativity of singer-songwriters such as Warren Barfield, Nicole Nordeman, Nicole C. Mullen, and Jason Gray, who write well-crafted songs that tackle the real issues of daily life from a Christian perspective. There is a growing resurgence of the use of traditional hymns in contemporary worship services. Writers such as Fernando Ortega, Stuart Townend, and Keith Getty are offering modern hymns that may well stand the test of time.

I have also seen recent indications that those firmly entrenched in the world of praise-and-worship music are beginning to admit the music they have been singing for the past 25 years is, for the most part, lacking in substance. In a recent open letter to worship songwriters, Brian McLaren, a noted author, speaker, and pastor offered this insight: "Too many of our [worship] lyrics are embarrassingly personalistic, about Jesus and me…It really feels like worship…has become all about 'me, me, me.'" (*Worship Leader Magazine* [www.worshipleader.com]).

In a March 4, 2007, interview with *Challenge Weekly* (New Zealand), songwriter Graham Kendrick (writer of "Shine, Jesus, Shine" and "The Servant King") said this:

Broadly speaking, the new wave of praise and worship, which I have been a part of, has tended to emphasize the positive. Those who criticize it would say that in many ways it's triumphalist, and there is an element of truth in that. We are singing songs as if everything's wonderful; because we have Jesus, life is perfect. Of course, that's not reality.

Harold Best, former dean of the School of Music at Wheaton College, puts it a little more bluntly: "The literature of the contemporary/praise-and-worship practices has so far done little to cover the full scope of God's workings, the human condition, and its responses" (*Exploring the Worship Spectrum*, p. 66). This comes from a book in which six noted Christian authors offer their insights and opposing views on current worship styles and trends. I found it interesting that Mr. Best received little opposition to his statement from those others in the book who are experts in praise-and-worship music. While in the past five or six years there has been an emergence of worship music with greater lyrical depth and breadth, there seems to be little argument that the first two decades of praise-and-worship music provided the church with little more than a few catchy melodies.

If there is to be such a return to better crafted, more-meaningful songs in Christendom, then those of us who write songs for the sake of the Kingdom must be about the business of improving our craft. We should be studying the art of writing, enlarging our vocabulary, and expanding our musical horizons. Otherwise, we settle for giving God less than our best, and that is a travesty. After all, how can we claim to know personally the Creator of All There Is, and yet not strive to be the most creative of His children? Sadly, all too often when the Father entrusts us with a song, we are tempted to settle for that brief moment of inspiration—proudly proclaiming, "God gave it to me"—and believe that's the end of the process. Those who stop there at the mysterious intersection where God gives His gift of music are missing out on the best part: the joy of giving back to God one's best efforts, toiling with the Lord until the song is as good as it can be. You see, I believe writing a song is not merely about penning another radio hit for the Kingdom or kicking out something that grooves well for the band in Sunday morning worship. The Lord of the Universe does not need our feeble help creating music. If God wanted, the rocks themselves would sing His praise. (Luke 19:40) Instead, I believe, like all worthwhile creative endeavors, writing a song is an opportunity for the writer to get a little closer to God. It is as if He is inviting the songwriter to come out and play, join in the fun, and experience firsthand what a wonder it is to be creative.

Here's to better songwriting.

ROBERT STERLING
May 2008

On Being a Christian Songwriter (A Few Not-So-Random Thoughts)

Are You a Songwriter?

How do you see yourself? Imagine being at a party, and someone casually says to you, "So, tell me about yourself." How do you respond?

I live in a town where half the restaurant waiters and house painters would say, "I'm a songwriter." Not "I wait tables," or "I paint houses," but "I'm a songwriter." That would be their honest, unflinching response. And that's also true of plenty of the cab drivers, plumbers, and sales clerks (and probably a few doctors and lawyers) that reside in and around Music City, USA. The primary creative energy in their lives is songwriting. They wait tables, paint houses, drive cabs, and unclog drains in order to pay the bills. But their first love—their passion—the reason they moved from Dallas, or Des Moines, or Dubuque, to Nashville, is writing songs. "I'm a songwriter," they say. Of course, that begs the follow-up question, "Have you written anything I might have heard?" Their answer? "Not yet—but one day. One day."

So let me ask you again—How do you see yourself? Since you are reading this book, your answer may be, "I'm a songwriter." And since you've chosen to read this particular tome, my guess is that you are also a Christian songwriter. But for the moment, let's leave that particular modifier out of the equation.

What does it mean to be a songwriter? If you don't have to make a living as a songwriter in order to think of yourself as a songwriter (and you definitely do not), then what is it that makes a person a songwriter? If you write one song, good or bad, do you qualify for the club? How about ten songs? Or a hundred? What if you write only words, or just music? Is there a secret handshake? A songwriter's oath of allegiance? Or is it something else altogether?

Put most simply, a writer writes. So for the songwriter it would be, a songwriter writes songs. If you write songs on a regular basis—whether or not you make any money from the effort, whether or not you receive any recognition from others, and whether or not the songs are any good—in my estimation, you are a songwriter. You may not be a great songwriter, but you are a songwriter, nonetheless. And if you are driven to improve your writing skills, if you study the craft of songwriting, if your next song is your best song ever, then you have more in common with the great songwriters than you might realize. It has been my discovery, as I have taught songwriting, spoken with dozens of professional songwriters, and read and studied to write this book, that almost every great songwriter is working to become a better writer. Great writers care about the craft of writing. And great writers are convinced that their best song is still somewhere inside them.

Are You a Christian Songwriter?

To complicate matters further, this book is all about the peculiar quirks of being a Christian songwriter. (Oh, brother, does that word "Christian" ever throw a wrench into the gears.) What does it mean to be a Christian songwriter? Does that mean you are a Christian who is a songwriter, or a songwriter who is a Christian? (There is a difference.) Must you write only praise-and-worship songs about Jesus and the cross to be a Christian songwriter? Can you be a Christian songwriter and write songs about love and life and human relationships? Andrew Osenga, former lead singer of The Normals and member of the band Caedmon's Call addressed the issue in an online interview this way:

> Just because you're Christian doesn't mean all you can write about is the cross. You can talk about … temptation, about nature, about a girl, about your own feelings. You can throw them all in a song … The very act of creating, in and of itself, is an act of worship, of obedience … To be a Christian artist you have to understand you have the ability to write about everything. Otherwise, your art isn't art. (cMusicWeb.com; November, 2000)

As I write this, Osenga's viewpoint is being challenged by the overwhelming dominance of worship music on Christian radio and throughout the Christian Music scene. According to a record executive for an independent Christian record label, the term *Christian music* is fast becoming synonymous with *worship music*. And by worship music, I mean musically and lyrically simplistic songs that are sung in the first person vertically to God. I find this development disheartening, not because I disdain worship music. Worship music is fine. It can be great, in fact. But Christian music used to be, and still should be, more than just praise-and-worship songs. I encourage you to explore beyond the relatively limiting boundaries of worship music as you learn to express your heart and faith in song.

One of the best pieces of advice that can be given to a writer is to write about what you know. Makes a lot of sense, doesn't it? Well, a Believer knows Jesus. And a songwriter who is a Believer is going to tend to write songs that are influenced by Jesus in one way or another. In some songs the Christian message may be blatant and out in the open for all to see. In others the message may be subtle, leaving the listener with unanswered questions to ponder. Either way, I'm convinced that if Jesus is in the heart of the songwriter, then Jesus will be at the heart of the songs. That's what makes a songwriter a Christian songwriter.

For the most part, the thing that separates Christian songs from all the other songs we hear day in and day out are the lyrics. Christian songwriters employ just about every musical style known to man, but the lyrics are what typically define a song as Christian. Today, most of the songs we would describe as Christian songs are blatant in their message. The current popularity of praise-and-worship music is funneling a lot of songwriting efforts in that particular direction. That has not always been the case. In the early 1990s, the goal of just about every professional Christian songwriter was to write a subtle *crossover* song, with the hope of it becoming a hit on one of Christian-music superstar Amy Grant's records. (A crossover song is a song with a lyric that could be talking about either God or your boyfriend.) The thing to remember is that the pendulum of popular Christian music is always swinging. No one knows at what point the pendulum will be tomorrow, let alone a decade from now. Regardless of whether you write songs with an obvious Christian message or songs that shade the Christian intent from plain view, both are valid approaches and each has its own set of limitations.

Christian Art: Implicit Versus Explicit

Reed Arvin is a wonderfully talented musician, author, and deep thinker. For several years, I had the good fortune to teach alongside him at the Academy of Gospel Music Arts. In his seminar talk "The Creative Christian Life," Reed defined the blatant and subtle approaches to Christian art as *explicit* and *implicit*, respectively. According to Arvin, art that is explicitly Christian speaks directly of the good news of Christ and the cross. It is aimed primarily at fellow Believers and at the Church body. Its intent is clearly Christian, whether it is to praise God, edify the Church, or share Jesus. The current Christian radio charts, the hymnals in church pews, and music folders of church choir members are filled with these explicitly Christian songs.

On the other hand, art that is implicitly Christian doesn't necessarily spell out the Four Spiritual Laws or the plan of salvation, but instead suggests a worldview that could come only from a Christian. Like the novels of C. S. Lewis, implicit Christian art is aimed at the world's mainstream culture. It implies the truth of Christianity, allowing observers to discover it for themselves. An implicitly Christian song shares God's Truth in a way that hopes to reach those who would otherwise never listen at all. The late Bob Briner, author of the book *Roaring Lambs*, promoted just this sort of approach for creative Christians. In the early 1990s, Amy Grant was coming under fire from some fellow Christians for crossing over to the secular market with records like *Lead Me On* and *Heart in Motion*. Here's how Mr. Briner answered those critics:

> Those who criticize [Amy Grant] for crossing over into the secular market with music that is not distinctly Christian forget one thing. Her music takes up the airtime that could have gone to one of the multitude of recordings offering only degradation and moral rot. Amy Grant is being salt in the world … One Amy Grant record provides more salt for a decaying world than a thousand sermons decrying the evils of popular music … We need more Amy Grants than we need reactionary sermons. We also need Christian musicians, talent managers, producers, and record-company executives to bring salt to the whole influential popular-music industry. (*Roaring Lambs*, p. 40)

Strong stuff!

I believe both the implicit and explicit approaches to Christian songwriting are valid, creative avenues to pursue. Certainly Christ and the cross are at the core of the Christian experience. In fact, there is no Christian experience without Christ and the cross, and Believers need to write about those things. On the other hand, the entire world can embrace many attitudes and ideas that spring from the Word of God—attitudes and ideas that are centered in Christ, but that are not exclusively Christian. In the Sermon on the Mount, Jesus taught us to be peacemakers, to love our fellow man, to be humble and forgiving. These are concepts everyone can understand, concepts that can make the world a better place to live in regardless of religion, concepts that the Christian songwriter can certainly illuminate—even if the songs don't mention Jesus by name.

Consider what the apostle Paul wrote in his letter to the church at Philippi: "Finally, brothers, whatever is true, whatever is noble, whatever is right, whatever is pure, whatever is lovely, whatever is admirable—if anything is excellent or praiseworthy—think about such things." (Phil. 4:8) Now there's a worthy list of adjectives for a Christian songwriter to aspire to: true, noble, right, lovely, admirable, excellent, and praiseworthy. These are all very high standards for any songwriter, Christian or not, to meet. Notice there's no mention of church, Jesus, or even God in that list. But the Christian knows that God is the author of the list, and that changes the way the Christian sees the world. (*Tools for Ministry and Career*, p. 79)

Know Your Audience

With every new song you tackle, you are faced with deciding which kind of song to write—one that is blatantly Christian in its message, or one that contains a subtle Christian message. Both have worthy purposes. And they are not mutually exclusive to the creative Christian. You may well explore both kinds of songs in your songwriting lifetime. Whichever you choose, you need to keep your audience in mind as you write. Why? Because the two approaches have different audiences. Just as you won't reach a rock 'n' roll audience with easy-listening songs, you can't reach the mainstream culture with churchy songs. And you're not likely to get a lot of positive feedback from the church if your song lyrics are so subtle that the listener can't tell if you're singing about God or your pet dog. It's important to know your audience.

If your goal is to write subtle, implicit Christian songs in hopes of reaching the nonbeliever, I say excellent! That is a laudable goal. There may well be no more effective way of reaching mainstream culture today than with popular music. Music is everywhere all the time—the constant, unrelenting backdrop to everyday life. It's on our TVs and our radios and our cell phones. It plays nonstop in our malls and elevators and theme parks. And no kid feels fully dressed today without his own portable MP3 player, loaded with literally thousands of his favorite songs. Commercial music is a perfect tool to introduce the Gospel to many who have never heard the Good News. But you cannot make lasting musical contact with nonbelievers without first knowing who they are and what they are concerned about. You can't preach the answers if you don't know their questions. Christian songs written for the mainstream culture should not sound arrogant and condemning. Instead, they must reflect an empathetic understanding of the hopes and fears of our fellow man. Too often, Christian songwriters attempt to venture into the mainstream culture with songs that shout with the fiery fervor of a revival preacher: "Sinner, get right with God!" Then those Christian songwriters are surprised when their songs land on deaf ears or, worse still, are rejected with outright anger by the mainstream audience.

A song with a subtle but Christ-centered message of love and understanding may open the door for another song that has a more direct message of Jesus. Or it may simply create the opportunity for someone else to speak to the listener of Jesus at some other time, long after the song has stopped playing. In fact, the Christian songwriter may never see what, if any, response her song elicits from its listeners. If you write with an implicitly Christian message, it's important to be content to let the song speak for itself, knowing that there may never be an immediate conversion response to the song. To use a tired Christian metaphor, but one that is still on target, the songwriter who writes using a subtle Christian message is a seed planter. It's an important job, but you may not be around to see the seeds grow to bear fruit.

Most Christian songwriters, especially beginners, choose to write songs that Arvin describes as explicitly Christian. If this is the case for you, you are in good company. So far as we know, King David focused on songs that praised God, leaving the pop music of his day to others. The same could be said of Charles Wesley, Isaac Watts, and Fanny J. Crosby, three of Christendom's greatest hymn writers. It's no big surprise that believing songwriters focus on songs that are blatantly Christian. When we consider how deeply Jesus touches the Believer, it's only natural that Christian songwriters would express themselves with songs that are explicit in their Christian message. Some writers feel called to write only songs that are explicitly Christian. That's fine. The Church needs songs that evangelize, speak to the Body, and give praise to God. Let me be more specific—the Church needs *well-crafted* songs that evangelize, speak to the Body, and give praise to God. And creating well-crafted songs is, in fact, the primary focus of this book.

In Their Own Words: How important is the craft of songwriting to you?

Craft is everything. Otherwise you end up with a great idea that never pays off.
　　　　　　　　　　　　　　　　　　　　　—TONY WOOD

Craft is not just important to songwriting; craft is songwriting. Anything less is personal journaling or improvisation.
　　　　　　　　　　　　　　　　　　—DEBORAH CRAIG-CLAAR

Being creative is not enough. Craft gives a song legitimacy.
　　　　　　　　　　　　　　　　　　—LOWELL ALEXANDER

Songwriting is a very deliberate and intentional process. First the songwriter must have the tools to write great songs; then the writer must know how to use those tools effectively.
　　　　　　　　　　　　　　　　　　　—BABBIE MASON

Jesus' Chairs (the Importance of Craft)

For hundreds and hundreds of years, Christian composers, painters, sculptors, and authors have proclaimed their faith through their art. The results are some of the most awe-inspiring works of art ever created—the music of Bach, Michelangelo's painting of the Sistine Chapel, the novels of C. S. Lewis. But there has also been a great deal of bad religious art created along the way. (I know. I've contributed my fair share.) In her book *Walking on Water—Reflections on Faith and Art*, Madeleine L'Engle writes, "Art is art; painting is painting; music is music … If it's bad art, it's bad religion, no matter how pious the subject." (p. 14)

Is it not enough for the Christian songwriter to write songs that pour from the heart, inspired by a relationship with the Lord? Or must he understand the craft and follow the rules of songwriting? Does the art form itself matter to the Christian songwriter, or is the relationship with Jesus all that matters? Giovanni Palestrina, a 16th-century composer, believed we should work diligently when we write music for the Lord. He put it this way: "If people take great pains to compose beautiful music for profane (secular) songs, they should devote at least as much thought to sacred song—nay, even more than to mere worldly matters." Well put, Giovanni.

The best answer I have for the question "Should craft and workmanship matter to the Christian songwriter?" is this: "Jesus' chairs."

"Jesus' chairs?" you ask. Yes. "Jesus' chairs." Allow me to explain.

According to scripture, Jesus was a carpenter (Mk. 6:3) and the son of a carpenter (Mt. 13:55). Carpentry was the family business, and Jesus almost certainly learned the trade from his father, Joseph. I can even imagine the sign that hung outside the shop—"Joseph and Son: Quality Carpentry Since 45 BC." Some very smart Bible scholars say a more accurate translation than "carpenter" would be "stonemason" or even "building contractor." Regardless, I am going out on a limb to assume Jesus and his earthly father built things for a living. And for the purposes of this particular illustration, I am going to stick with "carpenter."

Work with me here, and keep in mind I can provide no scriptural evidence for what I'm about to suggest. It's only a theory. But here goes: I believe that when the Creator of the Universe took the time to make a chair in his earthly father's carpentry shop, it would have been *the very best chair you could possibly get anywhere in Galilee.* Can you imagine Jesus building a chair with uneven legs that tilted annoyingly every time somebody sat on it? I can't. What I can imagine is people coming from miles around Nazareth to buy furniture from Joseph and Son. Their furniture must have been unbeatable. Beautiful. Well crafted. Built to last. I would have hated to be the competition across town.

So, as followers of Jesus, how should Christian songwriters write songs? The answer: We should write songs the way Jesus made chairs. They should be beautiful, well crafted, and written to last. To do that, we need to understand the craft of songwriting. Personally, I have no doubt that Jesus mastered the use of every carpentry tool in Joseph's workshop. Similarly, we must master all the song forms, know the intricacies of rhyme and poetic devices, and harness the power of melody and harmony—because these are the tools required to write great songs. I feel certain that Jesus toiled long and hard to make his work excellent. We need to understand that writing is often hard work, and that it's worth the effort.

Talent: The 800-Pound Gorilla

In all the books I've read about songwriting, there is one subject that gets very little specific mention: talent. Perhaps the authors assume their readers are all immensely talented. More likely, they didn't want to broach such a touchy subject. Talent is like the 800-pound gorilla in a room: we all know you need talent to write a good song, and who am I to judge your talent, so let's not disturb the big guy, okay?

I'm going to deal with talent briefly, and focus the remainder of the book on craft, which is where I see the greatest weaknesses currently in Christian music. Here's what I believe about talent:

- **God doesn't gift us all equally.** Jesus' parable about the talents makes it plain that God gives different things to different people for reasons that are His own. What we as individuals do with our gifts is what matters.

- **You do need talent to write good songs.** How much talent? That depends on how hard you are willing to work. It has been my experience that hard work can narrow the gap on raw talent.

- **With hard work, your natural talents may increase.** Practice may not make perfect, but practice certainly can make you better. It increases your confidence and draws out your natural talent. Will hard work turn you into the next Billy Joel? Probably not—unless you are naturally gifted to begin with. But far be it from me to say how high a person can or cannot reach in a lifetime of dedication to a craft.

I am not being falsely humble when I say I have never thought of myself as super-talented. I am talented enough, but I know lots of musicians and songwriters who are far more talented. For 30 years I've closed the gap on those folks and earned a living alongside them by applying myself to the work at hand, and demanding more of myself. Somewhere along the line, I learned not to be intimidated by more-talented musicians. Rather, I choose to surround myself with these people whom God has gifted so tremendously, and learn from them. My own skills have grown over the years partly, I believe, because of my associations with people who are more talented than I am.

The Parable of the Talents (Matt. 25:14–30) also makes it plain that God rewards those who use their abilities wisely. You may be a remarkably talented songwriter, or you may be only moderately talented. I am not concerned about that. I am concerned that you learn how to apply whatever musical talent the Lord has blessed you with to write better songs for the Kingdom.

Enough about talent. Back to craft.

The Four Stages of Competence

Every beginner, regardless of his or her level of talent, will write some bad songs. The typical not-so-talented beginner will write some really bad songs. Take heart. Experienced professional writers still kick out the occasional clunker. Fortunately, we live under grace and mercy, so the bad songs we write won't be held against us for eternity. Fortunately, God is capable of using even our lamest efforts for His Kingdom. But that's no excuse for ignoring the craft of songwriting. We should all strive to make our songs as excellent as we possibly can. (*Jesus' chairs*, remember?) But what is a realistic goal of excellence for the beginner, the amateur, the weekend writing warrior, to have? The answer is simple: to improve. Try to make every new song you compose better than the song that preceded it.

Psychologists refer to the Four Stages of Competence, which describe the typical progression of mastering most any skill. They are the following:

Stage 1   Unconscious incompetence. You are totally inept and completely unaware of your ineptness. This is also known as "blissful ignorance."

Stage 2   Conscious incompetence. You are still inept, but now you are aware that you are inept. This describes my golf game perfectly. It stinks, but at least I know it stinks. This can be a very frustrating place to be.

Stage 3   Conscious competence. You are competent for the task at hand, but must consciously think about the details of the work. This isn't a bad place to be at all. You've become adept at a skill, but still have to think about it. This is where most of us spend much of our lives.

Stage 4   Unconscious competence. You have reached the summit where you perform your work well without ever having to think about it. In the immortal words of Professor Henry Higgins in *My Fair Lady*: "It's second nature to me now / Like breathing out and breathing in." In other words, you are Michael Jordan shooting lay-ups.

As you search for your current placement on the competence scale, keep in mind most of us begin our songwriting journey at stage 1, or unconscious incompetence. We don't know a thing about the rules or the craft of writing, and we are blissfully unaware as to just how bad our first songs really are. The fact you are reading this book, however, suggests that you have moved at least from stage 1 to stage 2, conscious incompetence. You are now thinking about your writing and awakening to the flaws in your songs. You still haven't mastered the craft, but you are working on it.

Talented writers move pretty quickly to stage 3, conscious competence. At this stage, writing requires real thought and hard work, but the results are good, solid songs. A lot of professional writers spend much of their creative time at stage 3, because that is where most rewriting is accomplished. Stage 3 is the reachable goal that a serious beginning Christian songwriter should set for herself, if she wants to entertain the possibility of writing songs other people will want to hear over and again.

The final stage, unconscious competence, is very rare air. The best of writers get to visit stage 4, sometimes long enough to write a song or two. But most have to come back to the realities of stage 3 every now and again. Consider that even Tiger Woods has a coach and works daily to improve his skills. I see occasional glimmers of unconscious competence in my own work when I examine a song or a melody and wonder, "Where did that come from?"

As I said, stage 3 should be the attainable goal of any talented writer willing to work hard. The information and exercises in this book, and other books like it, will help you move toward that goal. But to further bring into focus the progression to better writing, I like what my friend and fellow songwriter Kyle Matthews had to offer amateur writers in his AGMA seminar called *The Life of the Songwriter*. In his seminar, Kyle boiled it down to Three E's: education, exposure, and experience. These Three E's apply to every writer, regardless of their talent or status. For the beginning writer, the Three E's would be the following:

Education: Learn the basics of music theory, song form, and song craft. Know how lyrics differ from other forms of creative writing. (The fact you are reading this book puts you well on this road.)

Exposure: Listen to songs—lots of songs. Analyze their language, styles, and structures. This will help you immensely as you develop your own creative voice.

Experience: The best way to write a good song is to write a lot of songs. Don't fixate on your early efforts and bog yourself down. Write, write, write. Keep writing. Keep moving forward. "The act of writing is your own best teacher." (*The Life of the Songwriter*, p. 24)

If you are serious at all about the craft of songwriting, you should always be about improving. Whether or not you are ever paid a dime for your songs, continually strive to become a better writer. Even after 30 years of professional songwriting, creative growth is still where I find the deepest satisfaction.

Accepting a Challenge

I would offer that writing a well-crafted explicitly Christian song might be a greater challenge than writing a well-crafted pop song. Why? Because there are limitations placed on the Christian song that would never apply to the pop song. Despite the ever-broadening acceptance of popular musical styles in worship, there are still certain styles of music that are generally considered inappropriate for most worship services. That's why you don't hear a lot of sultry jazz music at First Baptist Church on Sunday mornings. It just doesn't feel right to a lot of folks. And consider this: the pop lyricist is completely free to write about any subject, including those that might be sexually suggestive, politically charged, or simply nonsense. The Christian lyricist writing for a worship service is writing about the relationship of a Holy God and His creation—a much smaller target to aim at, wouldn't you agree?

It is more limiting to write a well-crafted Christian song than a well-crafted secular song, and Christian songwriters should accept this challenge gladly. Wouldn't it be amazing if the world were to turn to Christian songs as the pinnacle of good songwriting, rather than the other way around? Unfortunately, too many Christian songwriters accept these limitations and never consider how to stretch their creativity within those limitations. They repeatedly rely on safe music and familiar spiritual catchphrases, resulting in songs that sound tired and trite the moment they are written.

Take heart. It doesn't have to be that way. Christian songwriters haven't yet approached the point of exploring all the myriad creative ideas that God shares with us. There are endless ways remaining to express the insights He lays on our hearts every day. But make no mistake; we have to do our part of the work. We cannot be content to let God inspire us yet be unwilling to do our share of the heavy lifting. We must not glibly accept the privilege of creativity without also shouldering its burden. In Genesis, we read that when God created, he took the void of nothingness and made an orderly universe from it. And He said that it was good. (Gen. 1:31) Following the Father's example, we should take the chaos of our world and make sense of it somehow, not only with our lives but also with our songs. And our work should be good—very good, in fact.

When we create something of beauty, we honor God. When we write a well-crafted and artful song, it pleases Him. When our work is fresh and truthful, God delights in it. So, I challenge you to raise the bar on your own songwriting to a higher level. I encourage you to write songs that do not compromise in either their craftsmanship or their spiritual insight. And I trust you will strive daily to create art that is enduring and meaningful for the sake of our Savior.

Then, the next time someone says to you, "So, tell me about yourself," you can respond without hesitation, "I am a Christian songwriter."

Why Write Songs?

Perhaps the most important question in the world is "Why?" Answering the question "Why?" gives us the motivation we have for doing all the things we do every single day. When I was a kid, my parents always insisted on knowing why I did the dumb things I did before they punished me for doing them. Maybe if I had good intentions, there would be some mitigating mercy in their sentence. Since this is a book about songwriting, before we go much further, I have to ask: "Why do we write songs? I mean, really—*Why do we write songs?*" Songwriting is often difficult and frustrating, and I'm pretty sure it causes the early onset of gray hair and facial wrinkles. For most of us the financial rewards are slim to none. And even our friends and family often don't understand our obsessive preoccupation with composing the perfect three-and-a-half-minute radio hit. We eagerly show them our newest musical baby—only to have them say, "Gee, that's nice." "*Nice?*" you want to say to them. "Are you deaf? It's *great!*" So, I ask again, "Why do we write songs?"

I thought about that for a while, and came up with a short list of reasons that I call Robert's Top Five Reasons for Writing Songs. It is by no means a complete and definitive list. Feel free to scribble your own list in the margins (assuming you didn't borrow this book from the local library).

ROBERT'S TOP FIVE REASONS FOR WRITING SONGS

5. **Big money.** Not so fast. If you are reading this book, that means you are writing Christian songs, so scratch this from list.

4. **Worldwide fame.** Christian songwriters—see No. 5, above.

3. **Inspiration demands a creative response.** Maybe, maybe not. Lots of folks have figured out how to ignore inspiration and survived.

2. **Because you *have to*.** Now we're getting somewhere. But why do you *have to?* That's easy. It's because...

1. **You've got something to say.**

Aha! Now there it is—the real reason you write songs. That's why you struggle through the night to plunk out a tune that may never be heard, let alone be appreciated by the masses. That's why you own three different rhyming dictionaries and the latest programmable synthesizer with a built-in sequencer. That's why you willingly suffer the humiliation of rejection from friends, family, and perfect strangers. You have something to get off your chest. You shoulder a musical burden that can be lightened only by writing songs and sharing them with others. You need to connect with other people through music.

In Their Own Words:
Why do you write songs?

I write songs because I want to say something to people I love and music is such a good vehicle. —CHARLES F. BROWN

I write songs because I absolutely have to. I wrote them before I made money at it, and if the money all went away, I would write them still. —LOWELL ALEXANDER

Today there are more people than ever before trying to share what they have to say through music. That's no surprise. Anybody with a laptop and Apple's Garage Band can fancy him- or herself as the next Diane Warren. More important, everybody knows that music is an art form that communicates like no other. A great song can say in three minutes what a novelist takes 300 pages to communicate. A great song can make you feel more joy or more pain in a single verse and chorus than a mediocre movie can make you feel in two hours. A beautiful melody will spin in your head for days—to the point of driving you nuts—because it simply won't go away. Ever since the first caveman rhymed a few clever grunts to a three-note melody and pounded out a groove with dinosaur bones on a hollow log, mankind has known the power of a song.

You don't write because you want to say something. You write because you've got something to say. —F. SCOTT FITZGERALD

What Do You Have to Say?

So, now we know the No. 1 reason to write a song is because you have something to say. Let me ask this then—*What* do you have to say?

(I'll pause for a moment for you to ponder that question, and maybe even sweat a bit. Now I'll repeat it.) Exactly *what* do you have to say?

"Holy cow!" you may be thinking. "What do I have to say? My own dog won't even listen to me. What insight could I possibly offer to anyone anywhere on this planet?" If you struggle (and you should) with how to answer the question "What do you have to say?" there is hope. First, your reaction indicates a measure of humility, a quality you will need in order to deal with all the rejection a writer faces in life. Second, it demonstrates some self-doubt, an important character trait for any artist. Finally, it shows that you don't have all the answers, which is good. Writers generally have more questions than answers. In fact, your questions may be the most important things you have to offer. If you ask the right questions, your listener may discover the answers.

If it makes you feel any better, it is not our job to have all the answers. Furthermore, it's not our job as Christian songwriters to duplicate the Word. (The Bible really needs no help from us, after all.) Our job is to illuminate the Word, hopefully in ways that others might not have considered. We can best accomplish this goal of illuminating the Word by showing, not telling—by illustrating rather than preaching. Songwriters paint musical pictures using melody and metaphor, rhythm and rhyme—pictures that the listener will remember long after the sermon is over. So, rather than writing a new praise song that says, "I lift my hands to God because He is faithful," show the listener in your lyrics that God is faithful by relating what God has done. Or instead of writing a song that dryly intones, "Don't do drugs. Drugs are bad. Jesus is good," write a song that shows a life ravaged by the abuse of drugs, only to be changed by the love of Jesus. The listener will connect the dots without any more help than that. Trust in the imagination—both yours and your listener's—to do some of the work for you.

WHAT ABOUT SCRIPTURE SONGS?

But what, you ask, about scripture songs? A true scripture song quotes directly from the Bible and needs no help from us, right? Just pick a chapter and verse and set it to music. Not necessarily. The apostle Paul writes in 2 Timothy 3:16 that "All Scripture is God-breathed and is useful for teaching, rebuking, correcting, and training in righteousness." Please don't be offended by my next statement, but Paul says nothing about "singing." With the exception of the Psalms, the Scriptures were not written to be set to music. *The Scriptures are not lyrics.* They don't have regular meter. They don't rhyme. They don't employ the repetition and structure that a good song requires to be memorable. Most scriptures (including the Psalms) need some help from the songwriter to be effective songs. Without that help from the songwriter, the result is usually a bad song.

Here are three good examples of this sort of writing. First is "Thy Word," a simple but memorable song by Amy Grant and Michael W. Smith. The lyrics quote Psalm 119:105 directly for the A section of the song, and then carefully turns to the writer's own thoughts in the B section:

A   *Thy Word is a lamp unto my feet and a light unto my path.*
    Thy Word is a lamp unto my feet and a light unto my path

B   *When I feel afraid, think I've lost my way,*
    Still You're there right beside me

And nothing will I fear as long as You are near
Please be near me to the end.

(Repeat **A** section)

WORDS BY AMY GRANT; MUSIC BY MICHAEL W. SMITH
© 1984 by Meadowgreen Music and Bug and Bear Music

Psalm 8 is the inspiration for my other two examples. Linda Lee Johnson and Tom Fettke quoted almost this entire psalm for their enormously popular choral piece, "The Majesty and Glory of Your Name." (To date, nearly one million copies of its choral music have been sold.) But the authors added a stirring alleluia section to the end of the song in order to bring the music to a satisfying conclusion. In contrast, Michael W. Smith chose to quote only the last verse of Psalm 8 for his song "How Majestic Is Your Name," and again added his own words for the B section. (You can Google these songs if you're curious to see the entirety of their lyrics.)

When writing scripture-based songs, talented songwriters know that it is sometimes necessary to adapt the words in order to write a more memorable song. As for those few passages that can be set directly to music effectively, I believe that the music, if composed properly, will illuminate the scripture in the listener's mind. However, most really good scripture songs are the result of the writer molding the scripture somewhat to fit within the construct of a commercial song.

In Their Own Words: What is the most unique inspiration you've had for a song?

I wrote a song that actually grew out of an argument I had with my husband about another song. —SUE SMITH

It only takes a spark to get a fire going. —KURT KAISER (from "Pass It On")

Inspiration is the germ of an idea that starts us on our way. Beg, borrow, and steal inspiration from wherever you can find it. Just be sure you do something new with it. —KYLE MATTHEWS

Where Can I Get Some Good Ideas?

Sometimes the most difficult part of writing a song is deciding what to write about. Unless you're a songwriting prodigy or some sort of genius with creative superpowers, coming up with that first idea can be a tough hurdle to jump. Just getting started can be a genuine challenge. If you're lucky, you've got a collaborator to help grind out an idea. (If you're really lucky, you've got a collaborator who is full of good ideas and you can move right on to the fun part of songwriting—lunch!) A song, like every piece of art, begins with an idea. The idea is the "what" in "what you have to say." Sometimes the idea arrives in the way of a song title, a hook line, or a snippet of melody. Sometimes it's little more than a vague concept or a musical feel. But where exactly do song ideas come from? Do songwriters simply conjure them out of thin air? Is there some secret "idea" store where songwriters shop, or a mail-order "idea catalog" that only songwriters receive? If only that were so. As dull as it sounds, songwriters find their ideas and inspiration hiding in mundane, everyday things and places—in resources available to anyone willing to pay attention. Those same resources are all around you every day, and they fall into two general categories: reading and listening.

I don't mean to sound like a revolutionary, but you might try a diet
of good literature and poetry. You are what you eat.
—Pat Pattison in *Writing Better Lyrics*, p. 38

READING

Reading is perhaps a lyricist's best single source of ideas. I cannot imagine a good writer not being an avid reader. I'm not alone in that opinion. Alan and Marilyn Bergman are two of the finest and most successful lyricists in the world. Their list of hit songs is nothing short of awe inspiring ("The Windmills of Your Mind," "The Way We Were," "What Are You Doing the Rest of Your Life?," "How Do You Keep the Music Playing?"). In an interview for an ASCAP songwriting workshop, the Bergmans had the following to say about writing and reading:

Alan Bergman: You have to be a reader in order to be a writer, and we read a lot.

Marilyn Bergman: When I'm really stuck and feeling stupid, and feel that there are no more words anymore, and everything has been said, and everything has been said better—I'll read.

Alan Bergman: There's a wonderful story about writing. Richard Brooks is a wonderful director/writer who wrote and directed *Elmer Gantry, The Professionals, In Cold Blood*. He was a product of the Depression, and when he was 15 or 16 years old, he went on the rails from city to city, and he'd get off and try to write a story for the local newspaper for five dollars, and then go on. And one night he was in a typical hobo camp, sitting around with a can of soup, and a man said, "Hey kid, what do you do?" He said, "I'm a writer." The man said, "Have you ever read Dostoyevsky? Tolstoy? Nietzsche? Let me tell you something: for every word you write, read a thousand." So we read a lot: it stimulates writing. (http://www.ascap.com/musicbiz/bergman-part2.html)

So, look for song ideas and inspiration in your reading. But what do you read? Here are a few places to begin:

- **The Bible**—Duhhh.
- **Newspapers and magazines**—John Lennon wasn't being metaphorical when he wrote the opening line to "A Day in the Life": "I read the news today, oh boy." He was reading the paper and thought to write a song about what he read. Don't read just the front-page headlines and feature stories. Sometimes the best ideas are on page three of the Metro section.
- **Books**—Other than the Bible. Read great literature, history, and humor, too. You never know when a line will jump off the page at you as an idea for a song. In Rick Warren's book *The Purpose-Driven Life*, he writes in the first line: "It's not about you." That line struck me hard, and I almost immediately wrote the first verse and chorus to an acerbic song titled, "It's Not About Me." In *Walking on Water*, Madeleine L'Engle wrote that when Jesus "turned his steps toward Jerusalem, he was making a choice which led him to Calvary" (p. 26). The moment I read that sentence, I made a note in the margin of the book, which later led me to write the song "Turning My Steps to Jerusalem." Every professional writer I know has a dozen such stories.
- **Poetry**—Lyrics are not poetry (more about that later), but there is a wealth of ideas and inspiration to be found in poetry. Poems, especially those that tell a story, are ripe for adaptation into song. Like working with scripture, poems often require restructuring and editing to fit the strict meter, rhyme scheme, and lean nature of a commercial song.
- **Hymnals**—The hymnal in your church pew is an absolute treasure trove of rock-solid theology and inspired ideas—and they rhyme already! Don't get hung up on the use of archaic language or the occasional old-fashioned tune. Instead, dig into this wonderful book and try adapting a hymn, making the words your own, and writing a new melody. I have done this several times with success. Recently I borrowed phrases from Charles Wesley's hymn "Praise the Lord Who Reigns Above" for a song I wrote for church choirs titled "Soli Deo Gloria." A few years ago, I adapted Edwin Hatch's words to "Breathe on Me, Breath of God," making the lyrics more contemporary to fit a whole new musical setting. Some of the modern praise-and-worship writers have discovered the power of the hymnal, borrowing from it heavily and adding their own words and music. More power to them, I say.
- **Plays**—There's a reason we're still performing Shakespeare so long after his death. Stage drama is a powerful reflection of the human condition and how your fellow man sees the world. Read plays. Better yet, buy season tickets to your local community theater.

LISTENING

The other tried-and-true method of fishing for ideas is listening. Real listening has become something of a lost art. Most of us have learned to tune out the continual din of audio that bombards us every day. A good songwriter keeps his or her ears open to the sounds of life around them. Here are just a few places to pay special attention:

- **TV**—With 300 cable channels giving us 24/7 news and drama, there's bound to be an idea or two lurking inside the idiot box. Be selective.
- **Radio**—It's not just for listening to other people's hit songs. People say the craziest things on talk radio. Check it out.
- **Audio Recordings**—Other people's music can be a great source of ideas and inspiration, a jumping-off point for your own creativity. Be sure to add your own spin on things, creating something new. Otherwise, you'll be plagiarizing.
- **Movies**—Films have probably more influence on the general public than does any other art form today. Movies shape the way people think—right or wrong—about many issues. A songwriter needs to understand what the public is thinking. Go to the movies, buy a bucket of popcorn, and listen for song ideas.
- **Sermons**—You never know when the preacher is going to speak some little gem of a phrase that will turn into your next song. Keep a pencil handy in the pew. The pastor of a large suburban Nashville church once noticed the songwriters in his congregation scribbling notes. After learning there were songs springing from his sermons, he jokingly suggested from the pulpit that he get co-writing credit!
- **Conversations**—Eavesdropping is an underrated skill in the art of songwriting. Pay attention to what people around you are saying. There may be song titles in those conversations on the elevator. My friend and occasional co-writer Warren Sellers is especially adept at hearing a spoken phrase and molding it into a song idea or title. One such song we wrote together came from the line, "When I'm down on my knees, I haven't got far to fall."

Here's another good reason to listen to the radio and to other people's music: It is vital that you know what's out there in the world, so that you don't duplicate it. Smart writers study the songs that preceded their own so that they don't waste time chasing an idea that's already been a hit. There's no point writing a song called "The King Is Coming," no matter how good it might be. Why? Because Bill and Gloria Gaither's song by that same name is such a well-known standard that everyone will assume you stole the title. It won't matter that titles cannot be copyrighted or that your song is nothing like the Gaithers'. People will think you pilfered it. This happened to me with a musical I wrote for high-school kids. The title song, which I wrote with Michael W. Smith, was called "Living on the Edge." Just a week or two before the musical was released, Aerosmith hit the radio waves with a song called (you guessed it) "Living on the Edge." It was of no consequence that we wrote our song months earlier and had no possible knowledge of the Aerosmith song. There were still those people who assumed I took the title from the rock band.

THREE HOT TIPS

Here are three tips that will help you in your quest for what to write about. I warn you, these tips are so painfully obvious, so rudimentarily simple, you will want to slap your own forehead saying, "Now why didn't I think of that?" Well, you probably would have if I had given you another moment to think about it. So, here they are. Don't say I didn't warn you.

HOT TIP NO. 1: WRITE WHAT YOU KNOW

I wrote in chapter 1 that the best advice ever given to writers was to write what you know. It is obvious and simple advice, but it bears repeating. If you draw on your own life experiences, your own observations, and your own education, then your writing will be more authentic, honest, and true (all important qualities in any art form). When the Beach Boys sang about hot rods and surfing, we believed the words they were singing because they were Southern California boys who had grown up with hot rods and surfing. The Beatles sang about Penny Lane, which rang true in the song of the same name because the street was one they knew in real life. When Twila Paris pens another beautiful worship song, it has the ring of authenticity because it comes from a heart that loves God. So then—write about what you know.

> *We really got into the groove of imagining Penny Lane. It was just reliving childhood. Penny Lane is not only a street but it's a district—a suburban district—where, until age four, I lived with my mother and father.*
>
> —JOHN LENNON, on co-writing "Penny Lane"

HOT TIP NO. 2: WRITE ABOUT WHAT MATTERS TO YOU

You can speak with more authority, more depth, and more passion if you stick to subjects you care about. Robert Frost, arguably America's most famous poet, put it this way: "No tears in the writer, no tears in the reader." How can you expect your listeners to feel deeply about what you write if you don't feel that way, too? When looking for what to write about, look first at what is stirring your own heart. You may burn with conviction about evangelism, social injustice, or the plight of orphans. Whatever it may be, write about what matters to you. This is the driving force behind most Christian songwriters.

HOT TIP NO. 3: THINK OUTSIDE THE CHRISTIAN BOX

Not every song you write has to be a typical Christian song. By "typical" I mean songs that are imitative of what's currently playing on Christian radio and being sung during worship on Sunday mornings. There's nothing wrong with writing songs like that, but Christian songwriters need to feel free to broaden their definition of what a Christian song is and can be. In my own career I have written silly children's songs, show tunes, cowboy songs, and even light opera—all of which were aimed at Christian audiences. There are opportunities for composing songs with a Christian message (both implicit and explicit) that go beyond the confines of Christian radio. Hopefully, the variety of the songs analyzed in chapter 9 of this book will better demonstrate my point. Widen your creative vistas.

WHAT ABOUT ASSIGNMENT WRITING?

You may already have been fortunate enough (or unfortunate, as the case may be) to do some assignment writing. Perhaps you were tapped to write a song for your church's Easter service, or compose Thanksgiving music for a kid's choir, or pen a tune with a local recording artist. Assignment writing is almost always aimed at a very specific target. Sometimes the topic is something you know or care very little about. In those cases, how does my advice to write about what you know and what matters to you help out? Not much, I'm afraid. This is when it's good to be able to think outside the Christian box (see Hot Tip No. 3).

I've done a lot of assignment writing in my career. In the 1980s, I wrote a boatload of radio and TV jingles—all assignments, of course. I've also written songs at the request of specific artists, to fill a specific need. These days, I am occasionally commissioned to write an original piece of music for a particular church event. Also, many of the songs I write for choral musicals are aimed at specific needs within the musical itself. To be perfectly honest, many times I have lacked any great knowledge or passion for the assigned subject when I began the writing. Inevitably, though, I learn more about the subject matter as I write. The more I learn about something, the more I tend to care about it. And all the while, I am broadening my vistas, both creatively and personally.

So if a less-than-passionate assignment comes your way, don't turn it down without first giving it some thought; it will almost certainly be an opportunity to stretch your creative muscles. And perhaps with a little time and study, the assignment could become something you feel passionate about.

"I" Songs and "You" Songs: A Brief Detour

"I" SONGS

It may be my imagination, but it seems a lot of writers these days are content to gaze at their own navels and never write about anyone or anything else but themselves. There is an awful lot of "I" and "me" in today's Christian music and praise-and-worship songs. That's understandable to a degree. After all, songwriting is an intensely personal method of expression. It's only natural for there to be a lot of first-person point of view in our songs. Still, it's wise to occasionally peer outside your own world and write about something or someone other than yourself. Take a look at your most recent batch of lyrics. If they are all about "I" and "me," let me suggest that you take a different perspective in your next few songs. It will do your writing good.

"YOU" SONGS

Because Christian songwriters so often work in and alongside the church, it's easy to fall prey to the desire to preach in our writing. It's important to remember that we are musicians, not preachers. What happens when a Christian songwriter writes preachy songs? More often than not, the listener the writer wants most to reach is turned off. (Let's be honest—nobody enjoys being preached at.) Preachy songs often manifest themselves as what I call "you" songs. The lyrics in "you" songs say to the listener, "*You* better change. *You* need to get saved, otherwise *you* are going to hell." "You" songs almost always spring from a songwriter's sincere and heartfelt desire to share the Gospel and open the eyes of the world to sin. Both are worthy subjects. Unfortunately, the message that comes across to the listener in most "you" songs is this: "I'm better than you because I know Jesus." Is that really the most effective way to convince someone of Jesus' love? The more we shout and the more we accuse, the less people will listen. That's human nature.

What's the answer for the songwriter who wants to write songs that evangelize and expose the darkness of sin in this world? Try writing in the third person. Tell a story and *show* how sin ruins lives and how God's grace transforms lives. By changing the lyrical point of view from "you" to "he" or "she," you have spared the listener from feeling preached at. Instead, he or she is listening to a story, and hopefully identifying with the character in that story. This is exactly what I did in the first verse of my song "God Only Knows." (The lyrics are analyzed in chapter 7, "Writing Is Rewriting.") I changed "you" to "she" in the first verse to soften the message and draw the listener into the story. By the second verse, I shifted back to "you" without fear of sounding preachy, because the listener could hear the parallel to the first verse.

By the way, I know a little something about writing "you" songs. I wrote a lot of them in the early part of my career, including the first song I ever got recorded. Fortunately for me, that song can no longer be found anywhere.

Be Ready to Write

Since good ideas can be elusive, you should always be on the lookout for them, ready to capture them when they come your way. This may take some conscious effort at first, but over time you will begin to naturally see and hear life through a songwriter's filter. John Braheny calls this "developing a songwriter's consciousness" (*The Craft and Business of Songwriting*, p. 8). Observe the world around you with the focused intent to discover source material for your songs, and you'll be amazed at how many ideas suddenly come your way. The crazy thing is that the ideas were there all along—you just weren't noticing them. But with a keenly developed songwriter's sense, you'll spot ideas coming whether you are consciously looking for them or not. For the Christian songwriter, a regular quiet time of prayer and Bible study is an invaluable help in developing the sensitivity to see the world through a songwriter's eye.

Unfortunately, inspiration is an unpredictable thing. You never know when or where a good song idea is going to hit you. Your best ideas may come at inconvenient times—in the checkout line at Target, during a worship service, or right before you fall asleep. Experience teaches us that failure to jot your idea down immediately almost always results in a lost idea. Have you ever had a great late-night inspiration, only to find the inspired idea is no longer there when the alarm clock rings the next morning? Or maybe you've had an idea on the drive to work, but by the end of the workday it has vanished. Keep a notebook and pen handy. Make sure that the batteries in your microcassette recorder are fresh. Learn to politely excuse yourself from a conversation in order to discreetly jot down a great hook line that pops into your head. When your Bible study teacher says something that sparks an idea, write it in the margin of your Bible, or on an old church bulletin—anything you can get your hands on. Just make sure you capture the idea before the inspiration vanishes into the ether.

I loved the wacky character Michael Keaton played years ago in the movie *Night Shift*. He was always coming up with crazy moneymaking schemes and barking them into his portable cassette recorder. His most unique inspiration had to be his idea for instant tuna salad. "Feed mayonnaise to tuna. Call Starkist." Okay. So his ideas were nuts—but his method of capturing the moment of inspiration was as sane as could be.

Here in Nashville, a lot of country songwriters keep what they affectionately call their "hook book." Often nothing more than a simple spiral notebook, a hook book contains all the writer's song ideas, hook lines, and lyric phrases. The writer adds to his hook book whenever inspiration strikes. Then later, when he sits down to write or co-write with a collaborator, he has a supply of ready ideas. A prolific writer can fill up a hook book in a matter of months. One writer friend of mine has dozens of these notebooks, dating back for years. What a great way to document the progress of your work over time!

My own version of a hook book sits on my computer's hard drive in a file called Songs in Progress. It contains snippets of songs, pieces of lyrics, titles, and ideas that I have had neither the time nor inclination to finish. Every now and again I go back to that file and run through each fragment of a song. I can never predict when one of these dusty concepts will be perfect for the song I am writing today.

In Their Own Words

> *My lyrics seem to pop out of nowhere when I least expect them. That's why I keep an idea notebook going all the time, so I can catch little things as they spin past.* —Claire Cloninger

Discover Your Own Creative Process

Much has been written about the creative process—tons, in fact. There is no shortage of theories about it. Lots of folks have dissected it, analyzed it, and put their own spin on it. I'm going to boil it down to something very simple, and it's this: The creative process is a mystery to me. Okay, I know that there are stages to creativity. (I cover them later in this chapter.) I know that there are things one can do to get creatively fired up. But still, if we're being completely honest here—the process is a mystery. After all, where *did* that great idea come from? How on earth did I come up with this melody or that lyric? (The creative process may be some of the best evidence we'll ever see of the Holy Spirit at work.)

For many skilled writers, an effective creative process results from well-practiced craftsmanship and hard work. Like most skills, whether it is dentistry or small-engine repair, the more you work at it, the easier it gets. Every day in Nashville, there are writers who lock themselves into Music Row writer's rooms with the express intent of writing a hit song. These writers have mastered the craft of songwriting. They have developed a creative process that responds to focused effort and hard work. They blend their craftsmanship seamlessly with their creative talents, and a song is born. *Voila!*

For the beginning writer, it comes down to this: The more you write, the better the writer you are likely to become. Practice will lead to improvement. Your creative process will become smoother and more automatic if you take time to write something every day. "But that's impossible!" you tell me. "I work nine hours a day!" Okay then—find time to write something every other day, or at least once a week. And by "something," I don't mean that it has to be a song. You may spend the time writing a carefully worded letter to a friend, a thoughtful journal entry, or a grocery list that rhymes. If you're like most busy people these days, your entire life is scheduled in your date book or your personal digital assistant or the calendar on your refrigerator door. In that case, schedule time on your calendar to write. Block out an appointment for yourself, and honor that appointment just like you would a meeting with a client or a visit to the doctor. Even if you can carve out only 20 or 30 minutes a day to write, those brief sessions will help you keep your creative engine tuned up and ready to go.

No two songwriters I've ever known share the exact same creative process. Each has his or her peculiar method to get the creative juices flowing. For some professional writers, especially those in the Platinum world of pop and country music, their primary creative motivation is money. For them, it is either write hits or get a day job. These guys respond well to deadlines, black coffee, and adrenaline. If you are wired with that sort of creative mind-set, you might want to set your own deadline for finishing a song. Tell your friends that you're going to show them a great new song in three days. Then see if you can produce under pressure. Other writers like to work in a calm, relaxed atmosphere. They mull ideas over slowly and avoid working in the wee hours of the evening. I personally prefer to focus on one song at a time, and work uninterrupted until I've completed the song. If I get too many songs cooking at one time, they likely will all end up sounding the same. I know other writers that are completely comfortable working on several songs at a time, letting each one simmer awhile until it's finished. Some are at their creative best when they are left alone to write. Others need the electricity of a good collaborator.

If you are just beginning your journey as a songwriter, you may not yet know your own creative process. It may take some time for you to discover it. (Again, daily writing can be the key to unlocking your creative method.) There will likely be some trial and error involved, but it is important to learn which process suits you well. Once you know how you work best, you can avoid putting yourself into situations that will frustrate your creativity.

A word of caution: Once you've discovered your own creative process, don't turn down a creative opportunity simply because it isn't happening the way that is most comfortable for you. If you think of yourself as a Lone Ranger, don't miss out on the chance to meet Tonto just because you've never worked successfully with a collaborator. On the flip side, if you always work with a collaborator, don't assume it's impossible to work alone. Be open to expanding your creative process. Be willing to grow. Revel in the God-given mystery that is creativity.

In Their Own Words: Is there a particular creative process that suits you best?

I have found that it works best if you have a text from which to work, as opposed to forcing a text into a melody.   —KURT KAISER

I write five days a week. Generally three days are with co-writers and two days alone.   —TONY WOOD

I've found that composing in the car is the perfect setting. I turn off the cell phone and the radio and bask in the silence. I place a cassette player on the seat and let the tape roll while I brainstorm.
     —BABBIE MASON

I know that if I will just show up, walk into my office and close the door, start with a prayer, begin rhyming the rhymes, looking at the idea notebook, a song will draw near. If I will show up, God will meet me there. Songs will meet me there. It never fails.
     —CLAIRE CLONINGER

I keep all of my notes. All of them. It's amazing how many times you will want to retrace your steps.   —DEBORAH CRAIG-CLAAR

My creative process involves first getting enough sleep.
     —LOWELL ALEXANDER

The Stages of Creativity

The creative process can be broken down into stages. If you don't believe me, just do an Internet search on "stages of creativity." You will find experts from the fields of business, education, the arts, even child psychology offering insights on the subject. All these experts make great points about the creative process. Many of them draw their insights from the work of a French mathematician named Henri Poincare (1854 to 1912), who determined that there are four stages of creativity. Poincare's stages were originally used to analyze problem solving (after all, Henri was a math geek), but they apply very well to songwriting. So I am going to borrow Mr. Poincare's idea about the four stages of creativity for the next few paragraphs. According to Poincare, the four stages of creativity consist of the following:

1. Preparation

2. Incubation

3. Illumination

4. Verification

Each stage is unique and separate from the others. When you're in the thick of writing, you may pass from one stage to the next so quickly that you don't see it happen. Experienced writers pass from one stage to the next unconsciously. You may spend hours, or days, or even years on one stage, and yet only seconds on another. Still, as you nurse a song from its initial idea to a finished work, you will invariably travel through these stages. Let's examine them individually.

PREPARATION

Preparation, according to Poincare, is the time spent defining a problem. In the narrow context of writing a song, preparation is the time spent forming an idea and determining what to write. It is also the time for the writer to think about form and style. All this may happen in a flash of brilliance, or it could take several days of thought. In the broader context of your creative life, preparation includes your education (musical and otherwise), your reading, your life experiences, and the development of your worldview. Keep that last part in mind when you need an excuse to go to the movies or waste an afternoon listening to records. Both can be terrific "prep time." In a sense, preparation is in part what enables an experienced and gifted writer like Willie Nelson to pen a song like "Crazy" on the back of a napkin in a matter of minutes. Willie had been preparing for that moment of creativity his entire life.

In his book *Fearless Creating*, Eric Maisel offers there are six stages of creativity. He calls the first two stages "Wishing" and "Choosing." I like that. First, you have to want to create something—that's wishing. Then you have to decide what to create—that's choosing. It's easy to assume that the readers of this book have all chosen songwriting. But allow me to encourage you to occasionally choose other creative avenues, like painting, or scrapbooking, or videography. Expand your creative horizons, and you will become a better songwriter. In the past few years, I tried my hand at writing two children's books. The experience was by far the hardest creative work I have done in my life. Neither book is likely to ever be published, but I don't regret the hours (lots of them) I spent writing the books. I believe the effort made me a better songwriter.

INCUBATION

Just because you're not actually pounding away at the piano or scribbling lyrics on a legal pad doesn't mean that you aren't in the thick of the creative process. To the contrary, sometimes the best thing you can do is get away from the pencils and paper, the keyboards, and the rhyming dictionary and instead just stew on your song for a while. That is incubation. Incubation is the time you mull over the melody in the back of your mind, consider lyric options, and live with your idea for a while. This stage is a great excuse for puttering in the garden, taking a long walk, or hitting a bucket of balls at the driving range. These sorts of activities engage the conscious brain in something mundane and free up the subconscious brain to go exploring. Just be sure to take a notepad or portable recorder with you, in case you make a creative breakthrough strolling around your neighborhood.

Johnny Mercer was famous for his naps. This world-renowned lyricist ("Moon River," "Laura," "I'm an Old Cowhand from the Rio Grande," "That Old Black Magic," "The Days of Wine and Roses," to name just a few) would emerge from what his family thought was a prolonged nap only to write down complete lyrics that had been running through his head for hours. Sometimes he would dwell on a song for days before writing a word.

To the outside observer, incubation may look a lot like goofing off. Unless you're careful, it can become just that. There is a natural laziness in most of us that is never far from taking control of our day. A short stroll around the block can result in a two-hour chat with the neighbor across the street—and the creative process is shut down for the day. Creative incubation requires that you not stray too far from the job of writing. If the bright shiny things that wait outside your doorway easily distract you, you might want to keep the incubation stage indoors (metaphorically speaking). And remember, even if your family can't see what you're writing, you really *are* writing. You may have to occasionally remind them of that while you stretch out on the sofa to ponder your current creation. (Just try not to snore, or they'll know your writing has become napping.)

For many experienced writers, preparation and incubation happen very quickly. Since professional songwriters write almost every day, they remain in a near-constant state of preparation. Keep in mind that every song you write better prepares you for your next song. So, as you write more songs, preparation may shorten for you, too. For the writer with years of experience, the incubation stage may happen in a single flash leading to the final stages of creativity. But make no mistake—preparation and incubation both happen in the writing of every song, if only for a moment or two. Then the hard work begins.

ILLUMINATION

Illumination begins the moment you crank the creative engine and get started. Lyrics are written. A tune is composed. A groove is programmed, or guitar chords are hammered out. It is the most visible stage of the creative process—at least to the outside world. Illumination should feel spontaneous and free. In the business world, this sort of flow is called *brainstorming*. When you're working out a lyric, write down all the ideas that come to you—even the ones you think may lack potential. When collaborating with another writer, keep your comments positive and encouraging, so as not to shut off the flow of ideas. Keep criticism to a minimum. There will be plenty of time to fix things later. Illumination is the time for writing, not rewriting. Do not (I repeat: DO NOT) start editing your work before you even have a first draft of the words or a solid set of chord changes. Keep moving forward. Illumination is writing, writing, writing.

Maisel divides the illumination stage into two parts: *starting* and *working*. Starting is what separates the writers from the wannabe writers. There is nothing so exciting and yet so terrifying to most songwriters as the blank page. It waits expectantly for your creative brilliance to bring it to life. "C'mon," the blank page dares you. "Write something new, something fresh, something that nobody on the planet has ever thought of before in the history of mankind"—a daunting thought that has stopped many songwriters in their tracks before they ever really got started. Experienced writers know that if you don't start, you won't finish. There is no way around the requirement to settle down, pick up a pen or an instrument, and begin. For the part-time songwriter, there are hundreds of distractions to keep one from starting: kids, bills, TV, work.

"I'll get to the song when I'm finished with [insert your favorite excuse here]" is a classic roadblock to starting.

The second part of Maisel's version of illumination, or working, requires complete involvement and focus. If there is to be a free flow of ideas, the writer's greatest enemy at this stage is any element that would interrupt the flow. Making a quick phone call, answering an e-mail, or breaking away to watch a few minutes of television—any of these can destroy your creative process for the day. Creativity needs discipline to maintain focus. Achieving disciplined creativity is hard work. In an interview on the radio program *Fresh Air*, Richard Bausch, author of numerous novels including *Hello to the Cannibals*, said that there are two approaches to writing: *romantic* and *classical*. The romantic approach relies on inspiration—the need to feel the desire to write. In contrast, the classical approach relies on writing every day regardless of how you feel. Most songwriters are romantics at heart. We love inspiration. But the professional writer knows that inspiration is not enough. Real work is involved. Consider Johann Sebastian Bach. As a church organist and composer, it was Bach's job to write new music for the Sunday services every week. Because he took his work (and his art) seriously, we are now blessed with some of the greatest and most inspired music ever written.

VERIFICATION

Verification is the final stage in the creative process. Maisel calls this stage *completing*. I like to call it *perspiration*. Simply put, verification is finishing the work you started. Many beginner songwriters never reach this stage. They are content to stop at illumination and, as a result, never really complete their work. Imagine building an automobile, and stopping just short of painting it. Sure, the car will run down the highway, but it isn't really finished. The same goes for the first draft of a song. It may have two nice verses and a chorus that rhymes. But until it has been through the process of rewriting, the song isn't finished. Verification requires that you look at your work with an objective eye and determine what changes need to be made. And trust me—changes will need to be made. You may need to fix weak spots in the lyrics or try alternate chord changes in the bridge. You may want to experiment with the melody to be certain that it's absolutely right. But I can assure you that your song isn't finished yet. Most professional writers will tell you that verification is the most critical stage in the entire creative process. Rewriting is such an important part of writing that I devote an entire chapter of this book to the subject (see chapter 7).

Lots of writers have unfinished songs hidden away in old notebooks, gathering dust in the back of a closet—songs that never reached verification. That's not always a bad thing. Some songs don't need to be finished. We've all started songs with a creative fervor, only to run out of steam when we realize that the song idea wasn't as great as we initially thought it to be. That's okay. These songs provide learning experiences that make us better writers. But don't avoid finishing a song simply because you fear the song will fail. We all fail more often than we succeed. The more time you spend at the verification stage, the better your songs will become. Ironically, the better your songs become, the less time you'll need to spend at verification.

Coda

Some songs begin as lyrics in search of a melody. Others begin as a simple wordless tune. Some start as a lonely effort of a solitary writer and finish with the help of a collaborator. Some kick off in a room full of writers, and then it later falls to one brave soul to complete the task. Sometimes writing a song is a matter of slugging it out, just you and the muse and an old Martin guitar. No matter how a songs starts, there's no doubt that getting started can be the most daunting task the writer faces. All that said, sometimes the best thing to do is simply begin. That's right. Just start. Somewhere. Anywhere. An opening line for the first verse. A great set of chord changes. A clever hook line. A killer drum groove. You've got to start somewhere, and there is no right or wrong way to do that. The creative process is a mystery, remember? So go after it with a vengeance—because even a rotten beginning can be the start of something sweet.

The Shape of a Song (Thought and Form)

Art Versus Craft

If you spend any time around serious songwriters and musicians, more than likely you will hear someone refer to the music they write or perform as their "art." The more serious (or self-involved) the writer, the greater the chances are of the word "art" coming up in the conversation. And while there may indeed be some pretense in the word, it is true that there is a genuine art to songwriting. But if you hang around successful professional songwriters, it is more likely you will hear them speak of their "craft" and the "craft" of songwriting. So which is it? Is songwriting an art or a craft?

The answer is it's both. Songwriting is a wonderful blend of form and function and beauty. When a skilled craftsperson, such as a carpenter or a jeweler, blends originality and creativity into his work, they rise to a new level—to that unique combination of artist and craftsman—the artisan. The artisan puts her very best craftsmanship and complete creativity into her work. Christian songwriters should all strive to become artisans. We should do our dead-level best to write songs that are both well crafted and creative, songs that are classic in form and beautiful to the ear, songs that spring from the mastery of our own skills as well as from the inspiration of the Creator of All Things. We owe that to God.

To become an artisan, a worker must master the use of the tools of the trade. This process can take years. If you are a beginning songwriter, think of yourself as an apprentice—a student soaking up knowledge. This chapter is the first of several that will show you the tools you need to become an artisan.

Think Before You Write

Can you imagine a homebuilder working without plans…hammering and sawing away at random until a house was built? There is no telling what that house might look like when finished—if it is ever finished! As a rule, it's best to know what you're going to build before you start building it. For the songwriter, this means you should think before you write. An experienced builder works from a blueprint. Professional athletes envision the play before they execute it. Michelangelo, when facing a raw block of marble, saw the sculpture inside before he ever struck the rock with a chisel and hammer. "I saw the angel in the marble and carved until I set him free," he once said. For the artisan, thought precedes action.

Now, unless you are Mozart, no one expects you to completely know every detail of your song before you begin writing. That's why we have erasers—to make the inevitable changes as our songs develop. Many professional songwriters are so adept at the craft of writing that they can hammer out a good song in a matter of hours, armed from the start with nothing more than the basic idea of what the song will be about. But I recommend that the beginner take a little time and decide what he wants to build before starting in with the saws and hammers.

FIVE SIMPLE QUESTIONS

Here are five simple questions to consider as you begin your next song. If you answer them all before you write, chances are you will have less to rewrite when you finish your first draft. Consider them part of the incubation stage of creativity.

1. **What is the song's point of view?** Point of view (POV) is the particular voice from which the story of the song is told to the listener. It is determined by *who* is telling the story to *whom*. There are three voices to choose from, and they are the same three voices that David used for the Psalms, Shakespeare used for his sonnets, and Sondheim uses for his songs. They are easily identified by the choice of pronouns employed in the lyrics. They include the following:

   - **First-person POV:** The singer is the storyteller. The story is told from the "I" and "me" perspective. Look for these pronouns in the first-person POV: "I," "me," "mine," "we," "us," "our." This viewpoint is a favorite for love songs and songs that express a personal story. (Friendly reminder No. 1: In the previous chapter, I warned about the potential dangers of self-centered, navel-gazing "I" songs.)
   - **Second-person POV:** The singer is speaking to another person, giving direction, encouragement, advice, praise, and so on. This POV is sometimes referred to as *direct address*. The prominent pronouns in second-person POV are "you" (both singular and plural) and "your" (both singular and plural). The second-person viewpoint is great to use for speaking to a large audience (the plural "you"), so long as you stick to universal truths. Otherwise, someone in your audience might say, "That doesn't apply to me." (Friendly reminder No. 2: In the previous chapter, I also cautioned against preachy, finger-wagging "you" songs.)
   - **Third-person POV:** The singer is an observer of the action in the story, singing about other people. This viewpoint is excellent for dealing with sensitive or awkward subjects. The pronouns that identify the third-person POV are "he," "she," "they," "them," "his," "her," "their," and so on.

Pat Pattison tells us, "The point of view you choose controls the relationship between the singer and the audience. It sets the context for your ideas" (*Writing Better Lyrics,* p. 82). The first-person POV places the listener outside of the action, watching the subject sing about herself. The second-person POV makes the audience the recipient (the "you") of the singer's message. The third-person POV puts the singer and the audience on the same footing as observers of the action in the song. Because point of view creates the context for a song, it is extremely important that a song have a consistent point of view. If your song starts in the third person, don't suddenly shift to the first person. There are rare exceptions to this rule, but the beginner should focus on sticking to a single point of view in the song.

A common point-of-view error that occurs in too many praise-and-worship songs involves the way the writer refers to God. God is "He" in the verses (for example, "He is mighty. He is powerful."), then becomes "You" in the chorus ("We will praise You."). This is a shift from the third-person POV to the second-person POV. The writer may argue that the change in point of view doesn't matter, because the congregation understands what is being said. But I offer that the Christian songwriter's standards should be as high or higher than the secular songwriter's (*Jesus' chairs, Jesus' chairs*). Such wishy-washy shifts in point of view aren't acceptable in the secular world of songwriting. They should not be acceptable to the serious Christian songwriter.

"He" Versus "he"

The novice Christian songwriter should always remember that the listener cannot hear the difference between "he" and "He." The lowercase "he" can mean just about anybody, including your cat, Sparkles. The uppercase "He" is generally reserved to mean the Creator of the Universe, the Son of God, or the Holy Spirit. Any references to "he" or "He" should be kept consistent throughout the song. The listener should not have to rely on the printed lyrics in the CD case to understand who "he" (or "He") is.

2. **What one emotion do you want to convey?** A song is about *one thing*, so it should convey one primary emotion. Joy, sadness, hope, love, hate, anger—these are all powerful emotions for a writer to work with. Don't overload your listener by creating an emotional roller coaster that races up and down between joy and sorrow. If sadness is the core emotion of the song, don't fill the second verse with fear or anger. Stick to one overarching emotion. No doubt, a song can shift its emotional focus. A song that begins in despair can end in hope. But in that instance, the primary emotion of the song is hope, and despair is used to lead the listener toward hope.

3. **What is the specific setting of the song?** Envision the setting, the place, and time of your song, and try not to stray from that. Choose language and imagery that fits the setting. If your song is set on a lonely midnight highway in the 1950s, don't use a metaphor that refers to the Internet. The Internet didn't exist in the 1950s, and so even the most creative metaphor using the Internet is not going to fit your song's setting. Images that don't fit the song's setting serve only to weaken the song. This especially applies to songs that tell a story.

Not every song has an obvious time, place, or setting. But that doesn't mean the setting doesn't need to be considered. For example, at first glance, this little rule doesn't seem to apply to a lot of praise-and-worship songs. I believe, however, that many times they do—but in a subtle way. For instance, is the song in the present tense or in the past tense? (Time.) Does it spring from a wounded soul or a joyful heart? (Emotional setting.)

4. **What is the song's universal human theme?** A song is about one thing. Every song should have a single underlying theme that people can understand and identify with. What's more, the universal theme must be true. (Otherwise, it's not universal, is it?) This doesn't mean every song that springs from your guitar has to resound with some serious, heavyweight Truth. "Can't Buy Me Love" (John Lennon and Paul McCartney) is a catchy pop song, but it squarely hits the universal theme that money can't purchase a person's true affections.

There are dozens of great themes that are part of the universal human experience: Love conquers all. Hate destroys. Freedom demands sacrifice. Redemption comes at a cost. Power corrupts. The list goes on and on. Did you notice how all of the themes I listed sound like old familiar sayings? That's because they have all been around for hundreds and thousands of years. They have been stated and restated dozens of times in the Bible, in the works of countless playwrights, and in novels, songs, and movies. If you're looking for a new theme for your latest hit song, try reading something old. The books of Proverbs, Psalms, and Ecclesiastes are terrific resources for the Christian writer to find universal themes. Perhaps King Solomon said it best: "There is nothing new under the sun." (Ecclesiastes 1:9)

"Vertical" Songs

Beginning Christian songwriters too often fail to choose a strong underlying human theme. Perhaps that is because so many Christian songs these days have a "vertical" intent—that is, aimed at God as the audience. Keep in mind that vertical lyrics also have an earthly audience that hears and sings the songs. So even when the lyrics are aimed directly at God, make sure they speak to a theme that your fellow human beings can understand and appreciate.

5. **How will the song (or the story within the song) unfold?** Like a well-written short story, a song should unfold logically toward its primary point. It should have a strong start and progress to a satisfying conclusion. The verses should lead to the chorus. The second verse should provide details or ideas that naturally follow the material in the first verse. If there is a bridge in the song, it must provide new material that reasonably succeeds the information in the verses and connects the final choruses.

If the song tells a specific story, then it is important that the details of the story unfold in a commonsense fashion with an identifiable beginning, middle, and end. Don't spill the surprise in the first chorus, only to go back to the middle of your tale in the second verse. You wouldn't spring the punch line in the middle of a joke, would you?

The novice songwriter would do well to sketch out a quick outline of his or her song before getting too deep into the writing. The outline will keep the songwriter focused and help maintain the clarity of the song.

THE TV GUIDE TEST

Have you ever noticed how *TV Guide* magazine can take any movie or television program, no matter how complex, and distill its synopsis into one sentence? All three hours of the epic film *Gone with the Wind* are boiled down to something like "A Southern belle falls for a handsome carpetbagger during the Civil War." The heart-stopping thrills of *Jaws* are shrunk to "A man-eating shark wreaks havoc in the waters off a New England coastal village." Television episodes can be reduced to a mere handful of words: "Jerry looks for a new apartment." "Opie accidentally kills a mother bird." "The Dynamic Duo battles the Joker."

Here's a good way to check your song's blueprint, using the *TV Guide* test. Describe your song idea in a single sentence. If you can do that, then chances are that your song has a well-focused idea and an identifiable point of view. If your single sentence synopsis sounds intriguing, it's likely your song will be interesting to your listeners.

In Their Own Words: Is the decision to use a particular song form a conscious choice? Or does that happen instinctively when you write?

Choosing a song form is a conscious craft thing to me. I write in a particular form for the desired effect I am seeking.
—LOWELL ALEXANDER

Song form is instinctive. I cannot write a text without a melody in my head, and as a side benefit there is always a musical form in my lyrics.
—J. PAUL WILLIAMS

Often, it [the song form] becomes a choice based on what will have a better chance of getting cut.
—SUE SMITH

Choose a Song Form

In a 2007 interview with Craig Carnella, Broadway giant Stephen Sondheim said, "There is something about form in any art—in concert music, in painting, in novels…there is something about the conscious use of form that says to the reader or looker, 'This is worth saying.'" (ASCAP's *Playback* magazine, vol. 14, issue 3, p. 46) When artists limit themselves to the strictures of an art form, they are telling those that see or hear or touch their art that they have worked to compress and distill their thoughts and emotions into a single cogent statement. There are well-accepted forms in every type of art—forms that have evolved over years and years until they have been perfected. The mastery of the art form is foundational to successful creation in any artistic endeavor. Shakespeare accepted and excelled within the limitations of the 14-line form of the sonnet. Composers from Mozart to Stravinsky have been challenged by the restrictions of the sonata form or the rules of a well-written fugue. Serious playwrights learn how to properly construct a one-act, a two-act, and a three-act play. It is the same for songwriters. There are song forms to be mastered—three to be exact.

The three classic popular song forms we work with today did not appear overnight. They were not arbitrarily created by the charter members of ASCAP with the express purpose of frustrating novice songwriters in the 21st century. They were developed over many generations. In his book, *The Craft and Business of Songwriting*, John Braheny says, "People have an unconscious desire and need for symmetry, and the repetition of rhyme, melody, and form satisfies that need" (p. 67). Composers and lyricists long ago discovered that a certain degree of predictability in their music was a good thing. Audiences like music that has an understandable shape to it. Thus, over time three distinct song forms emerged—each with its own strengths, each with its own rules. Skilled songwriters master all three of the forms, learning the rules of each. Once the forms are mastered, the rules may be broken—not by accident, but with purpose and for a reason.

THE "HOOK"—A BRIEF DETOUR

Before we jump into song forms, let me give you a quick definition of a term that you've already seen in this book at least a dozen times and that you'll see a lot more: *hook*. The hook is the line in a song that hooks the listener's attention and sticks with him after the song is over. In most songs, the hook is the title of the song. Now, on with the show.

The AAA Song Form

EXAMINING THE AAA FORM

The first songs that migrated to America were hymns and the folk songs of English and Irish immigrants. These hymns and songs were composed mostly of a series of lyric verses (or *stanzas*) that were identical in length and set to the same melody. Each verse would begin or end with the same lyric line. This simple musical form is what we now call the AAA song form. It looks something like this:

A (verse 1; hook/title in first or last line)

A (verse 2; hook/title in first or last line)

A (verse 3; hook/title in first or last line)

The repetition of the music defines the form. There is no chorus and no bridge. Each music verse has the same form—an "A"—thus, for a three-verse song, the AAA song form. The tune is normally 8 to 16 bars long, constructed in 4-bar phrases. "I Walk the Line," by Johnny Cash, is a good example.

> *I keep a close watch on this heart of mine* (4 bars)
> *I keep my eyes wide open all the time* (4 bars)
> *I keep the ends out for the tie that binds* (4 bars)
> *Because you're mine I walk the line* (4 bars)
>
> WORDS AND MUSIC BY JOHN R. CASH
> © 1956 by Hi Lo Music

There are lots of notable exceptions to the 8- to 16-bar norm. Chris Rice's "Welcome to Our World" is built with 10 measures for each A section. "Ode to Billy Joe," by Bobbie Gentry, uses 24 measures for each verse. In the end, it is usually the song's story and its melody that determine the length of its verses.

The AAA form was a popular choice of folk-song writers in the 1950s and 1960s, perhaps because it is so effective at hammering home a direct message (something that hymn writers had discovered generations earlier). Pete Seeger's "Where Have All the Flowers Gone?" and Bob Dylan's "Blowin' in the Wind" became protest anthems for an entire generation of young people. The AAA song form is a natural fit for writers who want to tell a story. Each verse, or A section, acts like a scene in a play or a chapter in a book. The effect is like looking at a piece of panel art made up of separate screens. Each screen is a scene. Taken together, they tell a story.

The AAA song form may present a challenge to even the most gifted lyricist. To begin, the typical AAA song places the title or hook of the song in the first or the last line of every verse. That alone can be a demanding task. Further, the lyricist must keep the story moving, while always using the same hook line (or a slight variation) over and over. Finally, because there is no chorus to sum up the point of the song, each A section needs to reach a satisfying conclusion or resting place on its own. Every A section must somehow be a payoff for the listener, even if the song and the story are continuing.

Joni Mitchell's "Big Yellow Taxi" is a perfect example of how to make the AAA form pay off. In just four stanzas she examines the universal human theme of loss—from the loss of nature's resources to the loss of love. (Remember, a song is about *one thing*.) Mitchell closes each stanza with the following same lines:

> *Don't it always seem to go*
> *That you don't know what you've got 'til it's gone*
> *They paved paradise and put up a parking lot.*
>
> WORDS AND MUSIC BY JONI MITCHELL
> © 1970 by Siquomb Publishing

There are numerous creative variations of the AAA song form. Note that the title of Joni Mitchell's song above is "Big Yellow Taxi," but the hook line is "They paved paradise and put up a parking lot." As you study some of the great AAA songs, you will see that every writer has a way of nudging the form for his or her own purposes. In the hit song, "By the Time I Get to Phoenix," master songwriter Jimmy Webb made two significant alterations to the classic AAA form. First, he slightly altered the hook line in each verse to show the eastward journey of the storyteller: verse 1—"By the time I get to Phoenix"; verse 2—"By the time I make Albuquerque"; and verse 3—"By the time I make Oklahoma." The music remains the same, but the words change subtly. Webb also added a short coda, or tag line, to emphasize his final point: "She just didn't know / I would really go."

Another variation is to write a repeatable chorus that uses the same melody of the verses. "Born in the USA" (Bruce Springsteen) and "Achy Breaky Heart" (Don Van Tress) use this technique. Another trick for keeping the AAA song form interesting is to use a simple refrain to break the monotony of the repeated A section. Don Henley did this to good effect in "Dirty Laundry," his biting song about the news media. He wrote a repeated refrain, "Kick 'em when they're up / Kick 'em when they're down," to make his point. This technique bends the AAA song form, and makes it look a little like a song with a chorus. But the key to identifying Henley's song as having an AAA song form is that the hook/title line is at the very end of every verse, or A section.

When tackling an AAA song, a novice writer might wonder, "How many verses is enough? How many is too many?" Jimmy Webb needed only three verses to tell his story in "By the Time I Get to Phoenix." "Ode to Billy Joe" uses five verses. Chris Rice wrote six simple but elegant verses for his "Untitled Hymn (Come to Jesus)." A good AAA song typically has at least three verses (although many praise-and-worship songs make do with only two). The real determining factors should be 1) the demands of the story and 2) the patience of the listener. If the story demands five verses, or even six or seven, then go for it. Always keep in mind, however, your listener's willingness to continue listening. Don't wear out your welcome with six verses if you could have told the same story with only four. The tempo of the song may help when deciding how many verses is enough. Slower tempos will likely mean fewer verses. Faster tempos can accommodate more verses.

Though it is not used as much these days, the AAA song form is still a valid and effective one. Great writers like Chris Rice are still finding gems in this old mine. If you have never written an AAA song, make it your goal to tackle this tried-and-true song form. Study the great AAA songs of the past and see what you can create today.

AAA SONGS—AN INCOMPLETE LIST

Here are some AAA songs (writers in parentheses) that demonstrate the power and the flexibility of this simple song form.

"Amazing Grace" (John Newton)

"Big Yellow Taxi" (Joni Mitchell)

"Blowin' in the Wind" (Bob Dylan)

"Born in the USA" (Bruce Springsteen)

"By the Time I Get to Phoenix" (Jimmy Webb)

"The Downeaster Alexa" (Billy Joel)

"I Walk the Line" (Johnny Cash)

"Ode to Billy Joe" (Bobbie Gentry)

"On Broadway" (Leiber and Stoller)

"Scarborough Fair" (Paul Simon)

"Turn, Turn, Turn" (Pete Seeger)

"Welcome to Our World" (Chris Rice)

The AABA Song Form

Once upon a time, long ago and far away, there was a medieval troubadour and songwriter named Bruce of York who had grown weary of the simple AAA song form. Loitering about the castle one day, waiting to begin his next show for the king's Feast of the Full Moon, Bruce grumbled to his fellow musicians.

"Alas, it is always AAA," Bruce said. "Nothing but A's. It has become a royal drag to me."

His bandmates nodded in agreement. "We can dig it, Bruce. But pray tell what can we do about it? Three A's is the form we always play. And it has ever been thus."

Bruce of York replied, "Perhaps that it so. Still methinks I shall write a B section."

His buddies gasped, "A B section! Forsooth, dude, that has never been done before in the history of song!"

The innovator pondered for a moment. "'Tis true what you say. But after two times through the A section, I am bummed and I long for a variation in the melody. Dig? So I'll throw a B section in there, after the second A. After the B, I'll come back to the A one final time to cap things off."

"Righteous, my good man," the band responded. "Righteous."

Okay, so maybe that's not how the AABA song form came to be, but we do know it has been around for a long time. In the mid-1800s, Stephen Foster wrote "Beautiful Dreamer" and "I Dream of Jeannie with the Light Brown Hair," both of which have an expanded AABA form. In fact, from about 1910 to 1960 the AABA song form was the de facto standard for American songwriters, including Broadway and Tin Pan Alley masters such as Jerome Kern, George and Ira Gershwin, Irving Berlin, and Rodgers and Hammerstein. It is short and concise, built with four sections of eight measures each, for a total of 32 bars. It is melody-driven, making the song easy to remember. The AABA form was used in virtually every pop and country music standard written from 1930 to 1960. The American Film Institute's list of the Top 100 Movie Songs of the Past 100 Years is made up almost entirely of AABA songs.

AABA SONGS—AN INCOMPLETE LIST
There are literally thousands of famous titles to use as examples of this form. Here are a dozen you should study and learn:

"Crazy" (Willie Nelson)

"If I Loved You" (Rodgers and Hammerstein)

"Just the Way You Are" (Billy Joel)

"Mary Did You Know" (Mark Lowry and Buddy Green)

"On the Street Where You Live" (Lerner and Lowe)

"Over the Rainbow" (Harold Arlen and "Yip" Harburg)

"Raindrops Keep Falling on My Head" (Bacharach and David)

"Something" (George Harrison)

"This Day" (Lowell Alexander)

"To Make You Feel My Love" (Bob Dylan)

"The Way You Look Tonight" (Dorothy Fields and Jerome Kern)

"Yesterday" (Lennon and McCartney)

EXAMINING THE AABA FORM
Here is a simple diagram of the classic AABA song form:

A (8 bars; title/hook in the first or last line)

A (8 bars; same music with new words; title/hook in the first or last line)

B (8 bars; new music; lyric focus shifts)

A (8 bars; original tune w/new words; title/hook in first or last line)

The AABA form is elegant. Because it is melody-driven, the form flows. Sheila Davis puts it this way: "In contrast to the stop-start quality of both the AAA and the verse/chorus, the AABA expresses one moment's feeling in a fluid statement" (*The Craft of Lyric Writing,* p. 62). Expressing that "one moment's feeling" is the difficult job of the lyricist. Most AABA songs begin with the music, and lyrics are written to the tune. But unlike for the composer, who gets to repeat the A section, there is no repeating for the lyricist. Each section has new lyrics. Like its AAA cousin, the AABA creates a challenge for the lyricist to keep the story moving. There is no rest stop at the chorus, because there is no chorus.

Some people mistakenly refer to the B section as the chorus. The more accurate and common name for the B section is the *bridge*, or the *release*. Both names describe the function of the B section, which is to release from the second A and bridge back to the final A. Just as the music of the B section takes the listener someplace new, so should the lyrics of the B section. The B section is a perfect time to shift gears from the general to the specific, to change directions, draw a conclusion, or dig deeper into the subject of the song.

EXPANDING THE AABA

Like the AAA form, writers have created successful variations of the AABA. These variations keep the form fresh and alive. The most common alteration would be the expanded AABA (AABABA). By simply repeating the B section and the final A section, the song is stretched a bit. To the untrained ear, the end result can resemble the verse/chorus form. But don't be fooled. Check out the placement of the hook/title and the power of the A section's melody, and you'll know it's really an AABA song.

Twila Paris truly expanded the AABA form in her song "How Beautiful." The A sections are each made up of two smaller sections with an added extension. The B section is 20 measures long. Here's the form of the song:

A (a1 + a2 + extension)

A (a1 + a2 + extension)

B (20 measures)

A (a1 + a2 + extension)

Sometimes in the expanded AABA, new lyrics are written for the second B and/or the final A. Andrew Lloyd Webber and Trevor Nunn employed this expanded form in "Memory," from the musical *Cats*. It looks like this:

A – **A** – **B** – **A** – **B** (new lyric) – **A** (new lyric)

Hit machine extraordinaire, Carole Bayer Sager, expanded the AABA this way for Leo Sayer's big song "When I Need You":

A – **A** – **B** – **A** (repeat first A) - **B** (new lyric) – **A** (repeat second A)

In "Just the Way You Are," Billy Joel expanded the form still another way:

A – **A** – **musical interlude** – **A** – **A** - **B** – **A**

Gordon Sumner, aka "Sting," really opened up the form with "Every Breath You Take," by adding a C section to the song.

A – **A** – **B** – **A** – **C** – **B** – **A** (repeat third A)

It seems that hundreds of new praise-and-worship songs are being written every day. Because the writers want the songs to be easy to learn, simplicity is a key element in their construction. Frequently the writers compose only a single A section and a single B section. Instinctively, however, they almost always repeat the first A before going to the B, and then follow up with a final A. The end result feels like an AABA form. "Come, Now Is the Time to Worship," by Brian Doerksen, is a good illustration of this:

A – A (exact repeat) – **B – A** (repeat of 1st A)

It occurs to me that with a little more work in the lyric department, worship songs with this simplified structure could be made into a genuine AABA song, offering a deeper or more complete thought to the worshipper.

Many Christian songwriters never try their hand at composing a song with the AABA form. That's too bad, really. It is a wonderfully expressive, melodically powerful song form. If you haven't yet written an AABA song, you don't know what you're missing. Give it a try, and discover what great songwriters have known for generations.

The ABAB/ABAC Form

There is another song form so closely related to the AABA form that I am including it here as a sort of "first cousin" of the AABA form. The ABAB form and its own variation, of ABAC, have fallen out of vogue despite the substantial number of song standards crafted this way. The ABAB and ABAC normally have a 32-bar structure, built with two 16-bar sections "joined together rather like Siamese twins" (*The Craft of Lyric Writing*, p. 73). In the case of the ABAB, the two halves are musically identical. For the ABAC, the final C resembles the B but contains some variations. What makes this form so closely related to the AABA form is that, like the AABA, the lyrics represent a seamless continual thought. The B section, even though the music repeats, is definitely not a chorus.

"Fly Me to the Moon," by Bart Howard, is a classic example of the ABAB form, which looks something like this:

A (8 bars; title/hook generally in the first line)

B (8 bars; new music that "completes" the A; title/hook may be placed in the last line if it is not in the A section)

A–B (8 + 8 bars; repeat the form with new words; maintain title/hook placement)

The ABAC form is simply a variation of the ABAB. The C section is essentially an altered B section. Henry Mancini and Johnny Mercer used this form to win Oscars for their masterpieces "Moon River" and "The Days of Wine and Roses."

The Verse/Chorus Song Form

Since the early 1960s, the verse/chorus song form has come to dominate popular songwriting. That may be because the form, with its repetitive memorable chorus, is so "radio friendly." The vast majority of pop, country, and R&B hits written since 1960 use the verse/chorus song form. That is not to say that the verse/chorus form is new. It's been around a long time. The very first song to sell a million copies in America was a verse/chorus song called "After the Ball." Charles Harris wrote it in 1892. Keep in mind that this was prior to the advent of recording technology. The million copies sold were sheet music!

EXAMINING THE VERSE/CHORUS FORM

In its most basic form, the verse/chorus song is built from two distinct musical pieces: the verses, which tell the story of the song, and the chorus, which contains the title and/or hook. The chorus has distinctively different music from the verses, usually charged with more energy, and it is repeated between the verses. The verse/chorus form is sometimes mistakenly referred to as an ABAB form. But as you now know from the preceding definition of the ABAB form, they are two different song forms.

There are countless variations on the verse/chorus form, but this is what the basic version looks like:

A (verse 1)
B (chorus; title/hook in first and/or last line)
A (verse 2)
B (chorus; title/hook in first and/or last line)
B (chorus; title/hook in first and/or last line)

Here are some common variations of the verse/chorus form:

A (verse 1)
A (verse 2)
B (chorus; contains hook/title)
A (verse 3)
B (chorus; repeated two or more times)

Or

A (verse 1)
B (channel)
C (chorus; contains hook/title)
A (verse 2)
B (channel)
C (chorus; repeated ad infinitum)

Or how about:

A (verse 1)
B (chorus; contains hook/title)
A (verse 2)
B (chorus; contains hook/title)
C (bridge)
B (chorus; repeated ad nauseum)

The verse/chorus song can even begin with the chorus, like this:

A (chorus; contains hook/title)
B (verse 1)
A (chorus; contains hook/title)
B (verse 2)
A (chorus; contains hook/title)

There is almost no limit to the possible combinations for the verse/chorus song. It's kind of like eating at your favorite Mexican restaurant. Practically every dish on the menu uses the same five or six ingredients, but there are 300 items on the menu to choose from. Since there are so many variations of this form, let's take a look at the individual parts of a verse/chorus song and see how each piece functions within it. That way, you will better understand how to assemble your next verse/chorus song.

All verse/chorus songs are made up of four primary building blocks: the *verse*, the *chorus*, the *channel*, and the *bridge*. All verse/chorus songs use the first two blocks. The channel and the bridge are optional blocks for the songwriter to use to build a more complex song. Let's examine each building block in the order that it typically appears in a song's lyrics.

The Verse

SET UP THE CHORUS

The verses of a song contain the lion's share of the song's information. If there is a story being told, the verses do most of the storytelling. As each verse unfolds, it should lead directly to the chorus (or the channel, if the song uses a channel). The verse's job is to set up the chorus, making the chorus the inevitable result of the verse. The listener should be made to feel that the chorus is the only logical answer to the verse. That means every line of the verse should relate to the chorus somehow. When done well, the listener will almost be able to guess what the chorus will say (*almost*, but not quite.) If the verse isn't leading smoothly into the chorus (or channel), then it's not doing its job. In my role as a teacher and adjudicator for the Gospel Music Association, I have seen lots of songs that had good verses and good choruses. The problem was that the verses didn't have anything to do with the chorus! There was no logical connection. Imagine the verses from the Beatles' "Get Back" leading to the chorus of "All You Need Is Love." It just doesn't work. The verses must set up and connect to the chorus. In fact, every line of every verse should support and somehow lead directly to the chorus. Otherwise, the line is serving no purpose but to fill space.

> *Figuring out where to go after the first chorus is one of the hardest problems that songwriters face … It's called second-verse hell.*
> —PAT PATTISION, *Writing Better Lyrics*, p. 47

MULTIPLE VERSES, ONE CHORUS

It's essential for a songwriter to know how to write multiple verses that lead to the same chorus in different ways, thus making the chorus a nice surprise each time it comes around. The second verse cannot simply be a repeat of the first verse. (Yawn.) The second verse (and third, if there is one) must be a progression of the story or a new spin on the song's subject matter. Each verse must shine a different light (if only slightly different) on the chorus. That way, each repeated chorus has new meaning and a bigger payoff for the listener. You can accomplish this all-important technique in lots of ways. Some are more dramatic than others, but they are all effective. Here are a few methods that work, along with examples of songs that use them:

1. **From the general to the specific/personal.** If the first verse speaks in general terms to the point of the song, the second verse can speak in specific, or personal terms. The reverse also works—from the specific/personal to the general.

    Examples of this technique are "Life, Love, and Other Mysteries" (Regie Hamm and Joel Lindsey), "Honesty" (Billy Joel), "Where There Is Faith" (Billy Simon), "God of Wonders" (Steve Hindalong and Marc Byrd).

2. **The "next chapter."** This is aimed not so much at "story" songs, but at songs that are making a point about something without a specific narrative. (If a song is a "story" song, then each verse should tell a little more of the plot.) In the case of songs without a specific narrative, each verse expands the point of the song, fleshing it out further.

    Examples of this technique are "He Reigns" (Peter Furler and Steve Taylor), "Go West, Young Man" (Wayne Kirkpatrick and Michael W. Smith), "Speechless" (Steven Curtis Chapman), "We Shall Behold Him" (Dottie Rambo).

3. **The parallel image.** Verse 1 and verse 2 parallel, or mirror, one another. If verse 1 is about daytime, verse 2 is about night. If the first verse describes the actions of one individual, the second verse describes the similar actions of a completely different individual. If the first verse is about victory, the second is about loss.

    Examples of this technique are "Blue Skies" (Grant Cunningham and Matt Huesmann), "Love Enough" (Robert Sterling and Scott Williamson), "In Christ Alone" (Don Koch and Shawn Craig).

4. **The Bible story to modern application.** This is a popular technique of Christian songwriters. The first verse tells a familiar Bible story, and the chorus makes the point of the song. Then the second verse tells how the same applies to us today. The chorus has a modern application as well. Southern Gospel songwriters love using this technique. And it works in reverse, too.

   Examples of this technique are "One More Chance" (Robert Sterling and Tony Wood), "Samaritan's Heart" (Rodney Griffin), "For the Sake of the Call" (Steven Curtis Chapman).

5. **From personal story to application.** This is similar to the previous technique, except the writer tells a personal story in verse 1, and then makes a broader application in verse 2.

   Examples of this technique are: "No More Pain" (Geoff and Becky Thurman), "God Only Knows" (Robert Sterling).

6. **Surprise twist in the story.** A favorite of country songwriters, this technique can deliver a powerful emotional punch. A surprise twist in the story happens in verse 2 (or 3), which gives the repeated chorus new and deeper meaning.

   Examples of this technique are "Love, Me" (Collin Raye), "Where've You Been" (Jon Vezner), "Tie a Yellow Ribbon" (Russell Brown and Irwin Levine), "Butterfly Kisses" (Bob Carlisle and Randy Thomas).

MAKE THE VERSES MATCH

Logically, all the verses in a verse/chorus song should be the same length and use the same music. Why? Musical repetition is important in commercial songwriting. If the verses are not the same length and don't match one another rhythmically, then it will be impossible for the music to repeat. So, the words of all the verses of a song should pretty closely match one another in rhythm and duration. In the old days of Tin Pan Alley, songwriters made certain each verse was rhythmically identical to the others. Slight variations in the rhythm patterns of the verses were *verboten,* or forbidden. That is no longer the case with pop music. Minor rhythmic variations are perfectly acceptable. Note—I said *minor* variations. This is not an excuse for laziness. The rhythmic scheme of the lyrics (known as *scansion*) should match as closely as possible from one verse to the next. Also, a song's verses should all contain the same number of lines and use the same number of measures. If they don't match, it should be for a good reason—not because the writer wasn't paying attention.

HOW MANY IS TOO MANY? HOW LONG IS TOO LONG?

A verse/chorus song will have at least two verses, and sometimes three or more. In today's homogenized world of commercial radio, hit songs rarely have more than two verses. If the verses are short, the writer might choose to begin with two verses before going to the chorus. If the verses are longer, a single verse prior to the first chorus is probably plenty. If there is a story to tell, the lyricist might need two, or even three verses to get the narrative out before the first chorus. Don Francisco used a full *eight* (count 'em—eight!) verses in his epic song "He's Alive!" before he ever got to the chorus. I don't recommend that approach to the faint of heart.

There is no rule for the length of a verse. They come in every size. I suppose a classic song verse would be eight bars long, built of four lines of two bars each. There are, however, thousands of exceptions to that. (If your verses run over 16 measures, you probably should consider a little editing.) The tempo of the song can also affect the number and length of the verses. The old rule-of-thumb for radio hits was "Get to the chorus within 60 seconds from the downbeat of the song." I'm not so sure that's a hard-and-fast rule, but there is wisdom in it. These days, listener attention spans are shorter than ever before, and songs are spare and lean. The contemporary songwriter cannot afford to waste words. Don't take four verses to say what could have been said in three, or even two.

The Channel

The channel is a brief section that falls seamlessly between the verse and the chorus. It is also known as a *prechorus*, a *climb*, a *lift*, a *lead-in*, and probably some more names I can't recall right now. Each of these names is quite descriptive of the channel's place and purpose in the song: it "channels" or "lifts" the verse to the chorus and helps the song "climb" from the verse to the chorus. The channel's primary purpose is musical—to add excitement or to shift the song into a higher gear as it approaches the chorus. For the lyricist, the channel is an opportunity to wrap up the general information of the verse and make the transition into the specifics of the chorus. Just as the channel's music heightens the action or tension of the song, so should its lyrics. Typically, a channel is brief—only one or two lines long. The lyrics for the channel may be different for each verse, or they may be repeated with each verse. There is no set rule in that regard. A song with a prominent or significant channel often does not need a bridge.

The Chorus

The chorus is the centerpiece of the verse/chorus song form. It is the succinct, crystallizing, easy-to-remember "Aha!" moment when the song comes into complete focus. If a song is about *one thing* (and it is), then that *one thing* is summed up in the chorus. If your song has a point (and it should), then that point is made in the chorus.

The chorus almost always contains the hook line and/or title of the song. (The hook line and the title are usually the same.) There are rare successful exceptions to this, but don't use them as an excuse to misplace your hook in the bridge of your song. If the chorus is the focal point of the song, then the hook line is the focal point of the chorus. Just as every line of the verses should relate to the chorus, every line of the chorus should relate to the hook/title.

More often than not, the hook appears in the first or last line of the chorus, and sometimes in both. Some songs will place the hook in the middle of the chorus, as well. There is no set rule about the hook line/title placement. But it stands to reason that if the hook line is the focal point of the entire song, then it should land in a prominent spot. And there is no more prominent landing spot in a verse/chorus song than the first or the last line of the chorus.

Ideally, the chorus is exactly the same each time it is sung. We all want our songs to be memorable, and the repeating chorus is the tried-and-true way to accomplish that goal. Gifted songwriters occasionally make subtle changes in a chorus without burdening the listener's ears and memory. Generally, when a chorus changes in a verse/chorus song, it is the final chorus that is altered. Typically, the changes are made to accommodate a surprise in the story or to provide a special twist on the hook line. The beginning songwriter should work to master the use of one chorus per song before tackling the altered chorus.

The Bridge

Sometimes two verses and a killer chorus repeated a dozen times just aren't enough to satisfy. Sometimes you need a little something extra to ensure that the final chorus gets the lift it deserves. Sometimes you have one more thing you just *have* to say. Those are the times you need a bridge. A great bridge can elevate a song to new heights. A great bridge will surprise your listeners just when they think they've heard it all. A great bridge gives new energy to a song in its waning moments.

Typically, the bridge occurs near the end of a song. It is usually brief (only two to four lines long) and provides a contrast to the rest of the song. After all the verses have been sung, followed by the second (or third) chorus, the bridge is inserted before the final chorus.

Here is a simple diagram to illustrate:

A (verse 1)

B (chorus)

A (verse 2)

B (chorus)

C (bridge)

B (chorus—repeated)

For the lyricist, a bridge offers a final opportunity to say something new, to shine a light on the subject matter from a different perspective. It should connect to the rest of the song but somehow be an independent thought. The bridge can sum up the point of the song, but it should not simply restate what the chorus says.

There are those rare but effective exceptions when the bridge is placed somewhere other than the normal spot between two choruses. In the hit song "Undivided," writer Melodie Tunney created a new twist on the form by placing the bridge after the third verse and before the final choruses, like this: verse/verse/chorus/verse/bridge/chorus/chorus.

The most unique use of a bridge I have ever seen is in the song "The Year of Our Lord," by the late master songwriter, Gary Driskell. (Gary also wrote the Song of the Year Christian smash "Another Time, Another Place" for Sandi Patti.) In "The Year of Our Lord," the form goes as follows: verse-chorus-verse-chorus-interlude-bridge-bridge-bridge-bridge. In this case, the bridge serves almost as an additional "surprise chorus." Several artists have cut the song, and not all used the bridge in this manner, choosing instead to return to the chorus after one bridge. But I heard Gary's demo, and this unusual format was definitely the way he designed the song to be sung.

Not every song requires a bridge. I have written bridges for songs, only to decide later they were unnecessary. (What do you do with the bridge you're about to throw away? Put it in your song files. It might come in handy on another song.) Knowing when to use a bridge is entirely a matter of what feels right to the writer. If you reach the end of your song and it doesn't feel finished, maybe you need a bridge. If you've written a song with a bridge and the song feels too long, maybe the bridge needs to go. Let your instincts be your guide.

VERSE/CHORUS SONGS—AN INCOMPLETE LIST

There are no fewer than a thousand verse/chorus songs I could list as examples to demonstrate a great chorus with a truly memorable hook. Here are a dozen that you should know instantly. Study them.

"9 to 5" (Dolly Parton)

"Another Time, Another Place" (Gary Driskell)

"Awesome God" (Rich Mullins)

"Because He Lives" (Bill and Gloria Gaither)

"Change the World" (Gordon Kennedy, Wayne Kirkpatrick, and Tommy Sims)

"The Gambler" (Don Schlitz)

"Hotel California" (Don Felder, Glenn Frey, and Don Henley)

"In Christ Alone" (Shawn Craig and Don Koch)

"Keep the Candle Burning" (Lowell Alexander, Gayla Borders, and Jeff Borders)

"Let It Be" (Lennon and McCartney)

"Up Where We Belong" (Will Jennings, Jack Nitzsche, and Buffy Sainte-Marie)

"You've Lost That Lovin' Feeling" (Barry Mann, Phil Spector, and Cynthia Weil)

Coda

The greatest temptation for a beginning songwriter is to jump headlong into every song with complete abandon. Pure spontaneity equals pure joy. Unfettered creativity is bliss. Well, at the risk of tossing a wet blanket on your creative fire, let me encourage you to think for a bit before you throw yourself into writing. If it makes you feel any better, remind yourself that thinking is part of writing. (The preparation and incubation processes are just as important as illumination.) Before you fill up three pages of a legal pad with lyric ideas, answer the five preparation questions listed in the early part of this chapter. You'll write better songs if you do.

As for song form, I encourage you to work with all three forms and their variations. Too many beginners stick exclusively with the verse/chorus form and never discover the strength of the AAA form or the elegance of the AABA form. Conquer them all in their most basic state, and then you can alter them to suit your own creativity. Study the work of the masters—the songsmiths of Tin Pan Alley and Music City, USA; the writers of the American songbook; and the authors of our greatest hymns. Soon all three song forms will become second nature in your songwriting.

Lyrical Odds And Ends (Key Lines, Word Play, and Economy)

Leftovers

This chapter covers three important subjects that refused to fit neatly in any of the other chapters of this book. This is specific information that didn't belong in the big-picture concepts of chapters 1 and 2. Nor did this material want to snuggle up with the chapters on song form (chapter 3) and poetic devices (chapter 5). So, I had no choice but to build a home for this material. Do not skip over this chapter! There's plenty of good stuff here.

Key Lines

It would be true enough for me to say that every line of a song's lyric is important. After all, every line should be important to the lyricist—especially the Christian lyricist (*Jesus' chairs, Jesus' chairs, Jesus' chairs*). However, there are two lines that are arguably more important than the rest: the **opening line** of the lyrics and the **hook**.

In Their Own Words: What is the most intriguing opening line you've ever written?

When days of the year closely press one another
  The light, though as bright, is as cool as the dawn"

It was a Christmas song, and I was trying to set a mood of winter.
—CHARLES F. BROWN

You know that life is like a million miles of railroad
  And sometimes this train I'm taking seems to go much too fast.

It came from a picture in my head. I guess I like the romanticism and melancholy of trains.
—LOWELL ALEXANDER

THE OPENING LINE

The opening line is the writer's best and sometimes only opportunity to grab the audience's attention. If you don't get them with the first line, chances are they won't stay tuned for the terrific chorus you wrote. Your little song has to compete with 200 channels of cable TV, AM radio, FM radio, and now satellite radio for the attention of anyone who will listen. You gotta grab 'em with a solid opening line, and don't let go until your song is over.

The opening line is a crucial moment in a song. It creates the all-important first impression the listener will make of your work. It sets the stage for every word that follows, establishing an attitude or tone for the entire set of lyrics. Once, I agreed to write music for lyrics based on nothing more than the strength of their opening line. Terry Cox, the lyricist, started her song, called "A River Called Rubicon," with one of the most intriguing lines I had ever read: "Fear has a traitor's lips / It will twist the words you say." I didn't need to read any further. I knew after those few words that I wanted to work on the song with her. (The rest of the lyrics didn't let me down, either.)

Here are just a few well-written opening lines you should recognize. They are all good attention getters.

Yesterday all my troubles seemed so far away. —from "Yesterday," by Paul McCartney

They got little hands and little eyes / They walk around tellin' great big lies. —from "Short People," by Randy Newman

Some people stay far away from the door / If there's a chance of it opening up. —from "Innocent Man," by Billy Joel

Every evening sky, an invitation / To trace the patterned stars. —from "Every Season," by Nicole Nordeman

Things change, plans fail / And you look for love on a grander scale. —from "Jesus Will Still Be There," by Robert Sterling and John Mandeville

How do you keep the music playing? / How do you make it last? —from "How Do You Keep the Music Playing," by Marilyn and Alan Bergman and Michel LeGrand

Moon River, wider than a mile / I'm crossing you in style some day —from "Moon River," by Johnny Mercer and Henry Mancini

Take a moment and think of a few of your favorite songs. Chances are that they have interesting, maybe even arresting, opening lines.

In Their Own Words: What role does a good hook play in your writing process?

> *There's a reason people say certain songs "write themselves." Those are the ones that start with a truly great hook. Then you just have to get out of the way and not mess it up.* —SUE SMITH
>
> *I love having the title first. It makes the rest of the blank page a lot less intimidating.* —DEBORAH CRAIG-CLAAR
>
> *I generally don't start until I have the hook. I may have a couple of lines on a scrap of paper, but until I have my hook (or my North Star for that song) I don't know where those lines fit into the development of the idea.* —TONY WOOD
>
> *If I've got the hook, I'm home free.* —CLAIRE CLONINGER

THE HOOK LINE/TITLE

I briefly covered the term *hook* in the previous chapter in the discussion on song form. Now I'd like to go into a little more detail. Simply put, the term is a metaphor referring to the line in a song that grabs the listener's attention and sticks in the mind after the song is over. In 99 out of 100 verse/chorus songs, the hook is the title of the song. It is almost always placed prominently in the chorus, often in the first or the last line, and sometimes both. Experienced songwriters salivate over a great hook line. As all serious country songwriters know, a great hook is as good as gold—a gold record, that is. It's important that the lyric hook be linked to the strongest musical (the musical phrase that is also the most memorable) hook in the melody.

One identifying characteristic of a great hook is that the line is a microcosm of the entire song. In that one brief phrase, the writer sums up the point of the entire set of lyrics. Ironically, in the writing process it is the reverse that usually occurs; the writer usually begins with the hook and works backwards to write the lyrics. But once the song has been finished, it appears as though the words were seamlessly written in sequence, and that the only logical place to land was the hook itself.

Here are a handful of heavyweight hook lines/song titles memorable for both their lyrical clarity and their musical strength:

"Ain't No Mountain High Enough" (Nick Ashford and Valerie Simpson)

"Bridge Over Troubled Water" (Paul Simon)

"El Shaddai" (Michael Card and John Thompson)

"Friend of a Wounded Heart" (Claire Cloninger and Wayne Watson)

"Friends in Low Places" (Earl Bud Lee and DeWayne Blackwell)

"Keep the Candle Burning" (Lowell Alexander, Gayla Borders, and Jeff Borders)

"The Heart of Rock and Roll (Is Still Beating)" (Huey Lewis)

"King of the Road" (Roger Miller)

"Over the Rainbow" (Harold Arlen and E. Y. "Yip" Harburg)

"Takin' It to the Streets" (Michael McDonald)

"Welcome to Our World" (Chris Rice)

"Will You Still Love Me Tomorrow?" (Gerry Goffin and Carole King)

Again, take a moment and think of some of your favorite songs. My guess is most if not all of them will have strong hook lines and titles.

> *People need a headline before they'll commit to buying a newspaper.*
> *The title is the headline. Give it to them.*
> —MOLLY-ANN LEIKEN, *How to Write a Hit Song*, p. 43

There are plenty of exceptions to the rule about the hook and the title being one and the same. Many terrific songs have been written in which the title isn't the hook line. The most memorable line from "The Gambler," written by Don Schlitz and made famous by Kenny Rogers, is "You gotta know when to hold 'em / Know when to fold 'em." That's the real hook line in the song, but it isn't the title. In "The Living Years," by Mike Rutherford and B. A. Robertson, the title appears twice—at the end of the first verse and at the end of the last verse. The hook of the song is its chorus, which expresses the simple, childlike truth: "It's too late when we die / To admit we don't see eye to eye." When I first heard the Doobie Brothers' hit song "Long Train Running," by Tom Johnston, I thought the title was "Without Love, Where Would We Be Now," because that's the memorable line from the chorus. These exceptions demonstrate that once a talented songwriter has mastered the rules of songwriting, he can purposefully and successfully break those rules.

Words, Words, Words

THE BIG BOX OF CRAYONS

Here's another case where I am going to state the incredibly obvious because, believe it or not, it's not obvious to everybody—a good songwriter needs a healthy command of the English language. Any kid will tell you it's better to have the big box of 64 crayons to color with, rather than the small box of 8. More crayons mean more choices. More choices mean a more colorful drawing, and more fun. Unfortunately, too many songwriters are working with the small box of crayons when it comes to their vocabulary. They rely on the same basic blue, red, and green—a handful of adjectives, verbs, and nouns used over and over in their songs. They recycle favorite catchphrases and fail to dig for the occasional synonym that might liven up their song. For example, if a song makes repeated references to a rose, the writer should find as many ways to evoke the image of a rose without using the word "rose." "Thorny flower," "crimson bloom," "ruby petals"—there are three quick possibilities. The overuse of any word will tend to dull its significance. I am not suggesting that to be a good songwriter you must memorize the latest edition of *Merriam-Webster's* or have the vocabulary of William F. Buckley, Jr. I am suggesting, however, that the more words you know, the more clearly and more creatively you will be able to express yourself. In other words, splurge on the big box of crayons.

Novice Christian songwriters are as guilty of this language laziness as other songwriters. Too often they repeat the same "church words" over and over—words like "glorify" and "magnify" and "anointed." (More about church words later.) Suffice it to say, even words as rich in meaning as "glory" or "praise" or "mercy" can become all but meaningless if they are used incessantly and without distinction.

NOT-SO-ORDINARY ORDINARY WORDS

Most of the words we use in commercial song lyrics are simple everyday ones. That's a good thing. Songwriting is a contemporary commercial art form. Our audience is made up mostly of ordinary folks, and we should speak to them using ordinary words. However, a good songwriter knows how to use normal, everyday words in unexpected ways, turning an ordinary word into something special. The unexpected twist on an everyday word or phrase often results in a much-needed word picture, which makes the lyrics more memorable. In "People Need the Lord," Greg Nelson and Phill McHugh wrote this seemingly simple line in verse 1: "On they go through private pain / Living fear to fear." There are no unusual words in the phrase, but the writers certainly found a new way to use ordinary words. What a great twist on the phrase "living day to day" to change it to "living fear to fear." It creates a powerful word picture that strikes a nerve with the listener. Put new life in your lyrics. Use ordinary words in not-so-ordinary ways.

HEY, EVERYBODY—LOOK HOW SMART I AM!

As your vocabulary expands, you will find all sorts of unusual words that might work in your songs. Terrific! Words that are a little bit out of the ordinary can enhance a lyric, if they are used sparingly. Like spices in food, a little goes a long way. Unusual words should be placed in the lyrics with thought and care. Otherwise, they risk losing their effectiveness. For example, "repartee" is a clever and unusual word that means "witty conversation"; it is the kind of word that a smart songwriter will carefully use only once in a song. So be wise with the use of words that aren't so ordinary. A song is not the place to try out the Reader's Digest "Word of the Day." Audiences shouldn't need a dictionary to understand your lyrics.

Here is an excellent example of a lyric that employs mostly ordinary words in fresh ways, and then springs an unusual word, "paragon," on the listener. This is the first verse of Michael W. Smith's hit "Secret Ambition."

> *Young man up on the hillside teaching new ways*
> *Each word winning them over; each heart a kindled flame.*
> *Old men watching from the outside guarding their prey;*
> *They're threatened by the voice of the paragon*
> *Leading their lambs away.*

WORDS AND MUSIC BY WAYNE KIRKPATRICK, AMY GRANT, AND MICHAEL W. SMITH
© 1990 by Riverstone Music, Careers BMG Music Publishing, Sony/ATV Songs LLC

Two of the best tools lyricists have to make themselves instantly smarter are a quality dictionary and an easy-to-use thesaurus. There are dozens of these books to choose from at your local bookstore. Find the ones that suit you best. I prefer a modern thesaurus that is laid out dictionary-style to the original Roget's version. You may prefer to use a software-based online dictionary at your computer. Novice writers might consider these books a crutch. Not so. A quality dictionary and thesaurus are must-have tools for the serious writer. (A good rhyming dictionary is another must-have. More about that later in the discussion about rhyme in chapter 5, "Poetic Devices.")

Clichés—Words That Don't Cut Like a Knife

Beware the cliché, for it is a sneaky thing. At first glance, it sounds comfortable—maybe even clever or inventive. Clichés will slip into your lyrics and try to convince you that they "fit like a glove." The cliché fills you with the "false hope" that it is the lyric that will "see you through." Instead, when you learn "the awful truth," and realize that the cliché has "done you wrong," you can hardly "stand the pain." In desperation, you convince yourself that you "just can't go on."

All clichés were, at one time, fresh and new ideas. When they were first used, these phrases were innovative expressions. (That's why they caught on in the first place, I suppose.) Over time, many have become everyday conversational idioms. That makes them very easy to use in lyrics. But clichés become stale and commonplace from their constant use. They lose their power to create vibrant verbal pictures. They hide themselves effectively in lyrics because they give the false impression of substance. Don't be fooled. Clichés are empty and impotent. Occasionally, in the hands of a skilled songwriter, a cliché can be used to good effect. The beginner, however, would be well advised to avoid clichés "like the plague."

> *Clichés are other people's licks. They don't come from your emotions.*
> —PAT PATTISON, *Writing Better Lyrics*, p. 32

Church Words

Earlier I mentioned the use of church words. Church words are those many familiar words and phrases we use in church but not much anywhere else. Here are a few examples: *glorify, sanctify, anointed, washed in the blood, born again, righteous, exalted, Calvary, Golgotha, diadem, hosanna, alleluia.* The list goes on, but I think you know the words and phrases I'm talking about. I caution all Christian songwriters, beginners in particular, to be careful with the use of these phrases.

Why should we be careful with these words? After all, they are perfectly useable words, deep in meaning and rich in tradition. They are used liberally in hymns and praise-and-worship songs. They appear in many popular Southern gospel songs. I believe that there are two reasons to be concerned about using church words:

Reason 1   Some church words have been used so much that they have become tired and clichéd and are little more than familiar catchphrases. (See my previous warning about clichés.) We need to let them rest awhile before we use them again. We need to find new ways to say what these old chestnuts have said for so long. At the very least, we should use them more thoughtfully and sparingly.

Reason 2   While these church words may be potent to the church Body, they have very little meaning to folks less familiar with the idioms of the church. In fact, phrases such as "washed in the blood" sound positively barbaric to some. If you are writing implicit Christian songs and your intended audience is unfamiliar with traditional gospel music, or even the Gospel message, you may well find the use of church words works against you.

That said, these words and phrases still do have deep meaning for many who were raised in the church. If those are the people in your intended audience, go ahead and use these words. Still, I encourage you to find fresh ways to say the same things and avoid the most overused of these phrases.

Write Naturally

For the most part, good pop lyrics are conversational. We live in informal times, and we converse with one another informally. Our most popular songs reflect this. The beginning Christian songwriter should work to avoid stiff and stilted language that doesn't sound real. As Leiken writes, "Sing it the way you say it" (*How to Write a Hit Song*, p. 18). Steer clear of archaic language. Old and out-of-use words sound phony in lyrics, unless they are used deliberately and effectively. If lyrics sound conversational and believable when they're read aloud, chances are they will sing the same way.

There are times when it is completely appropriate to use a more elevated tone of language in a song, particularly when writing music for the church. I am noticing a trend toward loftier lyrics among certain writers who are composing modern hymns. They have discovered that casual language can sound fluffy and even irreverent when referring to God the Father, the Trinity, and other such weighty subjects. When you choose to write this way, be sure to be consistent. A lyric should have a unified tone. Don't move from lofty to casual and back to lofty. Choose an approach and stick with it throughout the song.

A good example of this sort of writing is the new hymn "In Christ Alone," by Stuart Townend and Keith Getty. They have written a serious and thoughtful hymn text without ever sounding preachy or churchy. Here is the first stanza, to demonstrate:

> *In Christ alone my hope is found.*
> *He is my light, my strength, my song.*
> *This Cornerstone, this solid ground,*
> *Firm through the fiercest drought and storm.*
> *What heights of love, what depths of peace,*
> *When fears are stilled, when strivings cease!*
> *My Comforter, my all in all,*
> *Here in the love of Christ I stand.*

WORDS AND MUSIC BY STUART TOWNEND AND KEITH GETTY
© 2002 Thankyou Music (admin. worldwide by Worshiptogether.com Songs)

With the possible exception of the phrase "my all in all," which has been done before, the writers used ordinary words in new ways. The lyrics are married appropriately to a stirring melody that sounds as though it could have been written 200 years ago.

SCANSION AND PROSODY

It's also important that the words of a song fit comfortably with the melody accompanying them. This particular discipline, known as scansion, is a burden that the lyricist must bear when the lyrics are written to fit an existing melody. The lyricist's choices are narrowed to the confines of the rhythm of the tune. It is up to the lyricist to see that the words sing naturally to the composer's melody. Obviously, the reverse is true when the music is written to fit the lyrics. (See more on this subject in chapter 6, "Musical Beginnings.") The natural accents of the lyrics need to fit the stressed beats in the melody. A lyric at ease with its melody is said to "scan" well. Another word used to describe this concept is "prosody," which is the study of the metrical structure of verse, whether lyrics or poetry.

Poor scansion hits the very best writers sometimes. It even sneaks into our hymnals. The very first line of the beloved hymn, "Blessed Be the Name," places the emphasis on the wrong syllable of its very first word—"Jesus" no less. The name Jesus is naturally stressed like this: *Je*-sus. But the hymn writer, for whatever reason, used the first syllable as a "pickup" note, and landed the second syllable squarely on the stressed downbeat, like this: "Je-*sus*, the name that calms my fears." It's awkward and clumsy, even if it is in a hundred different hymnals.

Like all songwriting rules, the rules of good scansion can be broken effectively if the writer knows what he or she is doing. The deliberate use of unusual, or even awkward, scansion may draw just the right attention to some lyrics. Singer-songwriter James Taylor has practically trademarked his quirky mispronunciation of the article "the," using the long *ee* sound when it would normally be pronounced *uh*. The rock band Mute Math broke all the rules of scansion in their song "Noticed," but it works because of the drive and syncopation of the song. Sometimes there is a fine line between clever syncopation and poor scansion. A good writer learns how to walk that line.

Economize: Less Is More

> *I have a few artistic principles, and one of them is 'Less is more.'*
> *Tolstoy would argue against me, but I don't think I could ever be*
> *swayed.*
> —STEPHEN SONDHEIM

It is famously rumored that in response to a challenge to write an entire story in six words, Ernest Hemingway wrote this economic piece of genius: "For sale: Baby shoes, never worn." It is also said that Hemingway believed those six words to be his very best work.

Most hit songwriters create a well-developed sense of economy in their lyrics. Not that I am suggesting we limit ourselves to a mere half-dozen words, but if you study the printed lyrics that accompany commercial CDs (and you should), you'll notice just how few words are in the lyrics of a typical song. Individual lyric lines are brief and to the point. Verses are often no more than four to eight lines long. Two verses, a chorus, and a short bridge are the norm. Commercial songs tend to be lyrically lean. Indeed, less is more. If your song has three verses, a double chorus that changes after each verse, a four-line channel, and a bridge, chances are you're song has too many words. You are running a serious risk of losing your listener long before you get to the bridge. As a rule, a good commercial lyric should fit nicely on a single typed page of paper (with room left over for the title, writer credits, and a copyright notice). Molly-Ann Leiken said it well: "A song is not a novel" (*How to Write a Hit Song*, p. 16).

A song may have only two verses and a single chorus and still be too wordy. If every line of the song extends the full width of the page, the song almost certainly would benefit from some careful editing. Remove extraneous verbiage that doesn't add to the meaning of the line. Often little pickup words that sit at the beginning of phrases can be dropped without hampering the listener's ability to follow the story. Short words like the articles "and" and "the" and the personal pronoun "I" don't always have to be sung. Often, their placement is understood without their even being said.

Tempo can be a factor in how long lyrics should be. A fast tempo can accommodate more words. It may also demand shorter words that are easier to sing. A slow tempo requires fewer words. In the slow song, the lyrics linger with the listener. And the words of a slow ballad can't hide in the shadow of a great groove the way that the lyrics of a fast-tempo song might. So, when writing a song with a slow tempo, there is a greater pressure on the lyricist to make sure that the words are interesting.

There are a couple of real benefits to lean lyrics. First, they're easier to sing. Fewer words leave the singer places to breathe. Second, fewer words make the lyrics easier to remember. This benefits both the singer and the listener. Of course, writing a few quality words is harder than writing lots of meaningless ones. Most professional writers will tell you that it is very hard work to make a song look easy.

> *It is only through hard work that I can give the impression of ease and simplicity.*
> —HENRI MATISSE

Coda

Some beginners, in an effort to bare their soul, write pages of lyrics for a single song. They fall in love with every word, convinced that each syllable is indispensable. If you are such a writer, begin working today to write leaner, more-economical lyrics. Make every word matter. You'll be a better songwriter for the effort.

Other beginners never explore the colors that are available to them through having a rich vocabulary. They are content to use the same 100 to 200 words over and over again in their songs. If this describes your writing, spend some more time reading good literature and well-written books. Madeleine L'Engle says, "We think because we have words, not the other way around. The more words we have, the better able we are to think conceptually" (*Walking on Water*, p. 38). Open your mind up to more words, and you will express yourself more clearly in your writing.

At the same time you expand your verbal horizons, examine your work for tired clichés worn thin with overuse. Find new words to replace trite phrases that have lost their power to create authentic verbal pictures. Avoid spiritual platitudes that once were fresh with meaning but no longer stir the listener's heart.

Finally, master the power of a great opening line and a memorable hook in your songwriting. Every line you write is important, but none are as crucial as the opening line and the hook. Strive to create opening lines that grab the listener's attention and hooks that won't let the listener go.

Poetic Devices (Sound Effects and Figures of Speech) 5

Sunday-School Lessons That Rhyme

This chapter is for the sake of all those Sunday-school lessons that rhyme. Let me explain. Part of my job as a songwriting instructor for the Academy of Gospel Music Arts was giving face-to-face song critiques to a room full of amateur Christian songwriters. By and large, these sessions were a fun and educational experience. Everyone was there to learn, and most had a good attitude about accepting honest, constructive criticism. I certainly admired the writers' courage to allow me to criticize their babies in front of a small crowd of strangers. I tried never to hurt anyone's feelings and, though there were occasional tears, nobody ever threatened me with bodily harm. During the sessions, time and again I listened to songs that could best be described (in the words of my friend, Dan Keen) as "Sunday-school lessons that rhyme." The lyrics were truthful, theologically sound and sometimes made a worthy point. But they lacked art. Short of a simple rhyme scheme, they were void of poetry. Not a single picture graced their lines. These songs may have been long on Truth, but they were short on Beauty. Regardless of their theology, and difficult as it is say, they were bad lyrics.

As I have emphasized in earlier chapters, an artisan has complete command of the tools of his trade. (*Jesus' chairs, Jesus' chairs, Jesus' chairs.*) Primary among those tools for the songwriter are poetic devices. Make no mistake: a lyric is not a poem. A poem is complete by itself. It exists to be read. A lyric is half of a song. It exists to be sung. Still, lyrics use many of the same literary devices found in poetry. These touches of poetry shouldn't shine a spotlight on themselves, but the song should be better for their presence. Cleverness is no substitute for content. Good writers don't force poetry into their songs. Instead, they work to incorporate these devices naturally, confident that the result will be a more effective and more powerful song—not another Sunday-school lesson that rhymes.

In Their Own Words: What are your thoughts on the use of poetic devices?

Many people make the mistake of thinking that a poetic device makes a lyric flowery or fancy. In reality, using a poetic device often means choosing a simpler word that means the right thing, and does what it was put in the lyric to do without calling attention to itself.
—SUE SMITH

Poetic devices are part of my vocabulary and come very naturally. I've made conscious efforts at times to speak a little more plainly. I think, though, that it was more effective to once say, "Hold the lamp to guide the traveler to the shore" rather than "Be a steadfast witness."
—CHARLES F. BROWN

The use of literary devices becomes less conscious with experience. The great songs seem to always include them. —LOWELL ALEXANDER

Rhyme: More Than Just Ear Candy

It is very hard to make things rhyme properly . . . and most songwriters today don't want to work that hard.
—STEPHEN SONDHEIM

WHY RHYME?

For many of you there will be a strong urge to skip past this segment on rhyme. That's understandable; after all, everybody knows about rhyme. It's old hat. To say that rhyme is a useful poetic device for songwriting is like saying one needs flour to bake a cake. Just another observation from the Encyclopedia of Things That Are Painfully Obvious, right? Actually, it has been my experience that many beginning songwriters display a genuine lack of understanding, let alone mastery, of the creative use of rhyme. So, I choose to begin this discussion of poetic devices with the one device songwriters most commonly use and abuse—rhyme.

Let's face it, even in a time when some consider rhyme less than cool, any impartial examination of the great songs of the day will reveal a healthy dose of it. Like a hammer in a carpenter's toolbox, rhyme is one of the basic tools every good songwriter must know how to wield accurately and efficiently. Otherwise, the result will be shoddy workmanship—a song that doesn't hold up. Rhyme acts as a song's verbal adhesive, bonding words to each other in the listener's ear, connecting lyrics across the span of a verse or chorus. A clearly structured rhyme scheme defines the framework of a song, creating an aural road map that makes the song easier to follow. And because rhyme is the repetition of key sounds in a lyric, rhyme also makes the song easier to remember. The childish rhymes of nursery songs seem simplistic to adult ears, but there is no denying that those little verses are memorable. Decades pass, but no one forgets the words to "Mary Had a Little Lamb." Effective use of rhyme holds the listener's attention and creates a sense of expectancy for the rhyme she knows is coming. A good songwriter understands that rhyme is pleasing, even comforting, to the ear. Finally, musical phrases that parallel each other often cry out for words that do the same. To ignore the rhyming demands of the melody is to weaken the power of the song.

A SONGWRITER'S DEFINITION OF RHYME

My well-worn paperback of *Merriam-Webster's* dictionary defines "rhyme" as the "agreement in the terminal sounds of words." This definition, however, allows for the inclusion of homonyms, which songwriters should avoid. A homonym, sometimes called an "identity," is made up of two words that are spelled differently but sound the same, as in "see" and "sea." When used as rhymes in a song, homonyms tend to sound dull and lifeless. I know that to be a fact, because I have made this error with "see" and "sea" myself in an otherwise good song, and it bothers me every time I hear it. Take a look:

> *Tell me, tell me how long will we keep on*
> *Pretending we do not see*
> *All the pain and the hurt that's all around us*
> *Like a mighty troubled sea?*

(From "The Secret of Life") WORDS AND MUSIC BY ROBERT STERLING AND JOHN MAYS
© 1997 by Word Music and Two Fine Boys Music

See what I mean?

So in our pursuit to become better songwriters, I will rely upon Sheila Davis's more specific definition of "rhyme" from her wonderful book, *The Craft of Lyric Writing*. Ms. Davis defines "rhyme" as two or more words that contain "the same final accented vowel and consonant sounds and a different consonant preceding that vowel" (p. 185). That means "peal" and "steal" do rhyme, but "repeal" and "appeal" do not. Why? Because the final accented sounds of "repeal" and "appeal" create an identity, not a rhyme. Got it? Good. Let's keep moving.

THE BASICS OF RHYME

Rhyme, as we all know, appears mostly at the ends of lines. There are three common types of this end-line rhyme, and they are exactly what their names suggest them to be. The first, **single rhyme** is also called **masculine rhyme**. This involves rhyming single syllables or the final syllable in multisyllable words. For example: *scheme/dream; snow/grow; graze/appraise*. It is by far the most common form of rhyme.

The second is **double rhyme**, also known as **feminine rhyme**. It occurs when the last two syllables of words agree, and the stress is on the first of the two syllables. Here are some examples of double rhyme: *traded/faded; cheaper/keeper; date you/hate you*. It is a little more difficult to create than is single rhyme, and it is less common. Note that double rhyme can be made by rhyming individual two-syllable words or by combining two single-syllable words.

Finally, **triple rhyme** is (you guessed it!) the rhyming of the last three syllables of words. A few examples of this feat are *call again/fall again; taking up/making up; drearily/wearily*. Like double rhyme, triple rhyme is often created by rhyming phrases, not just single words.

Not all rhyme occurs at the end of the line. A rhyme that spices up the inside of a line is known as **internal rhyme**. Here is an example of internal rhyme: "As I was *falling*, I kept *calling* out to you." Placing two rhyming words adjacent to each other in a line is called **contiguous rhyme**: "He comes from the *great state* of Texas." In the hands of a skilled lyricist, both internal rhyme and contiguous rhyme can offer a sort of bonus for the listener.

THE QUEST FOR PERFECTION

Should rhyme always be perfect rhyme? Is it okay to settle for an imperfect rhyme? If so, how close to perfect is close enough? For decades the standard for rhyme was simple: all rhymes were perfect—absolutely, dead-on perfect. The great craftsmen of Tin Pan Alley understood that the only way to rhyme was with a perfect rhyme. Anything less was bad songwriting. The writer seeking to rhyme the word "love" was pretty much limited to a handful of choices: "of," "dove," "glove," "shove," "above." Perfect rhyme is still the standard in theater music. In pop music, however, perfect rhyme is not always the cool thing to do. It can be sterile and predictable. And as we've just seen, perfect rhyme can be limiting to the point of hindering the writer.

Sometimes an imperfect rhyme can be the perfect solution to a writer's dilemma. **Imperfect rhyme** (also called **slant rhyme**, **near rhyme**, or **false rhyme**) is an almost-perfect rhyme. Close, but not exact. With imperfect rhyme, the writer's choices can be increased dramatically. Consider our "love" rhyme again. With imperfect rhyme, the writer has at least another dozen or so options to choose from, including words like "rough" "enough," "flood," "bug," and "tub." None of them are as strong as a perfect rhyme, but all are possible substitutes (although I can't imagine why anyone would write a song that would rhyme "love" and "tub"). A word of caution to any writer who genuinely wishes to improve their craft: Don't settle for an imperfect rhyme just because it's easier to do so. That's not good writing. That's laziness.

RHYME TIPS

Finally, here are ten tips that will help you to make the most of your rhymes. Use these tips as a checklist to determine whether you are utilizing rhyme creatively, or are instead settling for the same tired rhymes you used in your last three songs.

1. **Rhyme the important stuff.** Rhyme draws attention to the rhyming words, so try to land your rhymes on words that reinforce the song's message or atmosphere. If you rhyme unimportant words, you're telling the listener you've written an unimportant song. Make sure there's a reason for the rhymes you create.

2. **Save the stronger, more creative rhyme line for the second half of the rhyme.** Make your listeners wait for that great rhyming line. They will appreciate the payoff.

3. **Avoid predictable rhymes.** Predictable rhymes telegraph the lyrics ahead, telling the listener exactly what's coming, spoiling the surprise. Because double and triple rhymes have fewer obvious rhyme choices, they have a greater tendency to be predictable than do single rhymes.

4. **Avoid rhyming slang and trendy words.** Slang words put date stamps on your work. Just ask anybody who ever rhymed the word "rad" in a song. There's a time and a place for trendy words. Trendy language has an immediacy to it, and can sometimes be used for comic effect. But remember that all trends fade, and you may find yourself rewriting your song six months (if not six weeks) down the road.

5. **Vary the color of rhymes within a song.** Using only one kind of rhyme is boring. Mix up the use of single, double, and triple rhymes. Try slipping an internal rhyme in occasionally. Avoid the tedious overuse of the same rhyme vowel. If every rhyme in your first verse is a single rhyme using the long *ee* vowel sound, the listener may never move on to your second verse.

6. **Rhyme naturally.** A classic problem of novice writers is inverting words in a phrase to force a rhyme. I call this "Yoda speak," named after the little green character in the *Star Wars* movies, who spoke in awkward, sometimes backward, phrases ("With you the force is, Luke"). Better to write the words the way people actually speak, and look for a new rhyme. Also related to this problem among Christian songwriters is what I call "hymn talk," which refers to the use of using archaic language to make a rhyme work. For example, if you use the word "thou" to rhyme with "now," you have committed the sin of hymn talk. That might have worked for 19th-century hymnwriter Fanny J. Crosby (1820-1915), but it won't work for you.

7. **When you're stuck for a rhyme, try rephrasing the line.** Sometimes you can say the same thing another way and open up new rhyming possibilities. For example, the line "Love always ends that way" can be rephrased to "That's how love always ends," and suddenly you have a new rhyming word without changing the meaning or the message of the lyrics.

8. **Don't settle for sloppy rhyme.** Even imperfect rhymes shouldn't be weak. Rather than settle, dig a little deeper. You may find something terrific.

9. **Get a good rhyming dictionary.** Not even the most brilliant wordsmith can think of every possible rhyme for a line. A rhyming dictionary, whether an actual book or in software form, is the perfect tool for finding an elusive rhyme or for jump-starting the rhyming process.

10. **Every now and then, don't use rhyme.** That's right. After this entire discussion, remember that sometimes little or even no rhyme can be very effective if it is done purposefully and with solid craftsmanship. Michael McDonald and Kenny Loggins used almost no rhyme at all in their song "What a Fool Believes." But the lack of rhyme suits the unusual musical phrasing of the song.

Rhyme Scheme: Shaping Your Song with Rhyme

The **rhyme scheme** of a song is determined by the pattern of the end rhymes in the lyrics. Consider this familiar nursery rhyme, with its simple a-b-c-b rhyme scheme:

Mary had a little lamb	(a)
Its fleece was white as snow	(b)
And everywhere that Mary went	(c)
The lamb was sure to go.	(b)

Rhyme scheme is a refining factor in the shape of a song. It contours the lines, creating predictable patterns for the listener. Each musical section of the song (verse, chorus, bridge) will have its own unique rhyme scheme. The verse and the chorus should not have the same rhyme scheme. However, all the verses of a song should share a consistent rhyme scheme. The rhyme scheme of the second verse (and third, if there is one) should follow the pattern of the first verse. That rule extends to the use of single, double, and triple rhymes also. If the first verse has an a-a-b-b rhyme scheme, with the b rhymes being double rhymes, then each additional verse should follow that same pattern.

Listen to the music for deciding on your rhyme placement. The melody can be a powerful guide to the rhyme scheme. If musical phrases repeat every four bars, then perhaps the lyrics should rhyme at those points. Experiment with varied rhyme schemes in your writing. Don't settle for the same a-b-a-a-b single-syllable rhymes in all your songs.

The 12 songs analyzed in chapter 9 demonstrate a lot of different rhyme schemes. Study them for ideas of your own.

Are You Repeating Yourself? (Lyrical Sound Effects)

In addition to rhyme, serious songwriters also carry a few other sound-effects tricks in their toolbox. Like rhyme, these devices all involve repetition of sounds. However, because these effects are rarely featured as prominently as rhyme is, their impact is generally less obvious.

ALLITERATION: REPEATING CONSONANTS

Alliteration is the rapid repetition of consecutive consonants in a line of lyrics. (See what I did there?) Effective alliteration calls for subtlety (unlike my previous heavy-handed sentence). Also, excessive alliteration can sound silly. You'll find an excellent example of subtle alliteration in the opening line of "Via Dolorosa," by Niles Borop and Billy Sprague: "Down the Via Dolorosa in Jerusalem that day." The repeated *dee* consonant in the line doesn't jump out at you. It quietly reinforces the power of the lyric by making the words flow more smoothly.

ASSONANCE: REPEATING VOWELS

Assonance is the repetition of stressed vowel sounds in neighboring words. Less obvious in its effect than alliteration, assonance can add to the atmosphere and the warmth of a line. Greg Nelson and Phill McHugh used assonance very well in the title/hook line of their popular song "People Need the Lord." As that lyric is gently repeated in the chorus, the *ee* sound in "people" and in "need" adds to the warmth of the song. And to further strengthen the effect musically, the melody notes on those two syllables are the same pitch, which, I am sure, was no accident.

ANAPHORA: REPEATING WORDS

Anaphora is the repetition of a word or phrase at the beginning of successive lines in a song. This effect is more obvious than alliteration and assonance, and is often suggested by a melody or rhythm that repeats itself at the beginning of successive lines. Anaphora is a great tool for the writer to use to establish a feeling of familiarity and make a lyric quickly memorable. Used well, it can strengthen a song's structure and even focus the direction of the lyrics. In the first verse of the socially conscious song "How Long Will Be Too Long?" (by Wayne Kirkpatrick, Amy Grant, and Michael W. Smith), we see a terrific example of how anaphora sharpens the lyric and drives the song to the chorus.

> *Tell me, how long will we grovel at the feet of wealth and power?*
> *Tell me, how long will we bow down to the golden calf?*
> *Tell me now, how long will be too long?*

WORDS & MUSIC BY WAYNE KIRKPATRICK, AMY GRANT AND MICHAEL W. SMITH
© 1990 O'Ryan Music/Emily Boothe, Inc./Age to Age Music, Inc.

Figures of Speech
(High-School English Class Revisited)

"A picture is worth a thousand words" is a trite but true piece of wisdom, and it might seem a bit out of place in a discussion about lyric writing. After all, lyric writing is all about words, right? Yes and no. Great lyricists understand that lyric pictures, painted with figurative language, make the words of a song leap to life in the listener's mind. A single well-placed lyric picture can set a mood, create a believable character, or shed insight on the subject at hand. Experienced lyricists employ these devices instinctively. They understand the power of pictures in their songs. Word pictures show rather than tell.

Of course, nothing in the following discussion on figures of speech will be news to those of you who paid attention in high school English class. That's when everyone was, at least in theory, learning about metaphor and simile and other such riveting minutia. The problem is that most of us were concerned with more important stuff like, "Is my face gonna clear up before the weekend?" Or "Who do you think is better—the Beatles or the Stones?" So, for the benefit of the majority, let's take a brief ride in the Way Back Machine and revisit some vaguely familiar territory, and perhaps in the process discover you can actually use something you learned in high school for fun and profit. And, for the record, the Beatles were and always will be better than the Stones.

METAPHOR

A **metaphor** is a direct comparison of two things that are essentially unlike each other. The lyricist finds a piece of common ground between two dissimilar things and creates a verbal equation. In doing so, the writer expands the meaning of the object being compared. At the heart of every metaphor is conflict, because you're putting two things together that don't really belong together (*Writing Better Lyrics*, p. 12). When Paul Simon sang the words "I am a rock. I am an island," he used metaphor to expand the meaning of his own human condition. He is neither a rock nor an island, but isn't that a much better way to say, "I am a hard and lonely person who requires no one else in my life"? It certainly sings better.

The first verse of Bruce Carroll's hit song "Breaking the Law of Love" demonstrates how effectively a metaphor can crystallize the message of a lyric. The first two lines of the song take aim at the singer's spiritual life. The third line drives the point home with an artful metaphor, equating his life's version of righteousness with garbage and lies. There is a lot of conflict in the two halves of this metaphor: "righteousness" and "filthy rags and fiction." But the equation rings true because the previous two lines support the metaphor.

> *Lord, I'm laying down this life of contradictions*
> *All the Sunday resolutions and the Monday rationales.*
> *'Cause my righteousness is filthy rags and fiction*
> *When I'm talking love and charity and living something else.*

WORDS AND MUSIC BY BRUCE CARROLL, CLAIRE CLONINGER, AND MORGAN CRYER
© 1991 by Word Music and Sophie Elle Music Publishing

Even the simplest of metaphors can create a sharp and memorable word picture. Consider these lyrics from the familiar folk song: "You are my sunshine, my only sunshine. / You make me happy when skies are gray." In the first line, the writer uses a direct metaphor: the object of his affection is his "sunshine." In the next line, the writer uses an indirect metaphor of gray skies to mean sad times.

As is clear from the previous example, metaphor is not always directly stated in the form of a verbal equation. Occasionally it is hidden as a concept in a line. Here are few additional examples of hidden metaphor from song lyrics:

"Take these broken wings and learn to fly again" ("broken wings" = wounded romance)

("Broken Wings" by Steven George, John Lang, and Richard Page)

"I made it through the rain" ("rain" = troubled times)

("I Made It Through the Rain" by Gerard Kenny, Drey Shepperd, Barry Manilow, Jack Feldman, and Bruce Sussman).

"The watercolour ponies will one day ride away" ("watercolour ponies" = youth)

("Watercolour Ponies" by Wayne Watson)

Metaphor has been a trusted device for as long as people have been expressing themselves with words. The Bible is filled with metaphor. Every parable Jesus told was a metaphor for the Kingdom of God. David poured out his heart using metaphor. Examine the poetic beauty of the opening lines of Psalm 23 (KJV), in which David uses the metaphors of a good shepherd, verdant pastures, and restful waters to describe how God provides for the every need of His troubled servant: "The Lord is my shepherd. I shall not want. He maketh me to lie down in green pastures. He leadeth me beside still waters. He restoreth my soul."

Another powerful characteristic of metaphor is that it transfers focus from the first part of the verbal equation to the second part. The second half of any metaphor is the focal point of the statement. Lowell Alexander opens his touching song "Come Harvest Time" with this beautiful metaphor: "Planted by God in a field without worth / We are but seeds in his eyes."

You see? The focus is shifted from "we" in the first part of the metaphor to "seeds" in the second part. "Seeds" is the image that the listener remembers. The picture is made stronger by the image of the field in the preceding line. "Metaphor takes its second term very seriously … because that's what everyone will end up looking at" (*Writing Better Lyrics*, p. 21).

Because of this powerful transfer of focus, a single metaphor can color an entire set of lyrics. In fact, a song's lyrics can be one big metaphor. In his brilliantly crafted lines of "Luck Be a Lady" from the musical *Guys and Dolls*, Frank Loesser maintained the comparison of a gambler's good fortune to the whims of a well-heeled female throughout the song. With every phrase of the tender Christmas song "Rose of Bethlehem," Lowell Alexander artfully equated the qualities of a perfect red rose to the newborn baby Jesus and the sacrifice He would one day make for mankind. In the Jars of Clay hit "Flood," the writers likened the trials of life to a flood of Old Testament proportions. In all of these examples, the metaphor works through the entire song, constantly transferring the listener's focus to the conflicting image that somehow makes perfect sense.

SIMILE

A **simile** is a comparison of two things using the word "like," "as," or "than." Like a metaphor, a simile compares dissimilar things and, in doing so, expands meaning. Think of the simile as the first cousin to the metaphor. A good listener (and all good songwriters are good listeners) will hear similes occurring every day in the conversations of their funniest and most colorful friends. "She's as sweet as honey." "He's nuttier than a fruitcake." "He ran like a scalded dog." If you listen, you will hear phrases like these all around you. So, pay attention.

For a simile to be effective, it must be truthful. Jim Croce sang to us that Leroy Brown was "meaner than a junkyard dog." Nobody would have bought that record if Croce had said a "junkyard cat." In the Leiber and Stoller song "Ruby Baby," the protagonist tells us he's never going to give up on his unrequited love with the clever simile: "Like a ghost I'm gonna haunt you." In other words, he'll always be hanging around. In Jason Gray and Doug McKelvey's song "Sing Through Me," they describe the feeling of being beaten down by life with two appropriate similes:

These days are like a hammer
They can leave me feeling numb
Like I'm down beneath the table
And I'm fighting for the crumbs.

WORDS AND MUSIC BY JASON GRAY AND DOUG MCKELVEY
© 2007 by Centricity Music and Songs Only Dogs Hear

In the song "God Only Knows," I described a young girl's sadness by saying that her "tears still fall like summer rain." There's a gentle melancholy attitude in the line that felt truthful to me. No matter how clever or artful the simile, it needs to be truthful.

A significant difference between simile and its cousin, the metaphor, is that simile does not transfer focus to the second part of the comparison. Despite the colorful imagery, the focus of the line remains on the first part of the simile. Perhaps this is because the use of the words "like," "as," and "than" diffuses the comparison, softening the verbal equation. In the opening lines of the chorus of "River of Love," singer-songwriter Dana Glover writes: "Your love is like the river / My love is like the sea." Those are two strong similes, but the focus is not ultimately on "river" and "sea," but instead is on "your love" and "my love."

Is there a way to know when to use metaphor versus simile? I like Pat Pattison's suggestion in his book *Writing Better Lyrics*: "As a rule of thumb, when you have several comparisons in mind, use simile. When you're using only one, and you want to commit to it throughout the song, use metaphor" (p. 21).

PERSONIFICATION

Personification is the trick of giving human qualities to inanimate objects. The writer paints the picture by breathing life into something that is lifeless: "The walls laughed at me," "the whispering breeze," "a weeping midnight moon"—these are examples of personification. Occasionally, in a dramatic first-person point of view, the singer can become the inanimate object that is being personified. Barry Manilow sang to the entire world, "I am music, and I write the songs," and Bruce Johnston, who penned the tune, made a gazillion dollars (*The Craft of Lyric Writing*, p. 167).

Nicole Mullens used personification very sweetly in the opening lines of her song "Redeemer," when she paints the picture of God teaching and speaking to the sun, moon, and stars as though they were His children:

Who taught the sun where to stand in the morning?
And who told the ocean, "You can only come this far?"
And who showed the moon where to hide 'til evening?
Whose words alone can catch a falling star?

WORDS AND MUSIC BY NICOLE C. MULLEN
© 2000 by Lil' Jas' Music

SYNECDOCHE

Synecdoche is a counterpart to metaphor and simile. While metaphor and simile both expand meaning, synecdoche contracts the meaning by reducing the image of something to one significant characteristic or part, substituting the specific for the general. For example, a common use of synecdoche is found in the phrase "a new set of wheels," reducing a new car to one significant attribute—its wheels. Similarly, describing a police officer as a "badge," a bank as a "vault," or an Ivy League education as a "sheepskin from Harvard" is to use synecdoche. Years ago, my wife and I wrote a song called "He Hears Every Word." In it, we described a child's bedtime prayers with this line: "Her 'now I lay me down to sleep' the Father understands." We reduced the child's prayer to a single familiar line using synecdoche. Similarly, the title of Amy Grant's song "Breath of Heaven" reduces the enormity of God's Spirit to that one simple phrase.

Whenever we substitute a brand name for the general product, we employ synecdoche: "Coke" for all soft drinks, "Avon" for all makeup, or "Kleenex" for all facial tissues. For those of us who choose to face the challenge of writing songs that refer to an all-powerful and ever-present God, synecdoche is our friend. Think about it. Every time we refer to God as "Father" or "Creator" or "Savior" we are reducing Him to a single attribute, which makes it possible for our finite brains to deal with the infinite Creator of the universe, if only for a moment.

METONYMY

Like synecdoche, **metonymy** is another device that reduces meaning. It does so by substituting the subject with an appropriate symbol or icon. So when one uses the phrase "from the cradle to the grave," metonymy is employed three times. First, it represents birth with the symbol of a cradle. Next, it represents death with the picture of the grave. Finally, the two metonyms join together to symbolize the entirety of life. "The pen is mightier than the sword" uses two metonyms. "Pen" symbolizes the written word, and "sword" symbolizes military power. Because metonyms are symbols, they show rather than tell. As a result, they are particularly economical, using just a few words to say much. In the second verse of the song "One Love," Brent Bourgeois makes effective use of metonymy:

> *I can't imagine what I'd do*
> *Without my daily bread from you* [symbol for God's sustenance]
> *Your sweet manna from above* [symbol for God's love freely given]
> *Filling up my heart.*

WORDS AND MUSIC BY BRENT BOURGEOIS
© 1994 Adrian and Delaney Music/Maverick Music

Euphemisms that soften the bluntness of an image are a type of metonym. For example, when we refer to death as "passing," or to the crucified Christ as a "lamb," or to the cross as a "tree," we substitute a symbol for the harsher image. In doing so, we paint a picture.

IRONY

Irony is the method of making a point by emphasizing the opposite of what you mean. The most pervasive form of irony in today's culture is sarcasm, which is generally blunt and often hurtful. That is not what we're talking about here. Irony is the writer's best tool for expressing the complexity of life, the result often being bittersweet. In the timeless O. Henry short story "The Gift of the Magi," a young husband and wife, who are poor but very much in love, each secretly sought to purchase a special Christmas gift for the other. The husband sold his most prized possession, a gold pocket watch, to buy a set of combs for his wife's long, beautiful hair. At the same time, the wife cut off her hair and sold it to a wigmaker to buy her husband a chain for his watch. Sad, isn't it? And yet their love for each other became richer for their mutual self-sacrifice. That's irony.

Of all the poetic devices, irony may be the most difficult to express. It requires an intimate understanding of the truth that it carries, and it generally needs to be delivered in a subtle fashion. Like metaphor, irony can be assigned to a single line in a song, or it can embody the entire lyric. Here are three basic types of irony that a songwriter should be familiar with:

1. **Understatement** treats something significant in a casual manner. To say that Microsoft CEO Bill Gates has a little money set aside for a rainy day is an understatement of colossal proportions. In the song "Living for the City," Stevie Wonder underplayed the surroundings of a boy raised in the abject poverty of a ghetto with the lyrics "Surrounded by four walls that ain't so pretty."

2. **Hyperbole** is an extravagant overstatement, and it is the extreme opposite of understatement. In his song "Hold Me, Jesus," Rich Mullins uses hyperbole in the lines "It's so hot inside my soul there must be blisters on my heart." In Dan Fogelberg's romantic ballad "Longer," he sings to his lover that "Longer than there've been fishes in the ocean / I've been in love with you." That's a long time. That's hyperbole.

3. **Paradox** is a contradictory statement that is somehow still true. For example, I can say with all honesty that "The more I learn, the less I know," because I've discovered that increased knowledge always leads to a greater awareness of how much more I have yet to learn. In the song "She's Leaving Home," Lennon and McCartney wrote, "She's leaving home after living alone for so many years." How can someone live at home and still live alone? Anyone who has ever lived in a home where communication has completely failed understands the truth of that sad paradox. In "The Kingdom Song," Claire Cloninger captured the irony of God's kingdom with these words:

In the Father's Kingdom
Where His children dwell,
The rich all know their poverty,
The poor all know their wealth.

WORDS AND MUSIC BY CLAIRE CLONINGER AND ROBERT STERLING
© 1997 Word Music/Juniper Landing Music

CHARACTERIZATION

Characterization is simply the creation of convincing characters. This might involve only a line or two in some lyrics, or it might weave through an entire song as a story. Country songwriters, perhaps more than any other group, know the value of this device, because they create vivid characters that come to life in their music. Songs like "The Gambler" and "A Boy Named Sue" are character-driven songs that climb to the top of the country charts and put their writers in the Songwriters Hall of Fame. Of course, country songwriters don't own the exclusive rights to characterization.

In a song titled "Casual Observer," I described the character of a bag lady and the man who is her "casual observer" with these few lines:

A nameless woman wanders by him aimlessly,
The sum of her existence in a shopping bag from Sears.
She recites to him her well-worn lines of tragedy.
He nods to her and tries to look sincere.

WORDS AND MUSIC BY ROBERT STERLING
© 2000 by Two Fine Boys Music

In the heartbreaking pop song "Tea for One," by the late Kevin Gilbert, we meet the lonely Duncan, who is afraid to act on his true feelings. At the end of the song, when Duncan finally decides to tell the woman that he loves her, he learns he has waited too long to tell her. Here is the first verse of this remarkable song, where in just a few lines we learn much about this compelling character:

Duncan was always cautious
Never the one to take a stand
Convinced to the bone that he's happier alone
And to justify the part, keeps a closely guarded heart

WORDS AND MUSIC BY KEVIN GILBERT
© 1994 by Canvas Mattress Music

Many great writers know the power of believable characters. Billy Joel wrote about the Piano Man, Brenda and Eddie, the Big Shot, and Anthony and Mama Leone. Lennon and McCartney gave us Eleanor Rigby, Father McKenzie, and Lovely Rita the Meter Maid. Sting sang to us about an Englishman in New York. Donald Fagen introduced us to the Night Fly. Paul Simon sang to us of Mrs. Robinson and amused us with a song about a guy called Al. We remember these songs because we remember the characters in them.

How Colorful Are Your Lyrics?

Poetic language is colorful language. Just as a movie filmed in Technicolor is generally more stimulating to the eyes than a film shot in black-and-white, colorful lyrics are more interesting to the ears than are those that are verbally black-and-white. A song blessed with a metaphor or two, a creative rhyme scheme, or a touch of irony is more intriguing than a song littered with worn out rhymes, containing no word pictures or believable characters. I am not saying every lyric you write should be burdened with heavy metaphors and strained by acrobatic rhymes. A little can go a long way. Still, you will want to examine your work for these devices to see if you are writing colorful songs.

Here is a simple, effective exercise I discovered in Molly-Ann Leikin's book *How to Write a Hit Song* (p. 17). Get yourself a box of crayons or colored pencils. Assign a color to each of the different poetic devices and each of the different types of rhyme that are outlined in this chapter. (Blue for metaphor, red for irony, green for single rhyme, orange for internal rhyme—you get the idea.) Now grab a crayon and go through one of your song lyrics, and circle each occurrence of these poetic devices with the assigned color. When you're finished, you'll have a pretty good visual answer to the question, "How colorful are your lyrics?" If you've used three or four or more colors, terrific! But if your lyrics are a monochromatic picture, a coat of only one color, the desperate demonstration of a lone crayon, then chances are you need to do some rewriting.

Coda

I have thrown a lot of technical terms at you in this chapter—big, intimidating words like "synecdoche" and "metonymy" and "anaphora," which are hard to pronounce and even harder to spell. (I struggle with "metonymy" every time I type it.) I am not terribly concerned that you know the exact definitions and spellings of these words. I think it is much more important you master the writing tools these words represent. *(Show rather than tell. Show rather than tell. Show rather than tell.)* The effective use of poetic imagery and verbal sound effects are must-have skills for any songwriter desiring to be a true craftsman—an artisan. You may already be employing some, or even all, of these poetic devices in your writing, unaware of their official names and definitions. If so, then excellent. Bravo! Keep up the good work. If, like many beginning songwriters, you have been working with only a little bit of rhyme and no real imagery, I hope this is the start of a new phase in your writing life—one that explores the power of poetry in songwriting.

Musical Beginnings (Melody, Harmony, and Rhythm) 6

Music is the art of the prophets and the gift of God.
—MARTIN LUTHER

Let's Keep Things Simple, Shall We?

I suspect that music has been around as long as people have been. It seems whenever and wherever people gather, as a culture or a community, music emerges. It wouldn't surprise me to learn that Adam serenaded Eve in the Garden of Eden. So I think it's safe to say that music has been around for a long, *loooong* time. What's more, books about music—that is, how to read music, how to write music, how to play music—have been around for almost as long as music itself. That said, I have no grandiose dreams of writing the definitive text on musical composition. There are hundreds of good books, really big, impressive books, already dedicated to that task. And people much smarter than I wrote them. Here, I offer but one little chapter on writing music—just one. My hope is that this lone chapter will present some simple guidelines and helpful hints to aid the beginning songwriter. Read this chapter; absorb its contents. Then you'll have the rest of your natural-born life to study all those other books and master the art of composing music.

Melody + Harmony + Rhythm = Music

There are three (very obvious) elements to music: **melody**, **harmony**, and **rhythm**. I'll go into greater detail on each later, but suffice it to say, it's important you have a basic understanding of all three in order to write good songs. Here's a quick overview of these three essential elements.

Melody is the linear realization of musical pitch. A tune either goes up in pitch, or it goes down, or it repeats the same notes. Nothing to it, right?

Harmony is the vertical support of the melody line. The different pitches that lie underneath the melody define the harmonic progression of the song. Any melody can be harmonized in a number of different ways, but a good composer works to create an interesting and appropriate harmonization that will best suit the melody.

Rhythm is how melody is defined in the space of time. Are the notes long or short? Fast or slow? Rhythm is also what builds the underlying groove that drives most pop music today. In fact, rhythm has become the dominant element of pop music, pushing melody, and to some extent harmony, into the background.

In a well-written song, all of these elements work together to bring the words to life. A brilliant lyric set to an awkward rhythm or unsingable tune won't get far with any singer. A great melody coupled with boring chord changes and a dated rhythm groove is doomed to be ignored. Likewise, the world's hippest drum loop and coolest chord changes may get a song noticed, but without a compelling melody, the song won't be around for long. A good song is a marriage of lyrics and music, each part elevating the other. And good music has a memorable melody, interesting harmonies, and appropriate rhythm.

Let's examine each element of music in a little more detail.

Melody

All you need to do is remember a tune that nobody else has thought of.
—ROBERT SCHUMANN

IS MELODY DEAD?

If you were to examine the art of melody writing from the 1940s to today, it would be graphed as a sharp downward line. Compare the tunes of Richard Rodgers or George Gershwin or Duke Ellington to just about anything on pop radio, and it's clear: melody writing is not the cherished art it once was. As much as I like rock music and R&B, there is no denying the part they've played in devaluing melody. As rhythm became an increasingly important element in pop music, melody was pushed further and further into the musical background. That's true of almost all pop music, including popular Christian music. In the case of most hip-hop and rap songs, melody has all but disappeared. So have we heard the last of melody?

For all our sakes, and for the sakes of our children and grandchildren, let's hope not. There are still songwriters who know how to write memorable melodies. Country music and Broadway shows continue to value the importance of the tune. Pop stars like James Taylor, Josh Groban, and Celine Dion pack auditoriums by singing songs that rely on good melodies. In fact, artists that record songs with great melodies tend to stand out on the radio. (I think it's no coincidence that those same singers often enjoy longer careers as performing artists.) And though Christian music has lost some melodic ground in recent years with the repetitive simplicity of so many of the popular praise-and-worship songs, I believe there is hope for a return to better melodies in the church as well. We continue to sing "Amazing Grace" after all these many years because, in part, it has a powerful melody that the average pew sitter can sing. We Christian songwriters can still learn much from the great songs of our past as we work to write the melodies of the future.

In Their Own Words:
Where does melody come from?

Melody comes from experience.   —KURT KAISER

I rarely walk for any distance without some annoying tune starting to bug me.   —CHARLES F. BROWN

Listen to everything around you—and if you hear a melody in your head, sing it out loud until you can't forget it.   —PAUL SMITH

Sometimes I think melody floats like a muse on the wind, waiting for the writer to reach for it, capture it, and write it down before it disappears like a vapor through the mind's fingers.
                    —LOWELL ALEXANDER

WHERE DO MELODIES COME FROM?

Twelve notes. Twelve simple notes. That's all we have in our musical toolbox. Every melody ever written in Western civilization, from Bach to the Beastie Boys, has been composed with those same 12 notes. When you consider that there are only 12 notes to choose from, you would think that writing a melody would be a pretty simple thing to do, right? Anybody, even a small child, could hammer out a brilliant tune, given enough time. Computers could be programmed to play every conceivable melodic combination, and we could just choose a tune from a pull-down menu on our laptops. A thousand monkeys with a thousand pianos could eventually compose Mozart's *Requiem*. There are only 12 notes, after all. So why is it so difficult to write a memorable melody?

That's where God comes in. I think that composing a truly great tune is mostly a God-given talent—a gift. In my own writing, it's easy enough for me to spot the melodies I have hammered out—a product of pure technique. Those tunes may work, but they are often less than elegant. But my best melodies are unexplainable to me. They just happened. It's as if God placed them inside my head and waited patiently for me to notice them and write them down. Jimmy Webb offers this wisdom: "Great melody has an illusive [sic] consistency that is unteachable. If the heart is the bow and the soul is the violin and the brain is the musician, then melody is the fragile result of all three in love with the same idea" (*Tunesmith,* p. 181).

But if writing melodies is mostly talent—an *unteachable* gift from God—then is there any point in studying the craft of melody writing? The answer is—yes. Craftsmanship, when learned and applied properly, can enhance a writer's talent, and may even draw out hidden gifts. I believe that the human ear (the inner ear that "hears" music in the head) can be trained and strengthened and improved. The very best compositional teaching tools are the great melodies of our time. I cannot encourage you strongly enough to learn the tunes of the great songwriters whose melodies have shaped generations of popular music. I am talking about

George Gershwin, Richard Rodgers, Frederick Lowe, Frank Loesser, and Harold Arlen. I'm also talking about Lennon and McCartney, Paul Simon, Elton John, Burt Bacharach, and Henry Mancini. And let's not forget Hank Williams and Don Schlitz, or Dottie Rambo and Bill Gaither. That's just the briefest beginning. The list could go on for pages.

William Faulkner once wrote: "Read, read, read. Read everything, good and bad, and see how they do it—like a carpenter who works as an apprentice and studies the master." With apologies to Mr. Faulkner, I offer similar advice to the composer desiring to master the art of melody writing: "Listen, Listen, Listen. Listen to everything, good and bad, and see how they do it." If you want learn how to write great songs, then start listening to great songs.

WHAT MAKES A MELODY?

Simply put, a melody is a series of single notes or tones. There are no more rules than that. A melody might be 4 notes, or 5 notes, or 45 notes. That's up to you, the composer. But for certain, these notes will do at least one of three things. They will either:

1. **Ascend** (go up in pitch)

2. **Descend** (go down in pitch)

3. **Repeat** (stay the same in pitch)

And the notes will each have their own specific duration.

The entire challenge of writing a good pop melody is laid out by the choices the composer makes within those few simple parameters. Will the tune go up? How far up? Will it go down? How far down? Will it repeat? For how long will it repeat? And how long will each of those notes last? The successful composer knows that a good melody (like a good lyric) is a balanced combination of repetition, variation, and contrast.

REPETITION, VARIATION, AND CONTRAST

Most pop tunes are made up of relatively brief melodic phrases, repeated liberally. They are simple and, hopefully, memorable. As we learned in the lyric-writing chapters, **repetition** in pop songwriting is a good thing. It helps the listener remember the song. Too much repetition, however, will bore the listener. The key to writing an interesting melody is combining enough repetition to be memorable with enough variation and contrast to keep things interesting. Jimmy Webb put it this way: an interesting melody will "lead the ear in a path which is both pleasant and to some degree unexpected" (*Tunesmith*, p. 168). In other words, a good pop melody should be memorably repetitive with an occasional nice surprise thrown in.

Variation is not a complete change, but rather an alteration of what is expected. If you repeat an eight-bar musical phrase exactly, note for note, you risk boring the listener. However, if you alter the end of the repeated phrase even slightly, you've provided the listener with something unexpected. In a lecture at Harvard University, Leonard Bernstein said, "[Variation is a] manifestation of the mighty dramatic principle known as the Violation of Expectation.

What is expected is repetition, either literal or in the form of an answer. When those expectations are violated, you've got variation" (*Tunesmith,* p.172).

The principle of variation is common to most pop songs. Consider "Heart and Soul," by Hoagy Carmichael, which every kid in America learns to play on the piano by the age of ten. There is repetition in the shape of the opening phrases, but variation in their pitch. The second phrase is a third higher than the first. Or consider "Yesterday," by Paul McCartney. Compare the melody of the opening word "yesterday" with the tune used for the words at the end of the phrases: "far away" and "here to stay." They are the exact same shape and rhythm, placed in different positions on the scale. That is variation.

In those instances when the words are written before the music, the lyrics may influence the shape and repetition of certain melodic phrases. If a particular lyric phrase is repeated, the music would do well to do so the same—either as an exact repeat, or as a variation on the musical theme. (The reverse is also true. When the melody is written first, it will have an effect on the lyric's form and even the rhyme scheme.)

When the variation is extreme enough, a true departure from the phrases that precede it, the variation becomes a **contrast**, which may be exactly what the composer needs to begin a new section of the song. In fact, the sections of a song (verse, chorus, bridge, and so on) must show some distinct melodic contrasts in order for the listener to hear the sections happen. Pretty much the entire structure of the modern pop song is based on the idea of contrasting A and B sections. Of course, the contrasting sections of a song also need to complement one another, or the result will sound like two completely different songs.

How can you create contrast in your music? Here are three simple ideas, all of which are classic pop songwriting techniques:

1. **Change the level of the melodic line.** Make the chorus higher in pitch and/or intensity than the verse.

2. **Change the length of the musical phrase.** If the verse is made up of long phrases, the chorus can use short phrases. If the chorus is busy, keep the verses simple.

3. **Change the rhythm pattern.** If the verse is rhythmically straightforward, try more syncopation in the chorus.

THE HOOK REVISITED

The term *hook* has already been discussed in several chapters of this book. Previous mentions were directed largely to the lyric hook. But now it's time to talk about the music hook. The music hook is that brief portion of a song's melody that is the most memorable, and usually the most repeated. In the vast majority of pop songs, the lyric hook (which usually contains the title of the song) and the music hook occur simultaneously. That is because seasoned songwriters know that when the high point of the lyric coincides with the climax of the melody, the result is a powerful, sometimes unforgettable combination.

So where is that perfect place for the hook to happen? In the typical verse/chorus song, the hook falls on either the first line or the last line of the chorus—sometimes both. In the standard AABA song, the hook is normally placed in the first or last line of each A section. In an AAA song form, like the AABA, the hook typically appears in either the first or the last line of each A section. There are countless successful exceptions to those guidelines, but the beginning composer would be wise to learn to place the hook in these strong positions. Regardless, in a good melody it should be evident where the hook will go, because the whole melody will either lead to or spring from that point.

Just as the lyric hook should capture the listener's attention, the music hook must capture the listener's ear. This isn't always an easy thing to accomplish, considering that a hook is typically only a few notes long. Good composers know how powerful the right few notes can be when placed at the high point of a song. Consider these three standards: "Moon River" (by Henry Mancini), "Bali Hai" (by Richard Rodgers), and "Over the Rainbow" (by Harold Arlen). Each has a musical hook that has become part of popular music history. They are distinctive, elegant, and memorable. Similarly, the music hooks of "Born in the USA" (Bruce Springsteen), "How Can You Mend a Broken Heart" (Barry and Robin Gibb), and "You're So Vain" (Carly Simon) prove that the art of writing a memorable melodic hook didn't die with the passing of Tin Pan Alley.

As you study the melodies of great songwriters (and you must), take time to focus on the music hooks. Discover for yourself how this small but powerful tool can enhance your own songs.

INTERVALS

As I mentioned earlier, there are only 12 tones in the Western chromatic scale to work with—only 12! That means there are just so many intervals one can use. And since we are concerned with songwriting (which means we are concerned with music that can be sung), the number of effective intervals that a voice can leap is usually limited to within an octave. Basically, there are two options when it comes to forming melodic intervals:

1. A melody can move to an adjacent note (scale-wise in half steps or whole steps), or

2. A melody can skip notes (make leaps of a third or larger).

Too much of either in a tune is likely to get boring (and we're back to repetition and variation). Constantly running up and down the scale or repeatedly making acrobatic interval leaps gets old in a hurry. A good composer will instinctively use a combination of steps and skips and repeated notes to achieve a proper balance. A wonderful example of this sort of balance can be heard in the deceptively simple melody "Do-Re-Mi" (from *The Sound of Music*, by Richard Rodgers). The tune is built largely on scale steps, which makes for great text painting in a song that is about the musical scale. But Rodgers employs just enough skips to keep the tune interesting.

With regard to large interval leaps (of more than a fifth), my high school music-theory teacher taught me this simple rule of thumb: a significant melodic leap in any direction is generally followed by a move in the opposite direction. This basic rule has proven true in my own experience as a songwriter. I can't say why it works, but it does. Three excellent examples of this principle are found in the melodic hooks of the same three standards I mentioned earlier: "Moon River." "Bali Hai," and "Over the Rainbow." Check them out and see how the large leaps in the melody are always followed by a move in the opposite direction.

MELODIC RANGE

Several years ago, a particular praise song (that shall remain nameless) became enormously popular, sweeping the globe. Everybody sang it in church, and I do mean *everybody*. I was hired to do two different choral arrangements of this song, adding to the mountain of arrangements and recordings that were produced for it. Despite its enormous success, I believe that this particular song has a poorly constructed melody. Why? It was designed for use in congregational singing, but it has a range of an octave and a fourth. If we include the typical modulation that most congregations do when singing this tune, the range is expanded another full step to an octave and a fifth. (That is the same range as "The Star-Spangled Banner," by the way. Need I say more?) Almost no one in the pews can comfortably sing the song in its entirety. Either the opening lines will be too low or the peak of the chorus will be too high. Interestingly enough, by making one or two minor adjustments to the verse melody, the problem of the song's excessive range could have been solved. Fortunately for the writer, my opinion hasn't hurt the popularity of the song. (For the record, I think the chorus of the song is quite powerful.) Still, I contend that the range of the melody makes the song difficult to sing for all but the very best vocalists.

When writing a melody, you should always keep in mind the realistic limitations of the human voice. Most musical instruments have a three-octave range or greater. But the typical pop singer works within a very modest range of an octave, or an octave and a third. Some powerhouse female singers like Celine Dion and Sandi Patti command a larger range of an octave and a fifth, but they are few and far between. Male singers sometimes work with larger ranges, especially if they have control of their falsetto notes. But keep in mind that singers like David Phelps, Guy Penrod, and Andrea Bocelli are not your average singers. Just because their range spans more than two octaves doesn't mean a good melody needs to stretch out that far. Unless you are composing for trained opera singers, it is wise to keep the overall range of your melodies contained. In fact, many immortalized tunes are well within an octave or so. "Amazing Grace," "Heart and Soul," and "Over the Rainbow" all have a range of just one octave. Perhaps that is one of the keys to their longevity. Normal people can sing them.

RESTS

Speaking of normal people, remember—they have to breathe on occasion. If your melody is an unrelenting series of notes with no resting places, it will not only be impossible to sing, it will also be insanely boring. Rests are a crucial part of any melody. They give the singer the chance to take a breath and the listener the chance to let the words sink in.

Music is what happens between the rests.
—LEONARD BERNSTEIN

TEST THE TUNE

The best way to test your melodies is to sing them. The acid test of a good tune is, can it be sung by the average person? If you can't sing it comfortably, it probably needs to be rewritten. As you compose your songs, don't become addicted to the piano or the guitar. Occasionally work without the aid of an instrument. By working this way, *a cappella*, you will likely write melodies that are more singable and, as a result, more memorable.

TEXT PAINTING

One technique composers have used for generations to enhance lyrics is called text painting. Text painting is the deliberate use of melody and rhythm to match the music to the word pictures in the lyrics. As you write your next big hit, examine the lyrics for words or phrases that might lend themselves to a little text painting.

Here are a few examples from pop and theater songs:

1. *"Stop* [pause] *in the name of love"* (music stops)

2. *"Am I blue? You'd be, too…"* (melody sounds sad and forlorn)

3. *"The falling leaves drift by my window…"* (music "drifts" along)

4. *"Up, up, and away in my beautiful balloon…"* (melody soars)

5. *"Pick a little, talk a little / Cheep, cheep, cheep / Talk a lot, pick a little more"* (music mimics the sound of clucking hens)

A word of caution: Text painting is effective when used with discretion, but it can sound silly if overused. In the striving to marry your music with the lyrics, don't go overboard—unless, of course, your point is to be obvious, as with some novelty songs.

Harmony

BECOMING A CHORD JUNKIE

When I was first learning to write songs in high school, I became fascinated by the chord changes used by my favorite recording artists. As I explored the sheet music of the hit songs of the day, I discovered how a major seventh chord or a dominant seventh chord could completely alter the sound of the accompaniment and, as a result, change the sound of the song itself. Later, I learned the mysteries of the minor sixth and the "add 2/no 3rd" chords. Finally, there came the chord change of all chord changes—the "13th with the flat 9 and sharp 11" chord. Eureka! I had at long last reached the mountaintop!

Whether you are a chord junkie like me or not, having a basic understanding of harmonic structure is essential to becoming a good songwriter. Melody is the part of music that is instantly "hummable," but harmony is what gives a song its color. A typical melody can be harmonized in at least a dozen different ways. In the hands of a great arranger, even the simplest melody can be turned into an exotic harmonic adventure. But creating the original harmonization is up to the composer. Don't leave the harmonization of your melodies to others.

So how does one learn about the intricacies of harmony? The best way is to find a good teacher—either a piano teacher or a guitar teacher who understands pop music. The next best way is to play from sheet music at a piano or on the guitar, so that you can see and hear the chords at the same time. The worst way is with a book. The subject is too vast and does not lend itself to being taught from a book. (That's why I'm not going to go into any great detail about chord structure in this book.) Seriously, spend some money on music theory lessons with a teacher that understands pop music. It will be money well spent.

So if I can't teach harmony in one chapter, what shall I tell you? Let me try the shotgun approach. I'll fire off a lot of basic info, and hopefully, something will hit its target.

THE TRIAD

The basic building block of chord structure is the **triad**, or three notes in intervals of a third. Every triad has a root note, a third, and a fifth. Major chords are built upward with a root note, a major third, and a perfect fifth. A C triad, or a C chord, contains these notes: C, E, and G. Minor chords are built upward with a root note, a minor third, and a perfect fifth. Thus, a C minor chord (Cm) is spelled "C + E♭ + G." A diminished triad is built upward with a root note, a minor third, and a diminished (lowered) fifth. So a C diminished triad (C dim, or C°) is spelled "C + E♭ + G♭." See the following examples of triads built on C and G:

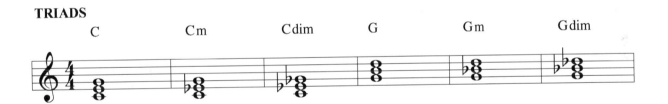

TRIADS

CHORD EXTENSIONS

Any triad may be extended by adding notes to it. Like the triad itself, extensions stack up in thirds: 1, 3, 5, 7, 9, 11, and 13. Since every triad contains a root, a third, and a fifth, the first (and by far the most common) extension is the next third in the sequence—the seventh. The seventh can be a major seventh, or a dominant seventh (lowered seventh). A C7 chord contains the lowered, dominant seventh; it is spelled "C + E + G + B♭." A C major 7 chord (C maj7) contains the major seventh and is spelled "C + E + G + B." These two chords, the C7 and the C maj7, are identical except for a simple half step on one note, but they sound and behave completely different from one another. Ah, the power of the extension.

The ninth chord follows next. A C9 chord assumes all the notes of a C7, plus the ninth—a D. The 11th and the 13th are the *superextensions*, creating very thick chords that jazz musicians love and pop musicians generally avoid.

Here are some examples of these extended chords. They are all written in the treble clef, from their root note up. In the real world of performance, these chords are usually spread out, or *voiced*, across the bass and treble clefs.

EXTENDED CHORDS

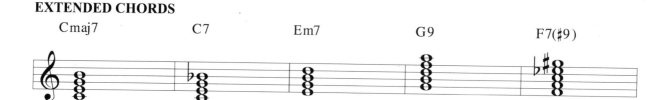

ADDED NOTES

Adding individual notes to a triad creates harmonic tension. If you want to thicken a C chord by adding the ninth without adding the seventh, you would call it a C (add 9). That same chord is also commonly called a C (add 2), or simply C2 by some. Why the "2"? Because the second and the ninth are the same note—a D.

Other commonly added notes are the sixth (C6), the suspended fourth (C sus4), and the raised fourth (C (♯4)). Each creates a unique tension that needs to be resolved. As you learn these chords, your ear will guide you toward the proper resolution.

Here are written examples of simple chords with added notes.

ADDED NOTES

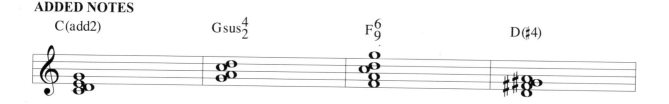

THREE CHORDS AND THE TRUTH

There is a familiar piece of Music City wisdom that says all you need in order to write a great country song is three chords and the truth. A bit simplistic, perhaps—but not wrong. Any melody that remains in a single diatonic major key can be harmonized with three chords—the I, the IV, and the V. In the key of C, that would be a C major chord, an F major chord, and a G major chord.

So as long as you are content to write songs that remain in a simple major key, you can write songs with the aid of only three chords. And trust me, hundreds of hit songs have been written with those three basic chords. However, if your melodies begin to venture out into the world of accidentals, chromatic tones, "blue" notes, "grease" notes, or modulations, you will need to expand your harmonic horizons with chord substitutions.

SUBSTITUTIONS

While most melodies can be effectively harmonized with no more than three chords, I do recommend that you study the structure of chords and the principle of chord substitutions. The more proficient you are with harmony and chords, the more interesting your songs are likely to be. This is the composer's corollary to the principle that a good lyricist should have a large vocabulary.

For every chord, there is a substitution. Sometimes there are three or four acceptable substitutions. Consider that for every note in the chromatic scale, there are at least a dozen chords that will harmonize that note. Do the math. The possible combinations of chords and substitute chords for any given melody are staggering. If you're just getting started as a songwriter, don't let that overwhelm you. There are some pretty standard substitute chords you can learn quickly.

So where does a beginning writer look for substitutions to replace a chord in a song's harmonic progression? It's not too difficult if you know this one thing: all chord substitutions share at least one common tone (sometimes two or three) with the original chord being replaced. Look for common notes in chords as a first clue for a possible substitution. Also, let the melody guide you. Any good substitute chord should suit the melody note (or notes) being harmonized.

EXAMPLES: CHORD SUBSTITUTIONS

Here are some basic substitutions for the I, IV, and V chords in the glorious key of C. Note that all the substitutions share at least one common tone with the original basic triad.

I chord (C chord): C maj7 + Am7 + Em7

(The Em7 is a bit of a stretch, but you see it does share one common tone.)

IV chord (F chord): F maj7 + Dm7 + Fm6 + B♭ maj9

V chord (G chord): G7 + Dm7/G + Em7 + B♭9

With a few simple chord substitutions, your latest song's harmonic structure will sound more sophisticated, without requiring you to have a degree in music theory.

ADEQUATE KEYBOARD OR GUITAR SKILLS

To be a nominally proficient songwriter, you need to develop adequate keyboard or guitar skills. Notice I said "adequate." You don't have to be a virtuoso pianist to write good songs. But if you can fumble out only three chords in one key, you are going to be repeating yourself—a lot. And that will get old. And you will get bored. And you will give up songwriting.

So spend some quality time developing adequate piano or guitar skills. What is "adequate"? You should be able to play in at least three major keys and three minor keys. Some technical proficiency will make you a more confident musician, which will also make you a more confident writer. You are never too old to take piano (or guitar) lessons.

And by the way, if you never studied music before, it's not too late to start. If you did study music, and stopped, you can always take it up again. It never hurts to continue your music education, whether it's music lessons, reading books, studying sheet music, or practicing some simple scales at the piano.

In Their Own Words

Every time I walk past the baby grand in my front room, I sigh and wish I could really play. Would it improve my songwriting? Actually, I think playing any instrument really well improves just about everything in life. —DEBORAH CRAIG-CLAAR

WHAT ABOUT KEYS?

When it came to playing in different keys, guitarists have had the capo bar at their disposal since the mid-1700s. And now, with the ability to transpose any modern electronic keyboard instrument into any key with the push of a button, today's songwriter has to be able to play in only one key, right? Just slap on the capo or hit the transpose button on the synthesizer, and choose any key you like. Irving Berlin, Tin Pan Alley superstar, writer of "White Christmas" and a hundred other standards, was a self-taught musician who could play only in the key of F♯. So he had a specially built piano that allowed him to shift the piano hammers to play in other keys, while staying on the black keys of the keyboard. (Imagine what Irving might have done with a rack of synthesizer gear and a digital audio workstation.)

There is a longstanding and widely held belief among musicians that different keys have different sonic characteristics and emotional qualities. (According to the infamous faux rock band Spinal Tap, D minor is the saddest of all keys. Music theorists are free to disagree.) Many musicians feel that the flatted keys are darker in their tonal quality than are the sharped keys. The key of A major seems brighter than ♭. No doubt, when writing at the guitar, keys like E and A and D that use more open strings will sound brighter than the key of F or D♭—especially when played without a capo.

Undeniably, the ability to play and write in more than one key will certainly broaden the composer's harmonic horizons. Besides, you never know when a modulation might come in handy.

HARMONIC BALANCE AND ECONOMY

It is important to find the right balance between harmonic activity and melodic activity. Too many chord changes happening too fast will sound manic. They may even distract from the melody. Too few chord changes might sound boring. As a rule a busy melody should not have busy chord changes. An elongated or sustained melody allows for more chord movement in support of the melody.

Now let's assume for a moment that you know all the great chords and their substitutions. You are simply dying to use them in your newest song. Hold on just a minute. It is also important to maintain a sense of economy. Don't try to use every hot chord change you know in every song you write. Save something for your next song.

COMPOSING FROM CHORD CHANGES

It is not unusual for some hit songwriters to begin writing with a drum groove and a great set of chord changes. That approach can be very successful in creating good songs with solid melodies. A great set of chord changes can even elicit a memorable melody. It's as if there are melodies hidden inside the changes and the writer has to draw the melody out. The chord changes act as a foundation on which you can build a melody. In fact, any given set of chord changes might inspire multiple melodies to choose from. John Lennon claimed his song "Because" (on the album *Abbey Road)* was inspired from the chords to Beethoven's "Moonlight Sonata"—played *backwards.*

When composing a chord progression, there can be a natural inclination to lead with your hands rather than your ears. Your fingers will automatically want to fall on familiar keys or comfortable strings, and you will soon be repeating yourself. As your knowledge of chord structure grows, so should the strength of your inner ear. Strive to hear the harmony before your fingers play a chord. As your musical confidence grows, you may find that your best work happens away from the piano or the guitar. That's right. You may want to try composing your music without the help of your trusty Martin or dusty Steinway.

ORIGINALITY

Every good musician begins by emulating others. Beethoven's early works were reminiscent of his hero, Mozart. Keith Richards of the Rolling Stones admits that he learned to play guitar by stealing Chuck Berry's riffs. We are all borrowing from those who came before us. It isn't criminal to mimic someone else's music, as long as you raise your work to a new level. A creative person learns to take from an existing piece and come up with something new. At some point you learn to use the things you like and put your own spin on it. Eventually, you sound like yourself.

Unfortunately, too many songwriters (Christian writers included) are content to remain at the mimicking stage, never moving on to create anything original. It is very difficult to break away from the magnetic influences of your favorite music to become your own creative person. I personally know this to be a fact. But Christian writers must work to find their own voice and to "sing unto the Lord a *new song.*" In his essay "The Role of Music in Worship," Harold Best cautions us: "The trouble with many Christian musicians is that they begin and continue imitating. Therefore, they have nothing new worth imitating... We have learned to cover this [imitating] up by calling it *ministry*" (*Tools for Ministry and Career,* p. 40).

Rhythm

The final musical element is **rhythm**. Rhythm has become all important in contemporary songwriting, pushing melody and harmony into the background. Having a great drum track and catchy rhythms can make the difference between a smash radio hit and a song that is never heard. But there is more to the use of rhythm in songwriting than the latest drum loop and percussion effects. Here, I want to discuss the several roles that rhythm can play in a song: the **prosody** of the lyrics, the **meter** and **tempo** of the song, and the overall **groove** of the music.

PROSODY AND SCANSION

The study of the metrical structure of verse is called **prosody**. The analysis of poetic verse into metrical patterns is **scansion**. Confused yet? *Prosody* and *scansion* are terms used by songwriters (sometimes interchangeably) to refer to the rhythmic agreement of words and music. Well-composed music has natural rhythmic stress points. As a melody flows by, certain notes are accented more than others. Some notes are longer in duration than others. Without these differences, music would be stiff and machinelike, not to mention boring. It is crucial that the stress points of the melody fit well with the natural rhythms of the lyric.

SOME SCANSION GUIDELINES

Here are a few simple guidelines for writing melodic rhythms that fit the lyrics well:

1. **The rhythm of the lyrics should "scan" naturally.** Don't place musical accents and stresses onto syllables that aren't stressed and accented in normal speech. As my mother taught me, the em*pha*sis should not fall on the wrong syl*lab*le.

2. **It sounds odd to stress small words like "the" or "and" or "a" in normal speech. It usually sounds just as odd to stress them in music.** Consider the opening lines to "The Best Things in Life Are Free" (DeSylva, Brown, and Henderson): *"The moon belongs to everyone. / The best things in life are free."* The musical stresses align perfectly with the natural spoken stresses of the line. How awkward it would have been to stress "the" and "to" and "in."

3. **To discover the secret to a lyric's natural rhythm, read the words aloud.** The lyric will immediately show you its own natural stress points.

4. **Save the long notes for words that matter more.** For example, consider holding a dramatic word at the end of a line for a longer duration, allowing the word's significance to sink in. Conversely, if a phrase might be spoken quickly in normal speech, then perhaps it should be sung quickly.

5. **Sometimes there are several ways to stress a lyric**—all of them natural. Which word (or words) you choose to stress in your melody can affect the interpretation of the line.

Take the simple line "I must go to the cross." Below are three legitimate and natural readings of the line. Each one changes the focus of the lyrics subtly.

- *I* must go to the *cross*.
- I must *go* to the *cross*.
- I *must* go to the cross.

6. **Not all single-syllable words are created equal.** A word like "choose," with its blended beginning "ch" sound and its "z" closing, takes longer to shape and sing than the word "hat," which can be spit out in no time. Don't assume because a word has just one syllable that it can be sung quickly, especially in

pickup phrases that lead to a major stress point in the melody. There are lots of single-syllable words that need a slightly longer note to sound natural. "You" and "your" are different by only one little letter on the written page. But from a singing standpoint, "your" is a much longer word than "you." "There" takes more time to enunciate than "the." "Can't" sounds like "can" when sung too fast. Pay attention to how your melody is treating the lyrics.

7. **Not all single-syllable words really are single-syllable words.** "Our" looks like a single-syllable word, but it is properly pronounced with two syllables: "ow-er."

8. **Writing more than one note per syllable is known as *melisma*.** Melisma can work wonderfully well, but it can also sound stilted and awkward when not done properly. Consider the stretched-out hook line of Dolly Parton's hit song *"I-ee-I-ee-I will always love you."* I'll let you decide if that's a good use of melisma, or bad. Just remember the axiom of Less Is More.

METER

Most pop music is in 4/4 (four-four) time—sometimes referred to simply as "four." Music geeks (like me) who studied music theory were also taught to call it "common time," because 4/4 is the most commonly used meter. You could probably have a successful career as a songwriter and never write in anything but 4/4. Still it would be a shame to never explore the worlds of 3/4, or 6/8, or 12/8. (And let's not even get into 5/4 and 7/8 and all the odd meters.) Much like your other songwriting tools, the broader your range of these time signatures, the more creative options you will have.

For the true beginner who may be wondering what all these numbers mean, there is an easy way to decipher the numeric code of any time signature. Simply put, 4/4 time means the song will be divided in measures of music that each contain four quarter notes or the equivalent of four quarter notes. Similarly, 3/4 time means that there are three quarter notes or their equivalent in each bar, 6/8 time means that there are six eighth notes or their equivalent per bar, and so on.

Every time signature has its own characteristics. For example, 4/4 time is the most straight-ahead meter. It is the time signature that the world moves to. It is natural. It is even. It is rock steady. Take it slow, and you can feel every 16th note in the accompaniment. Take it fast enough, and you've got a polka. The signature of 3/4 is more cerebral. You have to think about it a little more than 4/4. Take it fast enough, and 3/4 becomes a waltz, with a heavy downbeat followed by two lilting afterbeats. The time of 6/8 is usually felt in two beats—three eighths, plus three eighths. And 12/8 is the time signature of the blues: four beats made of three eighth notes each. Good songwriters feel at home using each of these four basic time signatures. The best way for a beginner to learn to apply them is to experiment. Don't worry about the odd meters like 5/4 and 7/8 for now. They are lots of fun to work with, but their application in the world of pop music is rare.

TEMPO

We all know the dilemma—finding the perfect tempo for our latest song demo. The tempo, or speed, at which a song is played can completely alter the feel of the song. Too fast, and the words feel rushed. Too slow, and the groove starts to drag. Sometimes the right tempo is immediately evident. Other times you might need to test several tempos to find the right pace. Here are a few tempo tips to keep in mind when you're working on your next magnum opus.

1. **Get yourself a quality metronome.** The new digital metronomes that offer eighth note, 16th note, and triplet subdivisions of the beat are great. They also have a tap tempo feature that allows you to tap in a basic tempo, which the metronome then captures for you.

2. **Experiment with the tempo.** The slightest change of one or two beats per minute (bpm) can make a significant difference in the feel of a song, especially at slower tempos. Sometimes a more extreme tempo change can be a surprising success. Slowing down a fast song gives it a whole new feel. You may discover you love it at the slower speed. Conversely, your latest ballad might find new energy at a faster tempo.

3. **When struggling to find the right tempo, try singing the chorus with no accompaniment.** Let the words settle into their natural rhythm, then try that tempo for the rest of the song.

It don't mean a thing if it ain't got that swing.
—Irving Mills and Duke Ellington

GROOVE

When musicians talk about groove, they are talking about the feel of a song—particularly its rhythmic feel. In the 1960s, the studio rhythm section of Motown Records, The Funk Brothers, created some of the most memorable and solid grooves ever recorded: "Papa Was a Rollin' Stone," "Signed, Sealed, Delivered, I'm Yours," "My Girl," "I Heard It Through the Grapevine," to name just a few. Largely dependent on solid drum and bass tracks, a great groove can be the defining sound of a hit record. Groove is what makes the listener want to move to the rhythm of the song. (My fellow Baptists beware—a great groove can lead to spontaneous dancing!)

Precisely because groove is all about the intangible feel of a song, the best way to study groove is to listen to records that have great grooves. Putting on just about any hit song from the Motown catalog would be a good place to start. Stevie Wonder and Stevie Winwood are both masters of groove. Tower of Power is a groove machine. Rufus (the group that made Chaka Khan famous) is as well. Kirk Franklin and Israel Houghton are no strangers to great groove. And the undisputed master of groove would have to be the late James Brown. But don't think that groove is limited to soul, R&B, and urban music. Rock musicians and country musicians know how to groove, too. Get out your records that make you feel like dancing. That's the best place to learn about groove.

Coda

A really good melody stands on its own, without lyrics. A quality melody is singable. It is memorable. But without the words, it's not quite a song. A great lyric is a pleasure to read on the page, but without the music it isn't quite alive. When music is coupled with the right words, the whole becomes greater than the sum of its parts. Each half elevates the other. The lyric is better for being with the music. The music is better for having the lyric attached. A good song is a marriage of words and music.

But how do you achieve that perfect marriage when setting music to words? It's vital that you capture the essence of the lyric. Pay attention to what the words are saying. Consider these questions:

- What is the overall emotion of the lyric? What sort of music will best express that feeling?
- Where are the peaks and valleys in the words? How can the music be shaped to fit the lyric's natural highs and lows?

It is not enough to slap any old tune onto the words. Nor can you force a cool musical groove onto a set of lyrics and hope for the best. Writing music to bring out the best in a lyric is an elusive art that involves experimentation, experience, and a gift from God.

The Perspiration Stage of Creativity

Remember the four stages of creativity outlined in chapter 2? It is in the third stage, illumination, that the most visible signs of writing occur. The words and music should pour out without a lot of second-guessing. Illumination is often driven by emotion, even inspiration. But after that, it is time for the hard work of verification or, in other words, rewriting. Where illumination is fueled by emotion (and black coffee), verification is guided by the intellect. Now is the time to be ruthlessly objective about your latest musical creation. This involves operating not from the "heart" but rather from the "head." It all sounds a little schizophrenic, I admit. But a good writer must make this shift from illumination to verification because without rewriting, the creative process is unfinished.

"But I have a song, and it's complete," you argue. "The creative process is finished for me." As I said in chapter 2, writing a song without ever rewriting it is sort of like building a car but never painting it. The car is complete in the sense that it has an engine, four tires, seats, and a steering wheel. It drives perfectly well. But with no paint job, the car isn't really finished. No one would want to buy that car. Unfortunately, too many beginning Christian songwriters are building cars with no paint job; they never reach the rewriting stage. They are content to stop at inspiration and never move on to the perspiration part of writing. If that has been your songwriting modus operandi, then this chapter is for you.

Rewrites? But the Song Wrote Itself!

It seems that every big-time songwriter has at least one story of a great song—a smash hit song—that was penned effortlessly in a matter of minutes.

"I'm tellin' you the absolute truth, Dave," they say to the Big Shot TV Talk Show Host. "The song just spilled out, complete and without flaw, while I was drinkin' a latte grande at the corner coffee bar. I took the song straight into the studio, and now it's my biggest hit single ever. Sold 5 gadrillion records."

And the songwriter still has the coffee-stained napkin covered with illegible lyrics to prove it. Stories of such songwriting derring-do lead the rest of us mortals to wonder if perhaps great songs are supposed to come easily. If we're working too hard at it, maybe we're doing something wrong. Occasionally, we are misled even further when the story of spontaneous inspiration is shared by one of our Christian brethren. "It just came to me straight from the Lord," the writer offers as she picks up her Dove Award for Song of the Year. There's not much arguing with that sort of inspiration, is there?

I am not going to deny that some truly terrific songs are penned quickly and with seemingly little effort. Some of my own best songs have happened in a flash of inspiration, so I know it can happen. Still, it's been my experience that this occurs mostly to talented people who spend a lot of hours working hard at their craft. These writers know how to draw deeply and quickly from the creative well without wasting time wondering where the well is. They devote most of their waking hours to being creative. They read incessantly. They observe people, nature, and life. They write on a regular basis. Much of what they write never gets past the trashcan. And every now and again, they write a great song in a matter of minutes.

Most seasoned professional writers require more than 15 minutes to write a well-crafted song. A good deal more. And the writing process invariably involves some degree of rewriting. The rewriting may be subtle—perhaps just some minor editing. It may be severe—throwing out entire verses and starting over. Successful songwriters know better than anyone that writing is rewriting.

In Their Own Words:
How important is rewriting to you?

> I believe rewriting is one of the greatest things that separates amateur writers from advanced writers. Amateurs spend 80 percent of their time writing and 20 percent rewriting. Pros spend 20 percent writing and 80 percent rewriting.
> —Tony Wood

> My biggest disappointments concerning songs I have written can all be attributed to an inadequate amount of rewriting.
> —Deborah Craig-Claar

> Rewriting is an absolute necessity!   —J. Paul Williams

> I always rewrite. I am an obsessive-compulsive rewriter.
> —Lowell Alexander

> Amateurs often believe their first drafts are divinely inspired. Pros know the humbling truth about lyric writing: There's always a better way to say it.
> —Kyle Matthews

Misconceptions About Rewriting

The commonly accepted folklore in Nashville is that Willie Nelson penned "Crazy" in a matter of minutes on a paper napkin at Tootsie's Lounge in downtown Nashville. He may well have done just that. Willie (notice how I casually refer to him on a first-name basis, as if I actually know the man—I don't) certainly is talented enough to whip out a major-league standard while downing a beer in a smoky honky-tonk. Yes, the song appeared on a barroom napkin in 15 minutes, but it took Willie 15 minutes, *plus the sum total of his creative life experience up to that moment* to write the song. The problem with these 15-minute-wonder-song stories is that they spawn some hard-to-shake misconceptions about songwriting. Here are two I'd like to clear up before we go any further.

MISCONCEPTION NO. 1:
THE BEST SONGS COME QUICKLY

Imagine this: you've just penned your latest song, and it came to you in a flash of unprecedented creative clarity. You think to yourself, "I wrote the song in 15 minutes. It must be brilliant. Willie Nelson would be proud." That's tempting to believe. But it's probably just the creative euphoria talking. Maybe it's a great song. Maybe it's not. All you know for sure is that you wrote it quickly. If it's truly a good song, it will still be a good song a week later when you look at it a little more objectively. Chances are it needs some rewriting.

I have lots of songs in my own catalog that were absolutely brilliant the day I wrote them. But over time they have become pretty average. Perhaps they were never as great as I thought they were in the first place.

MISCONCEPTION NO. 2:
INSPIRATION IS WHAT MAKES A SONG GREAT

In our little world of Christian music, a great deal of emphasis is placed on inspiration. (After all, another name for Christian music is Inspirational music.) When we are writing in times of deep prayer and meditation, it is very tempting to say about our creative efforts, "God gave me this song"—implying that the song is perfect because it came from God.

I am not about to deny that the Lord is in the inspiration business. I firmly believe He is. But I don't think songwriting means taking dictation from God. In fact, I believe God expects a little bit of effort on our part. (Otherwise, we shouldn't put our names on the songs we write, should we?) Inspiration is an important part of the creative process, but it is only a part—not the whole. Whenever I hear a novice Christian songwriter proudly announce, "God gave me this song," I am reminded of something a wise university professor once told me: "God gives us all breath. But sometimes it smells bad."

The Truth About Rewriting

The truth is that rewriting is an absolutely integral part of the writing process. I repeat—*writing is rewriting*. If you do not go through some sort of rewriting process, the chances are very high that your songs are not as good as they could be.

The truth about rewriting is that fast or slow doesn't matter. How long it takes to write a song is no reflection on the quality of the song. Fast simply means you are quick, not necessarily good.   Keep in mind the "Willie Nelson factor": You may have penned the song in a matter of minutes, but you may also have been thinking about the song for months.

The truth is that the writing struggle may take days, even weeks, to complete. Ernest Hemingway rewrote the novel *A Farewell to Arms* 39 times before he was satisfied with the results. When asked why he made so many rewrites, he said he wanted to get the words right. Granted, a song is not a novel. But if Hemingway was willing to rewrite, then we should be, too. It is not unusual for me to write a song in a single day. Inevitably, however, each time I go through the song, I discover small improvements to be made for at least a few days. The changes are sometimes miniscule: deleting the word "and," or changing a single note of the melody, or altering a chord in the bridge. And sometimes the changes are huge: deleting the bridge, or rearranging the order of the verses, or rewriting the chorus. Big or small, these changes are necessary to make so that the song becomes the best it can be.

Lowell Alexander is one of my favorite co-writers, and he is a relentless rewriter. Once, days after we had completed a song, he called me, suggesting a couple of small changes to the lyrics. He hadn't slept the night before because a tiny flaw in the words had kept him awake! We made the changes, and the song was the better for them. The truth is most amateur songwriters stop working the moment they write the last word of the bridge or chorus. And most professional songwriters know that their initial effort is nothing but a first draft, and their work has just begun.

The First Draft

The sooner you can accept the idea that your first draft is indeed a first draft and not the finished song, the sooner you will begin to see your own work in an objective critical light. And it is crucial you learn to be ruthlessly honest about your own work. It's better if you discover your song's weaknesses and correct them than if your publisher (or your spouse, or your chiropractor, or your plumber) has to point them out to you. Measure your work by professional standards, because that's how it will be measured in the marketplace.

CHECK, CHECK— 1, 2, 3...

So, how do you examine your own song objectively? It can be very difficult to criticize your baby. Over time, it will become an easier, more natural process. In *The Craft of Lyric Writing*, Sheila Davis offers five detailed checklists to follow when rewriting, covering everything from form to emotional content (pp. 290 through 292). Hers is a wonderful book, and I recommend you read it. However, if you don't own her book yet, here is a single shorter list of questions to consider as a good starting place for rewriting:

1. **Does the song have a well-constructed form?** It can be tempting to ignore the rules of song form. But as I discussed in chapter 3, the accepted song forms have lasted as long as they have for one reason: they work. As you grow as a songwriter, there will be opportunities to bend, even break, the rules. But as a beginner, you should discipline your writing to follow the forms. Do the verses match one another in length and shape? Is the rhyme scheme consistent? Is the hook line placed in a strong position? Does the melody lift at the chorus? Do the various musical sections of the song work well together? Examine the form of your song carefully.

2. **Are the key lines strong?** As discussed in chapter 4, examine the importance of the two key lines of a song—the hook and the opening line. Does the opening line grab the listener's attention? Is the hook memorable? Is it placed prominently in the chorus, or in the first or last line of the A section? If either line is weak, it's time to rewrite.

3. **Is the song about one thing?** A song is about *one thing*. It has one point to make. That single point is usually reflected in the song's title or its hook. Everything in the lyrics should support that point. The verses should support the chorus. The chorus should support the hook. The bridge should connect back to the chorus seamlessly.

    Even the imagery in the lyrics should have a connection to the one point of the song. If your song is were about being on fire for the Lord, then lyrical images of heat and flame and spiritual passion would all work well. But you wouldn't want to use word pictures that were gentle and breezy. They wouldn't fit the overall concept of your song.

4. **Is the song understandable?** In his essay "The Principles of Rewriting," Rick Beresford notes: "Songwriting is 'flash art.' Everything must be understood, make sense, lyrically and melodically, the instant it's heard" (*Songwriting and the Creative Process*, p. 88). So if your brother-in-law fails to understand your latest song after he's heard it three times, either your sister married an idiot or your song needs rewriting.

    Many songs have an underlying story or concept; this needs to unfold logically, or else the listener will become lost or confused. Check your lyrics to be certain the progression of events are never out of sequence. For example, if someone dies in the first chorus, he or she shouldn't be alive in the second verse. (Okay—you know I'm not referring to Jesus here.)

5. **Is the song memorable?** This is all about the effective use of repetition. A good pop song relies on repetition to make it memorable. This applies to both the lyrics and the music. Is there enough repetition in your song that a first-time listener can at least sing the hook line?

6. **Is the song interesting?** Repetition makes a song memorable. Too much repetition makes a song boring. Variation in the music and the lyrics is essential if you want your song to be interesting. Examine your song for the right balance of repetition and variation. Too much or too little of either weakens the song.

    Now is also the time to check your lyrics for the use of interesting rhyme and poetic devices. Is there metaphor or simile in the song? What about irony or an interesting character? Does the song *show* the listener something, or is it merely telling?

7. **Have you been consistent?** Good writers maintain a consistent point of view. Any change in point of view should be obvious to the listener without the aid of a lyric sheet. Better yet, don't change point of view at all.

    Good writers stick to a consistent language style. Don't mix archaic church words with hip, trendy street language.

    Consistency plays into the music side of things as well. The tone of the music needs to be compatible and consistent with the tone of the lyrics.

8. **Do the words and music make a good marriage?** The words should make the music better. The music should make the words better. If the words scan awkwardly when they are sung, you need to rewrite. If the range of the melody is difficult to sing, you need to rewrite. If there is no place for the singer to breathe, you need to rewrite. The combination of the music and lyrics should feel natural, even inevitable. If it doesn't feel that way, then (you guessed it) you need to rewrite.

9. **Does your song pay off?** Every song should go somewhere. From the opening line to the closing notes, a good song builds to a satisfying payoff for the listener. You might take your listeners to a surprise "Aha!" moment. Or you might lead them to a quiet, sentimental conclusion. You might lift them to a musical peak, or leave them in breathless quiet. What you must not do is write a song with an emotional "flat line." If you do, the song will be dead.

    This emotional climb becomes a greater challenge if the first chorus contains a significant payoff. In that case, it becomes important for any verses that follow the first chorus to set up the chorus to pay off again, but in a new way—each time the chorus rolls around.

10. **Is your theology accurate?** Christian songwriters have an added layer to their writing that secular writers don't have to deal with—theology. As you rewrite your song, examine the theological and spiritual content of your lyrics for Biblical accuracy and consistency. I am not suggesting that your lyrics be purely scriptural or that they be sermons. I am advising you to be careful not to put misleading or inaccurate theology in your lyrics.

The question of accurate theology isn't a new concern for Christian songwriters. Generations of Christians have received some of their most bedrock theology from the hymns they learned in church. They may not have been able to quote scripture and verse, but believers in the late 1800s learned that God the Father is "Immortal, invisible, God only wise / In Light inaccessible, hid from our eyes" when they sang Walter Chalmers Smith's brilliant hymn text. A child who has never read John 3:16 can know that Jesus loves her, when she sings the simple truth "for the Bible tells me so." Today's churchgoers learn basic Bible truths from the songs they sing in worship. Whether you realize it or not, you carry a heavy responsibility to be sure that your songs are theologically sound.

As a record producer for Point of Grace, the Talleys, and other Christian artists, I have run across a few songs written by professional Christian songwriters that had small theological inaccuracies. These problems were always fixable, and the writers, once made aware of the problems, were always willing to correct things. Why hadn't these writers seen the problems themselves when they wrote the song? Perhaps it was nothing more than they were too close to the song to see the problem. There is a lesson in this for you: find a qualified objective Bible scholar whom you trust to take a quick look at your lyrics. Perhaps your pastor or a minister could help you with this. Remember, you are seeking their input on the theological content of your lyrics, not on the art of your song. Still, you want to make certain that your art is also good theology.

TRUE CONFESSIONS

I recently served as a choral clinician at a music conference where one of my older songs was featured in a session. This particular song is more than 25 years old, and I had not heard it in a long time. The effect for me was almost as though I was hearing the song for the first time. So imagine my surprise when I spotted a potential theology problem in my own lyrics as the last two lines of the second verse rolled back around into the chorus. (Okay, it's only a problem if the listener hears the lyrics a certain way. But that doesn't change the fact that the lyrics could be misleading.) Here are the last lines of the second verse and the opening lines of the chorus. See if you think there is a theology problem.

> (verse)
> *God gave to us His only Son,*
> *The selfless sacrifice.*
> *How can we pay for all He's done*
> *When Jesus paid the price?*
> (chorus)
> *We will serve Him for the rest of our days.*
> *We will serve Him with the highest of praise…*
>
> "WE WILL SERVE HIM" WORDS AND MUSIC BY ROBERT STERLING AND CHRIS MACHEN
> © GlorySound Music

On the page, the question asked in the end of the verse is clearly rhetorical. The implied answer is we cannot ever pay for all Jesus has done. However, the listener hears the verse move straight into the chorus and may well miss the rhetorical nature of the question. The listener may think I am saying we can pay for Jesus' sacrifice by serving Him—a blatant theological gaffe.

If I were writing this song today, I would change the end of the second verse to avoid the possibility of such a serious theological misunderstanding. Live and learn.

> *I've found over the years that people of faith tend to accept what they hear in religious music as truth, and that scares the snot out of me. Had I known ahead of time that some of my songs would be in print several million times, I would not have had the courage to make them public.*
> —CHARLES F. BROWN

Time to Rewrite

> *A writer's best friend is the wastepaper basket.*
> —ISAAC BASHEVIS SINGER

So now you've gone through your first draft, examined it in the harsh light of day, and found some places needing improvement. Good. Now comes the hard part: fixing what doesn't work. Here are two approaches to consider as you rewrite:

WHEN IN DOUBT, THROW IT OUT

You must not be afraid to toss out a line or a word or a rhyme that is not serving the song. This may be difficult to do at first, especially if you lack the confidence that you can replace the line with something better. But nobody ever said writing a well-crafted song was easy. That goes especially for writing a well-crafted Christian song.

One step in this process is to toss out lyrics that are mediocre and trite. This requires objectivity and some experience, because mediocrity is so … mediocre. Mediocre lyrics just sort of "sit there," filling up space. Often, they're not all that terribly wrong. They're just not right. To fix mediocre lines, you have to dig deep to find something more creative to go in their place. This can be difficult, but once you write the improved lyrics, you will be glad you made the effort.

Another step is to trim the lyrical fat from your song. In the lean, mean world of contemporary music, where "less is more," there is little room for words that aren't absolutely necessary. This includes entire lines of lyrics as well as individual words, and even syllables, within a given line of lyrics. For example, if the lyrics to the bridge don't contribute something new to a song, perhaps you don't need the bridge at all. Connecting words, like "and" and "but," can often be dropped. "Because" can be reduced to "'cause." The missing words or syllables will still be implied in the line, without the rhythmic clutter. I am not suggesting that all contemporary music be lyrically anorexic. But most songs do not benefit from words that act as little more than filler.

Occasionally, you will run across a well-written line, a line you really like, that needs to be replaced because it doesn't support the song. This goes for the clever triple rhyme in the second verse that doesn't lead to the chorus, and for the cool, artsy phrase in the bridge that nobody but you understands. No matter how much you love these lines, you need to remove them and work to replace them with words that are just as creative and which do support the song. (Take the old lines and put them in your ideas file, and give them the chance of finding a home in a future song.) If it makes you feel any better, think of this as building character. A seasoned songwriter builds a lot of character.

The job of replacing a weak line with something better is not an easy one. When replacing lyrics, the music dictates the length of the phrase, the number of words or syllables, and sometimes even the rhyme scheme. These are limitations you just have to deal with. However, replacing the faulty line will be easier if you know what you want to communicate and you stick to the point. Don't waste time chasing lines that don't say what you need to say. Write down in simple prose what needs to be said in that space, and refer to that as you drag out your thesaurus, dictionary, and rhyming dictionary in search of the perfect replacement.

EXAMINE YOUR WORK FROM ANOTHER ANGLE

Don't automatically assume that the first verse you write for a song will remain the first verse; maybe it will be the second verse. And maybe the second verse is a better bridge than it is a second verse. Similarly, you may find that the first verse is stronger when its third and fourth lines are flipped to be the first and second lines. When rewriting a song, it's smart to be open to any possibility of improving your song. And that means you must be willing to turn your song inside out and look at it from different angles.

In my experience critiquing beginner's songs for the Gospel Music Association, I heard dozens of songs that could have been improved by simply moving things around a bit. A song is not a jigsaw puzzle, but it may be worth the effort to see if the lyrics work better in a different sequence than you originally imagined. In my own writing, I have turned bridges into verses, verses into choruses, and channels into bridges. I have cannibalized material from one song and put it successfully into another. I have edited two verses down to one. I have relocated a rhyme in order to put the stronger image at the end of the rhyme. The important lesson is that everything is open to change when rewriting. And in order to see those potential changes, sometimes it helps to look at your song from a fresh perspective.

> *Don't show your song to anyone too soon. After you've rewritten it*
> *until you think it's just perfect, put it in a drawer and leave it for a*
> *week. Then get it out and have another try at it.*
> —CLAIRE CLONINGER

Some Words of Encouragement and Advice

One of the coolest things to happen in the history of songwriting came about when I was a teenager. Recording artists began having the words to their songs printed on their records' album sleeves. (If you are younger than 30 years of age, you probably have never seen an album sleeve. Just think of it as a prehistoric version of the booklet that comes in a CD jewel box.) This was great, because I could study and learn from the lyrics of my favorite songwriters while I listened to their records. However, this terrific teaching tool came with a downside. Seeing the lyrics printed out all nice and neat made it all look so easy, as if the songwriter wrote it down like that the very first time. When my own songs didn't spill from my pen in such a finished manner, I felt reason to be discouraged. Maybe I wasn't a real songwriter. It never occurred to me back then that the song might have been rewritten a time or two before it was printed on the album sleeve. So allow me to close this chapter with some gentle words of advice and encouragement.

1. **Don't be deceived by someone else's finished song.** Almost certainly the song didn't start out the way you hear it on the record. It has probably been through the rewrite grinder. What's more, the rewrite may well have come at the cost of a few nights' sleep and a large bottle of Pepto-Bismol. So take heart as you rewrite. Even the most hardened professionals have to go through the same ordeal.

    Last summer, I visited the Morgan Library and Museum in New York City. There I saw the original manuscript of Beethoven's Piano Trio in D Major, op. 70, no. 1. What struck me is that this remarkable genius had scribbles and scratch-outs on his music, reminding me that even brilliant writers rewrite.

2. **Aim for progress, not perfection.** If you are a beginning songwriter, your number-one goal should be to improve. (I cannot say that enough times in this book.) The more you work at the craft of songwriting, the better you will become. If anybody should understand this struggle, it should be Christian songwriters, who already know we are all works in progress. Well, so are your songs. Adopt the attitude that your best song ever will be your *next* song.

3. **Seek qualified, honest criticism.** It is better to be saved by honest criticism than damned by faint praise. We all want people to like our songs. And most of us get plenty of ego-building compliments from our family and friends at church. But unless your grandmother is Marilyn Bergman or your best church buddy is Steven Curtis Chapman, chances are your family and friends aren't really qualified to offer worthwhile criticism of your work. If you want to improve as a writer, you must seek the objective criticism of writers and musicians who are better than you. If you are not fortunate enough to know any qualified writers and musicians, there are songwriting competitions and online services that offer song critiques. The GMA Academy (gospelmusic.org) is one that focuses entirely on Christian music.

    Here's the important part: Once you ask for this sort of criticism, you must be willing to take the bad with the good. Sure, it's difficult to hear someone tell you that your song needs work, but don't take it personally. Learn from the experience and grow.

Songs are like children. It's hard for a parent to look into the crib and say, 'My baby is ugly.' Find a brave soul with experience that is not afraid to tell you your baby is ugly. —LOWELL ALEXANDER

4. **Songwriting is a process.** Becoming a good songwriter takes time. It takes patience. And if you ever want to be successful at it, becoming a good songwriter takes the willingness to rewrite.

A Real-Life Rewriting Example

What follows is a handful of examples, re-creating a portion of the rewrites one of my recent songs went through before reaching its final stage. The song is now titled "Let Us Not Forget." It began as "May We Not Forget."

Of the five examples that follow, the first two are scans of my handwriting on legal pads. (*Scribbling* is perhaps a better word.) I am a prehistoric writer who still works with pencil and paper. I prefer to work on a legal pad with a mechanical pencil. But if those tools aren't available, I literally begin on whatever paper I can find in the immediate vicinity, and with whatever writing utensil is handy—from a No. 2 pencil to a dull Crayola. I move to the computer when I think the lyrics are pretty much done, and then continue editing from there. One reason I write on paper, at least in the early stages, is that it is so tactile and immediate. I can "feel" the words as I write them. Writing by hand also allows me to quickly jot down lyric snippets, ideas, possible rhymes, and word pictures anywhere on the page that is convenient. Sometimes those tidbits make it into the lyric. Sometimes they don't.

The last three examples are versions of the lyrics that made it into my computer. You'll see the first of my "finished" lyrics. After that are the lyrics I sent to Regi Stone when he was writing the music, complete with lyric options. The last example shows what came to be the final lyrics Regi Stone set to music.

IN THE BEGINNING ...

"Let Us Not Forget" began as a submission for use in a choral musical. The musical's theme was "praying for our country." There was a specific need for a song, a musical prayer of remembrance, for those brave people who defend our nation. I began with the title "May We Not Forget." I quickly wrote an ABA focusing on the sacrifice of those who give their lives in the defense of others. I originally figured I would write an AABA, but that didn't happen until some eight versions later. As is almost always the case when I start a song with the lyrics, I wrote with a simple tune in my head. This helps me stick to a form and know if the words "sing" well. Later I developed the melody more completely, only to ultimately toss it out. More about the music rewrites later.

Example 1 is the very first draft page of "May We Not Forget." It contains the skeletal lyric work that became the initial ABA form. In this brainstorming stage, words may pop into my head. I write them down and a form emerges. This is a spontaneous process, and the page sometimes is used for more-mundane things besides just lyrics. (Notice the reminder in the top left-hand corner that I had a ten o'clock haircut appointment on Thursday.) My first drafts sometimes include appointments, phone messages, reminders, and who-knows-what dashed alongside my lyrics. This part of the process is ugly and messy. Frankly, it's a wonder I can later decipher what I've written.

If you can read my scribbling, you'll see that the first A section is pretty much formed from the start. The two double rhymes hidden inside the stanza became a shaping factor of the song ("others/brothers"; "pleasures/treasures"). These initial raw lines served as the form for subsequent A sections. Right away, you see me questioning, scratching out, and changing things. I left space below the first A section for a second A section, which I assumed I would later write but never did; apparently, the idea for the B section came to me, and I worked on that instead. (See the scribbling about halfway down the page that starts with "Running t'ward the fray.") The concluding A section begins at the bottom of the page, and it continued onto the back of that same piece of paper (not shown).

Along the right-hand side of the page, you'll see lists of words I jotted down as possible rhymes for the last line of the B section. At the top of the page in the right corner is a couplet that must have hit me. I wrote it down, and it almost made it into the finished lyrics.

EXAMPLE 1. FIRST DRAFT OF INITIAL ABA
(THE PORTION OF THE LYRICS ABOUT SOLDIERS)

HOW ABOUT TRYING IT THIS WAY?

After completing the initial ABA about the sacrifice of those soldiers who fought and died for us, it occurred to me that I could write another ABA mirroring the first, focusing on Jesus' sacrifice for us. (Brilliant, yes? Maybe not.) Example 2 is more hen scratching on the legal pad, showing the initial stage of the development of this particular idea. (Best of luck to you deciphering the scribbles, by the way.) Look past the two names near the top of the page, and you will see the basic structure of the first A section and the B section. Both are marked with boxes around them, indicating that those pieces were the ones I would transfer to the next stage of writing, whether onto another piece of paper or into the computer. Along the outside fringes of the page are word experiments, couplets, phrases, and ideas that I toyed with before settling on the lyrics.

The remainder of the draft of this ABA was on another page of paper (not reproduced here). That page looks a lot like the one that follows—pretty much illegible to anyone but myself. But between the two pages, I believed I had the second half of the song completed.

Of course, I was wrong.

EXAMPLE 2. EARLY DRAFT OF THE SECOND ABA
(THE JESUS PORTION OF THE LYRICS)

MY GENIUS IS IGNORED

So, by this time, I had what I believed was a finished set of lyrics with a most unusual form: ABA–ABA. Two ABAs. Parallel halves of the same song. Half devoted to the sacrifice of American soldiers, the other half to the sacrifice of Jesus. Innovative, or so I thought. The music I composed for it was very open and "American." Remember, I was still pitching this song to be part of a patriotic choral musical.

I typed up the full lyrics in all their ABA–ABA glory. I prepared a lead sheet and recorded a simple piano-vocal demo. I pitched the song to the choral music company that was seeking songs for its musical.

They passed.

Why? Why did they pass? Could they not see that I had created something unique, maybe even brand new? I've never seen a song before or since with this unique form. Did they not "get" how cool it was that I had managed to write two mini-songs and combine them together into one, hitting two emotional hot spots with one song? What was the matter with those guys, anyway?

Example 3 below shows the lyrics that I pitched to the choral company. Read the lyrics carefully and see if you come to any conclusions about an inherent weakness in them.

EXAMPLE 3. THE FIRST "FINISHED" DRAFT OF LYRICS

MAY WE NOT FORGET
Words and music by Robert Sterling

A

May we not forget the sacrifice of others,
Our sisters and our brothers, who answered duty's call.
Willingly they served and set aside life's pleasures,
Its triumphs and its treasures, to freely give their all.

B

Running t'ward the fray where others dare not tread
Purchasing our freedom with wounds of crimson red.
Face into the fire, true courage without bound,
They fought and never faltered, and died on sacred ground.

A

So may we not forget as memory grows older
We stand upon the shoulders of those who've gone before.
Almighty God, please bless this humble, sovereign nation,
And grant our invocation of peace forevermore.

A

May we not forget the mercy Jesus gave us,
And how He died to save us upon a rugged tree.
Willingly He bore our shame and our transgression.
With love's unmatched expression, He set the captive free.

B
> Stretched upon a cross, Christ suffered, bled, and died,
> The Lamb upon the altar, sinless, crucified.
> The weight of ev'ry sin, the cruel sting of death
> Were borne away and conquered with Jesus' final breath.

A
> So may we not forget His tender love that sought us,
> His precious blood that bought us so we might be His own—
> Bold and unafraid to show to ev'ry nation
> The path to true salvation is Christ and Christ alone.

REJECTED? REWRITE—AGAIN!

After my standard period of moping and whining for not getting picked, I took another look at the song. I was still convinced that the elements of the song, both halves of the lyrics, and the music were all well written. But I began to wonder if what I had written was actually two songs, not one. And then my confidence in the music began to flag. I needed professional help. So I sought out the counsel of wiser souls. I sent the lyrics to two trusted collaborators, Deborah Craig-Claar and Lowell Alexander, and asked for their honest opinions. What I wanted to hear from them was, "The song is perfect. Brilliant, in fact." What I needed to hear was the unvarnished truth. Deborah and Lowell both said the same thing: "It is two songs. Pick one." They also said some very nice things about my use of language and imagery, blah, blah, blah. But most important, they confirmed I had broken the "one thing" rule, and the song didn't work because of that. So right now, imagine me slapping myself in the forehead as I remind us all about the "one thing" rule: A song is about *one thing*.

Now I was left to decide which of the two songs I would focus on: the "soldier" song or the "Jesus" song. It wasn't simply a matter of using one half of the existing song. Either half was going to require another A section to turn it into a complete AABA song. While I thought that there were some really stirring words in the "soldier" half of the lyrics, I chose to work on the "Jesus" song for personal and practical reasons. Personally, there's nothing more important in my life than the sacrifice Jesus made for me. And in purely practical terms, I would have a much better shot of placing a song about Jesus' sacrifice into print. So I set aside the soldier lyrics and once again went to work on "May We Not Forget." (And who knows when or where the "soldier" lyrics may be used in the future?)

Somewhere along the line, I decided to change the title to "Let Us Not Forget." It felt a little more "King James-ish" to me. I'm sure that I could have been swayed back to the original title if the change would have made a difference in the song being recorded or placed in print. It was a small change, except for the fact that it was the *title of the song*. After that, I wrote an additional A section (now the second A), and once again I had a finished song.

WHAT I REALLY NEED IS A COLLABORATOR

Did I say I had a finished song? Not so fast there, pardner. Remember how I had gotten a little disenchanted with my own music? Well, now that the song was purely about Jesus, the "American"-sounding music no longer seemed to fit. I was too close to my original tune to come up with something significantly different. I needed a collaborator—a tunesmith. I needed a fresh set of ears. I asked Regi Stone if he would consider writing a tune for the lyrics. I sent him the version in example 4. Notice that, with the exception of the second A section, the words are almost the same as the back half of the two-headed ABA song. Also, I gave Regi a couple of lyric options in parentheses and italics. I wanted his input on which of the options might sing better.

EXAMPLE 4. DRAFT OF "LET US NOT FORGET" SUBMITTED TO REGI STONE FOR MUSIC

LET US NOT FORGET
 Words by Robert Sterling; music by ???

Let us not forget the mercy Jesus gave us,
And how He *died* (came?) to save us upon a rugged tree.
Willingly He bore our shame and our transgression—
God's unmatched expression of love for you and me.

And let us not forget His body, bruised and bleeding,
His anguished painful pleading, "Father, please forgive."
He chose to give His life, an offering unswerving
To us, the undeserving, so we might choose to live.

Stretched upon a cross, He suffered and He died, *(or: His power cast aside?)*
The Lamb upon the altar, sinless, crucified.
The weight of ev'ry sin, the cruel sting of death
Was lifted from our shoulders with Jesus' final breath.

So let us not forget the selfless love that sought us,
The precious blood that bought us so we might be His own.
The old is gone away. We are a new creation,
A living celebration of Christ and Christ alone.

BUT WAIT—THERE'S MORE!

Regi wrote a beautiful melody for the lyrics. (A demo of the song is posted at robertsterlingmusic .com.) He made a rough piano-vocal demo, but only after a few more changes were made to the lyrics. Example 5 shows the final lyrics. They are nearly identical to the version in example 4. The changes are all in the first two lines of the B section. They are small but significant. Take a careful look at the differences between examples 4 and 5.

EXAMPLE 5. FINAL LYRICS FOR "LET US NOT FORGET"

LET US NOT FORGET
  Words by Robert Sterling; music by Regi Stone

Let us not forget the mercy Jesus gave us,
And how He died to save us upon a rugged tree.
Willingly He bore our shame and our transgression—
God's unmatched expression of love for you and me.

And let us not forget His body, bruised and bleeding,
His anguished painful pleading, "Father, please forgive."
He chose to give His life, an offering unswerving
To us, the undeserving, so we might choose to live.

May we now remember His awful sacrifice—
A lamb upon the altar, sinless, crucified.
The weight of ev'ry sin, the cruel sting of death
Was lifted from our shoulders with Jesus' final breath.

So let us not forget the selfless love that sought us,
The precious blood that bought us so we might be His own.
The old is gone away. We are a new creation,
A living celebration of Christ and Christ alone.

I THINK WE'RE DONE NOW

Just as there is no set way to write a song, there is no set way to rewrite one, either. The rewriting process on "Let Us Not Forget" is not some sort of standard by which to measure all rewrites. Nor is it out of the ordinary, as rewrites go. Granted, it's not often I write two songs as one, split them apart, and write a new song from the spare parts. This song may have undergone more drastic changes than most of my songs. But please notice how significant some of the smallest changes were. A great rewrite is in the details. The last 20 percent of a great song is often found hiding in the smallest of details.

Happy rewriting.

Collaboration (The Two-Headed Writing Monster)

Try It—You'll Like It

If you examine the writing credits of the current crop of hit songs (pop, country, Christian, or otherwise), you'll see that most of the songs were written by two or more people. This is so often the case that it would seem collaboration is a prerequisite for writing a hit song. If you go back a generation or two on the Hit Parade, you will find that collaboration is nothing new. Only the names have changed. In fact, there are so many famous writing duos that their names are almost inseparable from each other: (Richard) Rodgers and (Oscar) Hammerstein, (Alan) Lerner and (Frederick) Lowe, (John) Lennon and (Paul) McCartney, (Carole) King and (Gerry) Goffin, (Barry) Mann and (Cynthia) Weill, (Hal) David and (Burt) Bacharach, (Jerry) Leiber and (Mike) Stoller, Elton John and Bernie Taupin, and George and Ira Gershwin.

Collaboration is not unique to the pop and country music worlds. Christian songwriters often collaborate. Paul Baloche writes with Brenton Brown. Chris Tomlin sometimes shares the heavy lifting with Matt Redman. Michael W. Smith teamed up with Wayne Kirkpatrick throughout the 1990s. Greg Nelson wrote a grocery list of CCM standards in the 1980s with Phil McHugh and Bob Farrell. Bill and Gloria Gaither have shared writing credits on dozens of huge Christian songs.

My first co-writer was my late mother, Sarah. She was a talented, self-taught lyricist who allowed her teenaged son to write music for her words. My very first recorded song was one she and I wrote together: "Nothing to Lose." (Don't try to find it in the record bins. It's long gone.) In the years since, I have had successful writing partnerships with Chris Machen, John Mandeville, Lowell Alexander, Claire Cloninger, Michael W. Smith, and Deborah Craig-Claar, to name a few. Besides collaborating on creating two wonderful sons, I have also written some successful songs with my wife, Cindy. In fact, Cindy co-wrote her first song with me when she was in her early 30s. Steve Archer recorded the song called "If You Were the Only One," and it rose to No. 2 on the Contemporary Christian radio charts. Ever since that initial success, Cindy has been disappointed when any song she wrote didn't go straight to the top of the charts. Although I often write alone, I fully appreciate all that a good collaborator brings to the writing process. Much of my best work has been created with co-writers.

Most professional songwriters eagerly seek out collaborators. Most beginners write alone. Beginners often don't know how to go about building a co-writing relationship and may not understand the many advantages of co-writing. Allow me a few pages to wax poetic on the virtues of collaboration in the wonderful world of songwriting.

Why Collaborate?

There are lots of reasons to write with another person.

Perhaps your co-writer has musical strengths or lyrical insights that complement your own particular talents. Her abilities as a composer or lyricist, her musical skills or production experience—all these may benefit your growth as a writer.

Perhaps your co-writer has a way of looking at a song that is totally different from the way you do. The lyric may progress in an entirely new and innovative direction with a single suggestion from a good co-writer. The music may change style. Your original idea may spin into an entirely new concept. And that can be a good thing, an exciting thing.

Maybe your co-writer has business or publishing contacts that will enlarge the circle of people promoting your song. A co-writer may bring a publisher, or a producer, or even a recording artist—people you otherwise might never have met—into contact with you and your songs.

There are lots of reasons to write with another person, but they all come down to one thing: a good co-writer expands your horizons. For a beginning songwriter whose primary goal is to improve, this is significant. Never pass up the opportunity to write with a well-matched co-writer, regardless what the outcome may be. The experience holds great promise for professional and personal growth. If you have yet to venture into the world of collaboration, perhaps now is the time to dive in.

> *He provided a lightness, an optimism, while I would always go for the sadness, the discords, a certain bluesy edge.*
> —JOHN LENNON, on co-writing with PAUL McCARTNEY

What Makes a Successful Writing Team?

Did you notice in the previous paragraph that I said a *well-matched co-writer?* Like any good relationship, it is important that each collaborator complement the other's abilities. Gifted lyricists need talented tunesmiths. A big-idea person needs a solid craftsman. Starters need finishers.

Early in my career I struck up a successful collaboration with Chris Machen. Chris and I instantly hit it off as friends. Friendship helps, but isn't imperative. History tells us that William Gilbert and Sir Arthur Sullivan didn't care for one another all that much. Still, they managed to write *The Pirates of Penzance, The Mikado, HMS Pinafore,* and so on. What made Chris and I click as co-writers (besides a mutual love of Tex-Mex food and an off-beat sense of humor) was that he is a natural starter and I am a finisher. He would come to me with an idea, a title, some lyrics, and maybe part of a tune. I would complete the song, focusing mostly on the music. Often, we worked on a song apart from each other. Later in our writing relationship, as we grew more comfortable together, we occasionally reversed those roles. Now, years later, it is humbling to see that several of our songs have become standards for church choirs around the world.

In my various collaborations, I have sometimes been the lyricist and other times the composer. When I write with Claire Cloninger, she typically writes the lyrics first, and I set them to music (with rewrites occurring along the way). When writing certain types of musical theater songs with Deborah Craig-Claar, the music is created first, with the lyrics written to fit the tune. When I write with Lowell Alexander, we both contribute simultaneously to words and music. "Jesus Will Still Be There" (recorded by Point of Grace) started as a finished set of lyrics I wrote and faxed to John Mandeville, whom I had never met. He composed the music and played it for me over the phone. I met John for the first time when I went to his home to pick up the cassette demo tape.

My point here is that there is no single right way to collaborate on a song. Each of my collaborative relationships is unique from the others. But they all have two things in common: creative chemistry and mutual respect that elevates the work of both writers. Without this chemistry and respect, I can't see how any collaboration will produce much good music. It isn't too difficult to determine if you have creative respect for another writer; all you have to do is listen to some of their work. If you find yourself thinking, "I wish I had written that," then you may have found a prospective collaborator. Unfortunately, you won't know if there is any creative chemistry until you work together a time or two. A first-time collaboration is not unlike a blind date. Maybe it will result in true love, and maybe it will end in disaster. You will never know until you try. Approach each new collaboration with an open mind and a positive attitude, and give it your best shot. If nothing comes of it, then enjoy a nice lunch together, shake hands, and part friends.

In Their Own Words:
What makes for a successful collaboration?

Trust, a willingness to be vulnerable, commitment. —SUE SMITH

A safe environment to think aloud in, the same goal, respect.
—TONY WOOD

Being sure that each of you does at least one thing better than the other one does. —DEBORAH CRAIG-CLAAR

No egos and wanting only the very best regardless whose idea it is.
—J. PAUL WILLIAMS

A shared sense of humor. —CLAIRE CLONINGER

The ability to be critical and say "That's a terrible idea" to their face, and have them still feel loved! And vice versa!
—LOWELL ALEXANDER

Finding a Collaborator

If you've never collaborated with another songwriter, you may be wondering: Who do I choose? Where do I look to find that person? How do I ask them? What if he (or she) says "no"? How will I ever deal with the rejection? There is definitely something akin to a blind date in a first-time collaboration and nobody much likes blind dates. But one thing is for certain: if you don't ever ask, you will never know what the collaboration might have yielded.

WHOM DO I CHOOSE TO WRITE WITH?

When seeking a writing partner, look for someone who has different strengths than your own. Are you an expert at building killer tracks but you can't rhyme "blue" and "true"? Then look for a lyricist. Do you have a dozen legal pads filled with hooks and lyric ideas but you don't know flats from sharps? Search for a composer. Are you spilling over with great ideas but you have difficulty completing songs? Hunt for a solid song craftsman that can take your idea to the finish line.

Study the work of the songwriters in your area. Get to know their writing, and you will better be able to find someone whose talents will broaden your abilities. Whenever possible, collaborate with writers who will challenge you to grow as a songwriter. Even the most experienced writers want to work with writers that have a more impressive track record than their own, but this goal is especially important for novice writers. After all, your primary goal is to improve. What better way to do that than to write with someone with more experience and success?

WHERE DO I FIND A COLLABORATOR?

The best place to begin looking for a co-writer is right where you are. The fact is that lots of successful collaborations have initially sprung from nothing more than proximity—the writers lived near one another. Start with people you already know, and expand from there. If you are truly alone in your writing endeavors, then here are some ideas that may help you find a partner:

1. **Go to a local "writer's night."** Bookstores and coffeehouses are prime places for evenings of (often free) entertainment by local songwriters who just want to be heard. If your town doesn't have a writer's night, maybe you should start one.

2. **Visit area churches that feature singer-songwriters in the services.**

3. **Contact local and national songwriters organizations.** Nashville isn't the only town with a songwriters association. If your town doesn't have an association, check with national organizations. ASCAP, BMI, GMA (Gospel Music Association), and NSAI (Nashville Songwriters Association International) all have regional workshops and seminars at which you could meet any number of writers from your own area. All these organizations have Websites loaded with information.

4. **Get the word out that you are looking for a writing partner.** Put up a notice on the bulletin board of your local music store. Place a note in your church bulletin. Let all your musician friends know you want to co-write.

Once you meet someone you think might be a good collaborator, all that's left to do is to say: "I really like what you're writing these days. You wanna try to write a song with me sometime?" If the answer is no, thank them anyway. If the answer is yes, then you're on your way. Just make sure that you show up at the writing session with several great ideas!

The Co-Writing Session

Always expect the unexpected and allow for the possibility of pure musical magic. —from SONGWRITING FOR DUMMIES, p. 235

Chemistry between two writers doesn't always happen instantly. It may be wise for new collaborators to get together for coffee prior to the writing session. Give yourselves the chance to get to know each other before you get into a room and begin shooting holes in the other guy's ideas. Talk about music, church, family, whatever. Find out something about each other as people. All this will ease the awkwardness of your first session together.

NEARLY TEN TIPS FOR A HAPPY, HEALTHY CO-WRITING SESSION

Once you get together for your writing session, here are a few guidelines that may make your time more productive and pleasant:

1. **Come prepared.** Show up to the session with at least three or four solid song ideas. If you both do that, you will have six to eight ideas to start working from.

2. **Choose an idea and get to work.** Sometimes a single idea will grab you both. Other times, your co-writer will be much more passionate about an idea than you are. In that case, give serious consideration to her point of view. Remember, you chose to work with this person because you believe in her talent and ideas.

3. **Consider the writing room a "safe zone."** There are no dumb ideas. Both writers need to feel free to express whatever comes to mind without fear of hurtful criticism. The wrong idea may lead to the right idea. Lyrics that don't fit the verse may work in the chorus. A casual remark by one writer may result in a brilliant insight from the other.

4. **Be honest with each other, but remain kind.** There's nothing gained in saying that a lyric or a melody is brilliant if it is, in fact, mediocre. Condescension won't make the song better. Speak your mind without being harsh. Whenever you say "no" to an idea, try to offer an alternative.
   "We've used that rhyme sound already in the verse. Why don't we look for a different word?" "The bridge feels a little long to me. Do you think we could shorten it a bit?" "The music is working all right, but maybe it could soar a little more at the chorus."

5. **Encourage one another.** Songwriters are an insecure lot. We need to know if somebody likes our work. Let your co-writer know you appreciate his talent.

6. **Pull your own weight.** Make sure you are working every bit as hard as your co-writer is. There are stories in Nashville about people who received co-writing credit on a song for simply being in the room when it was written. Don't be one of those people.

7. **Share.** Don't hold back your ideas for fear that your collaborator will steal them. That's not a good way to build a creative partnership.

8. **Keep the goal of a finished song in front of you.** Stay focused on your work. Don't allow unimportant things (cell phones, e-mails, the lack of a nearby Starbucks) to keep you from actually working. The most important thing is to write a song that you are both satisfied with.

9. **Be generous with the credit.** There are no hard rules about how to split the credit on a co-written song. The assumption is generally that the credit will be split 50-50 unless otherwise discussed. But once a song has been recorded, those assumptions can be quickly forgotten as writers start thinking about future royalties. To be safe, settle the split in advance or as soon as the song is completed. Put it in writing, if need be.

And keep this in mind when you are tempted to want more than 50 percent of the credit: Even if you wrote all the music and half the lyrics, the song still wouldn't be complete if it weren't for your collaborator's contribution. Be generous with your co-writers. Doing so will make them want to write with you again.

WHAT IF YOU FAIL CHEMISTRY 101?

Co-writing is like any human relationship. Sometimes it simply doesn't work. Not everybody can be your best friend. Not every writer can be an effective collaborator. Be open to co-writing with anyone at least once, but don't feel pressure to stay in an unproductive writing relationship. That doesn't help either writer to grow. Learn from the experience and move on with no hard feelings.

> *The education I received from co-writing was equally valuable those*
> *times when the chemistry was bad as when we wrote a hit.*
> —from KYLE MATTHEWS's *Songwriting 101*, p. 14

Long-Distance Collaboration

The stereotypical Nashville writing session is two people squirreled away in a publisher's nondescript writer's room with a guitar, a boombox, a couple of legal pads, and a lot of coffee.

They work for three or four hours at a stretch, break for lunch, then return to finish the song. That scenario still plays out many times every day all over this city, but it certainly isn't the only way to collaborate on a song. With all the instant-communication technology available today, collaborators no longer need to be in the same room, or even the same city.

I live in suburban Nashville, but I have worked with co-writers who live in Mobile, Kansas City, Dallas, Los Angeles, and upstate New York. We work over the phone and via e-mail. I can send a quick MP3 or a lyric file over the Internet and get an almost instant response. Using a VOIP (Voice Over Internet Protocol) telephone, I can speak for literally hours at a time with a long-distance co-writer and never worry about having to pay long-distance phone charges or using cellular minutes. It's not the same as being in the room with my co-writer, but it's close.

This arrangement works best, of course, if you've already established an in-person relationship. In that case, the long-distance writing becomes an extension of the in-person relationship. I know a couple of songwriters who periodically journey to Nashville from other cities to work for a few days at a time. Because songwriting isn't a science and the Muse doesn't always cooperate, sometimes the songs they begin in Nashville have to be finished after they return home. Long-distance collaboration makes that possible.

So as you seek out collaborators, be open to finding someone in another city. All the same rules apply as when you work together in person, with one difference: in a long-distance collaboration, you never have to leave your house or change out of your bathrobe.

Becoming a Better Collaborator

Becoming a better collaborator is really pretty simple. It's like anything else: the more you work at it, the better you become. So if the idea of being a good songwriting collaborator appeals to you, then collaborate more often. If you are fortunate enough to have more than one writing partner, that's great. Working with more than one person may teach you a broader range of writing skills.

It is also beneficial if you can speak your co-writer's language, and I don't mean French or German or Spanish. If you write the lyrics and your co-writer composes the music, then you should learn the basics of music. Take a class or read a book about the rudiments of chord structure and melody. If your partner is the lyricist, then take some time to study the fundamentals of lyric writing. Your co-writer will appreciate it and your communication will improve, hopefully leading to better songs.

Two wonderful things will happen as you improve your collaboration skills:

1. You will write better songs. And that means...

2. You will be asked to co-write more, which will make you a better collaborator, which will help you write better songs, which will get you asked to co-write more, which will make you a better collaborator, which will help you write better songs, which will get you asked to co-write more...

Coda

It can be tempting to want to go it alone as a songwriter, and many great writers have done just that. Collaboration is certainly no requirement for success. There are no creative differences and no royalty splits to deal with when you write a song by yourself. Still, I think that every songwriter, especially beginning writers, should at least give co-writing a try. The potential for growth is too great to ignore. Plus, there is another benefit to collaboration beyond becoming a better songwriter—friendship. Sharing time in the songwriting trenches forges a unique bond between two people that often develops into a close friendship. I consider my collaborators among my very best and closest friends, and my life is richer for knowing and working with each of them.

Critical Thinking (Song Analysis 101)

Learning from Others

One of the best methods to hone the craft of songwriting is to study the work of other writers. By focusing a critical eye and ear on a well-written song, students (and we are all students) can learn techniques to apply in their own writing. This calls for objective analysis, not just casual listening. You can learn from the genius of others. You can also learn from their mistakes—and even the best writers make mistakes. Hopefully, in the process you will become more objectively critical of your own songs.

To aid you in this mighty endeavor, I have assembled a set of my own songs for analysis. I chose these songs not because I think they are the best songs of all time, but because they demonstrate many of the things I've preached about in this book: proper form, the use of poetic imagery, interesting rhyme schemes, and so on. Because I wrote (or co-wrote) these songs, I know the particulars of how and when they came to be written. I know their flaws. I can pass judgment on them without sounding petty about someone else's work. And it gives me a chance at some shameless self-promotion. To keep things interesting, I've selected a wide variety of musical styles and purposes: pop/CCM songs, theater songs, children's songs, choral songs, praise-and-worship songs, and so on. For a number of publishing and legal reasons, the majority of songs that follow have never been recorded beyond the demo stage. However, I hope you discover that a song's hit status and its musical genre don't affect the rules of good craftsmanship.

Putting the Song Under a Microscope

Since there are no graphs, calculators, or mathematical systems to rate a tune or its lyrics and give it a score, we must use subjective measurements when we analyze a song. And we should not be fooled by a song's retail success or its status on radio airplay charts. (That sort of success has as much to do with solid marketing and good timing as with craftsmanship and creative writing.) Hopefully, if you've made it this far into the book, you are more concerned right now with writing well-crafted songs than writing hits. (*Jesus' chairs*, remember? *Jesus' chairs*.) So, what are those subjective measuring sticks? What are some common characteristics of well-written songs? What are the hints and signs we should look for?

UNIVERSAL THEME

A good song generally relates to lots of people. It strikes a chord in the hearts of its listeners. At its core is a universal theme human beings can understand and appreciate. By far, the most common theme in popular songwriting is romantic love. In today's Christian-music climate, the most common theme is the praiseworthiness of God, yet there are so many more themes for Christian writers to tackle and explore. Here are just a few examples that you might not have considered:

1. Love (not just romantic love, but agape love)

2. Freedom

3. Sacrifice

4. Revenge (or its counterpart, Forgiveness)

5. Family

6. Friendship

7. Money and Greed

8. Politics and Power

9. Bigotry and Hatred

10. Redemption

As you look over that list, consider how many of those topics Jesus spoke about in the parables and the lessons he taught his disciples. If a topic was important enough for Jesus to preach about, it should be more than good enough for his followers to write about.

HONESTY

Well-written songs are believable, not phony. Characters in great songs speak and act like real people. Emotions are genuine. Troubles are real. Every problem doesn't come with a prepackaged Sunday school solution. Consider the soul-baring openness of Wayne Watson's "Would I Know You?" The singer questions the depth and motivations of his own faith with unflinching honesty. Here is the second stanza:

> *Would I know You now if You walked into this place?*
> *Would I cause You shame? Would my games be Your disgrace?*
> *Or would I worship You, fall down upon my face?*
> *I wonder if I'd know You now.*

WORDS AND MUSIC BY WAYNE WATSON
© 1992 by Word Music

Good songs may ask more questions than they give answers, because that's how life sometimes works. Good songs are honest.

SHOW—DON'T TELL

Good songs use imagery to paint pictures that remain in the listener's mind after the song is over. They show rather than tell. They use metaphor and simile and poetic devices to spark the imagination. Too many Christian songs are guilty of preaching, which is a turnoff for many listeners .

Here is the passage about winter in Nicole Nordeman's touching song "Every Season." Notice how her words work together to paint a melancholy picture of the coldest season of the year:

> *And everything in time and under heaven finally falls asleep*
> *Wrapped in blankets white. All creation shivers underneath.*
> *And I still notice You when branches crack*
> *And in my breath on frosted glass*
> *Even now in death, You open doors for life to enter*
> *You are winter.*

WORDS AND MUSIC BY NICOLE NORDEMAN
© 2000 by Ariose Music Group

SIMPLICITY

Well-crafted songs are often deceptively simple, and rarely complex. Don't let that fool you—simple is difficult. It is not easy to tell a compelling story in two short verses and a chorus. Good songs are generally concise and to the point.

The country standard "Blue Eyes Crying in the Rain," by Fred Rose, is the picture of lyric economy. It is a compelling picture of a lifelong love that is told in just two verses, with a simple repeated hook line. Similarly, Jimmy Webb needed only two very brief verses and a one-line chorus to tell the story of the "Wichita Lineman."

Keep it simple.

INTRIGUING TITLE

An intriguing title is one of the first signs of a good song. It is generally an indicator of a catchy hook, as well. A great title makes you want to smack yourself in the forehead saying, "Why didn't I think of that?" And the crazy thing is, great titles happen around us every day, if we would just pay attention.

"Jesus Take the Wheel" (by Brett James, Hillary Lindsey, and Gordie Sampson) is one of those titles that grabbed the attention of every radio listener in America for the better part of a year. In four short words, the writers encapsulated the desperate need that most of us feel for God to be in charge of our out-of-control lives. On the other hand, titles like "Commitment Song" or "Wedding Song" or "Fill-in-the-blank Song" are often indicators of an unfocused idea or a weak hook. Trust me, I know. I co-wrote "Commitment Song."

A STRONG START

Alan Jackson captured the attention of almost every Christian person in America when he sang, "Where were you when the world stopped turning on that September day?" Such is the power of a strong opening line. Good songs get off to a good start. They grab you right away and don't let go. I cannot emphasize enough how important a strong opening is for a song. It's like a good breakfast: it gets your entire songwriting day off to a good start. Review the list of opening lines in chapter 4, and then examine the opening lines of your own songs to see if they get off to a great start.

A SATISFYING PAYOFF

Like any good story, a well-written song leads to a satisfying conclusion. If the song tells a story, the end must be believable and even seem inevitable. A good writer convinces the listener the song couldn't have possibly ended any other way. Even if the song ends with a question or an unexpected surprise, the outcome must satisfy the listener.

Songs like "Bad, Bad Leroy Brown" (Jim Croce), "Where've You Been? (Don Henry and Jon Vezner), and "Rise Again" (Dallas Holm) are good examples of songs with strong payoffs.

AN APPROPRIATE AND WELL-CRAFTED SONG FORM

A well-written song has a form that suits the song well. (Not every song is best served by a verse/chorus form.) What's more, the song's form will be well crafted. If it breaks the rules of form, there will be a creative reason for doing so, and not just because the writer couldn't figure out how to make the verses match in length.

Take another look at Wayne Watson's "Would I Know You." He appropriately chose an AABA form for the song, framing each A section with his title. The lyrics contain a series of soul-searching questions that would have never been suited to the repetition of a verse/chorus form. On the other hand, a song like "Friends in Low Places" (Earl Bud Lee and DeWayne Blackwell) is perfect for the fun repetition of the verse/chorus form.

GREAT MUSIC

A great song has memorable music. The melody is a good marriage with the lyrics. The harmonies suit the tune, and the rhythms fit the words. There is an old musical-theater saying that illustrates the power of music: "No matter how brilliant the set design may have been, the audience doesn't leave the theater humming the scenery." Music is the magical element that makes many songs so amazingly powerful.

"Bring Him Home" (Alain Boublil, Herbert Kretzmer & Claude-Michel Schonberg) from *Les Miserables,* "Go Rest High on That Mountain" by Vince Gill, "Unchained Melody" by Alex North and Hy Zaret, "Praise the Lord" by the Imperials, "Easter Song" by Second Chapter of Acts...The list of songs goes on and on, in which music not only completes the lyrics, but elevates the song itself.

In Their Own Words:
What makes a song great?

A great song is memorable—something the listener does not easily forget.
                                              —PAUL SMITH

The combination of a lyric and melody that moves you and makes you want to hear it again and again.
                                              —SUE SMITH

Large royalty checks.   —CHARLES F. BROWN

That is the million dollar unanswerable question. If somebody could bottle the answer to that, we'd all be drinking it.
                                              —LOWELL ALEXANDER

Coda

No matter how many measuring sticks we use for determining the value of a song, it is the individual listener who ultimately decides if, say, "Moon River" is a better song than "The Macarena." (In case you are wondering, "Moon River" is the better song.) As I wrote earlier, the songs I've chosen to use as examples are not the ultimate best songs of all time, but they do represent a variety of styles and forms, and will hopefully illustrate how a well-written song can take on any shape or style as long as it communicates its meaning to the listener.

As you examine the lyrics of the following songs (or of your own songs, or of anybody's songs), use the characteristics listed above as you look for these things:

1. What is the **theme** of the song?

2. What is the **song form** used?

3. Is there a good **marriage of music and lyrics**? Do they elevate each other?

4. **Where is the poetry** in the lyrics? Look for pictures and verbal sound effects.

5. Does the song **get off to strong start**?

6. Does it have a **satisfying conclusion**?

7. Does it have an **intriguing title**? Is it memorable?

I hope you enjoy studying these songs. More important, I hope you learn something from them that you can apply to improve your own writing.

THE LISTENING ELEMENT

Needless to say, it is always better to listen to a song while studying it. Unfortunately, it was legally and economically prohibitive to provide a recording of all these songs along with this book. The good news is that I have posted as many of these songs as I could on my Website at robertsterlingmusic.com, as streaming audio. I encourage you to avail yourself of the recordings in order to get the most out of studying these songs.

For Your Criticizing Pleasure: 12 Songs

For each of the songs I've chosen, I've recounted a brief history of why and how the song was written, followed by some of the points of craft worth noting for that particular song. The full set of lyrics is then printed, with some thoughts on form, rhyme, and other tidbits added alongside the lyrics.

Now it's time for you to be critical of me. Please be kind.

SONG 1: "JESUS WILL STILL BE THERE"

This song is, to date, the biggest hit I've written. It became a standard for Point of Grace after it reached No. 1 on all the Christian radio charts in 1994. I was fortunate to be the group's first producer, along with a very talented guy named Scott Williamson. We were in a preproduction meeting with the executive producer and the girls in the group, and Terry Lang said something to the effect of, "We don't have any songs that talk about Jesus. We want to sing a song about Jesus." I took that to heart and went home and wrote the lyrics to "Jesus Will Still Be There" the next day.

Rather than write the music myself, I asked John Mandeville if he would take a look at the lyrics. John and I had never met. I knew and respected his work, and Point of Grace had already chosen another of John's songs for the record. I faxed the lyrics across town to John, and he called me back within a day to play a rough piano-vocal demo over the phone. He made a small change to the lyrics in the chorus. He also made a minor change to the lyrics in the second verse, and I asked him to make a small change in the melody to accommodate a rewrite. It all happened very quickly. The two of us met for the first time when I picked up a cassette demo at his house the next day. Point of Grace loved the song, and they did a great job of making it their own when we recorded it about a month later. The next time I saw John was at the party our publishers threw for us when the song became a hit.

The theme of "Jesus Will Still Be There" is directly stated in the title. No matter how our lives change and fall apart, Jesus is constant and his love is unchanging. The theme is hope, based on faith. Beyond that, the lyrics deal with some pretty universal human troubles in very simple language. The words of the first verse are true regardless of whether the listener is a Christian. It isn't until the chorus that the focus is turned to Jesus. The second verse acknowledges that we can grow, but we still slip and fall. We still need the love of Jesus. The song is an explicitly Christian song without being preachy. It offers a solution, but it doesn't demand that the listener take it.

"Jesus Will Still Be There" uses a typical verse/chorus song form. It has two short verses that are lyrically economical. There is a repeated channel that leads from each verse to the chorus. The chorus is hooked in the first and the last line. The lack of a bridge (John and I never felt it needed one) left room for a big modulation on the last chorus. The rhyme scheme is obvious, and it is consistent in the two verses: a-a-b-b (channel) c-c-c.

The use of metaphor matches the lyrics, and it is economic and simple. In the first verse I used "storms" as a metaphor for life's troubles. Similarly, in the second verse "lose your foothold" is a metaphor for slipping away from God. In the chorus you'll find the simile "sure as a steady rain." I also employed several familiar short phrases in new ways to catch the listener's ear: "When the going gets tough," "place your bets," "haven't got a prayer," "Time flies." One could make the argument that any of those phrases is overused or trite. They worked for me, and I'll stand by them.

John's music totally captures the economy of the lyrics. The tune is melancholy in the verse and lifts up to become reassuring at the chorus. The channel music is a steady build from the low point of the verse to the high point of the chorus. He then dials it all back down at the end of the first and last choruses, matching the sound of the intro. This accomplishes two things: first, it funnels the listener back to verse 2, and second, it musically bookends the song. It finishes as tenderly as it began.

"Jesus Will Still Be There" is available on several recordings. Most notably, Point of Grace released it on their debut recording, *Point of Grace* (Word Records, 1993), as well as on their collection of No. 1 singles, which is called *24* (Word Records, 2003).

Note: Here are a few guidelines to help you better understand how I chose to analyze the lyrics that follow. Rhyme scheme is indicated to the right of the lyric in lowercase letters. Verse structure and song form are indicated in bold at the beginning of each section. Instances of poetic devices are in italics with the particular device (also in italics) noted at the end of the lyric line. A song's hook is in bold type and noted next to the lyric line. General comments appear in parentheses near or after the appropriate lyric line. Because each song has a unique analytical purpose, I chose not to mark every single poetic device, rhyme scheme, song form, and so on for each song. With careful examination, you should find more items to analyze and criticize with each of the lyrics.

JESUS WILL STILL BE THERE
Words and music by Robert Sterling and John Mandeville

VERSE 1	**RHYME SCHEME**
Things change. Plans fail.	a
You look for love on a grander scale.	a
Storms rise. Hopes fade *(metaphor)*	b
And you place your bets on another day.	b

CHANNEL

When the going gets tough,   c

When the ride's too rough,   c

When you're just not sure enough …   c

CHORUS

Jesus will still be there. (hook)

His love will never change,

Sure *as a steady rain. (simile)*

Jesus will still be there. (hook)

When no one else is true,

He'll still be loving you.

When it looks like you've lost it all,

And you haven't got a prayer,

Jesus will still be there. (hook)

RHYME SCHEME
MATCHES VERSE 1

VERSE 2

Time flies. Hearts turn

A little bit wiser from lessons learned.

But sometimes *weakness wins* (alliteration—*w*)

And you *lose your foothold* once again. *(metaphor)*

CHANNEL

When the going gets tough,

When the ride's too rough,

When you're just not sure enough …

(repeat chorus two times)

SONG 2: "DECEMBER THROUGH MY WINDOW"

"December Through My Window" began as a melody in search of lyrics. I was in the middle of writing songs for a choral project, and this tune just sort of happened. (I don't know about you, but sometimes some lyrics or a tune will weasel its way into my brain, uninvited.) The melody didn't fit the project, but I liked the music and wrote it down, so as not to forget it. I continued to refine it for a few more days, with not a single word popping into my head to go along with the melody. Since the tune sounded Christmassy to me, I gave it the stunningly creative title: "Winter Song 1." Why the "1"? Because it was the first of three such wordless wonders I wrote that same week. The other two songs became "Winter Song 2" and "Winter Song 3." (So who says it's hard to come up with a great title?)

After living with the song for a while and realizing that no words were forthcoming from my own creative well, I decided to call Lowell Alexander. I called Lowell for three reasons: he loves Christmas, he appreciates a challenge, and he is perhaps the best wordsmith I know. I played the music for Lowell and told him I thought it sounded like winter. He agreed and set out to write a lyric. He called me back a week or so later with an essentially finished, faultless lyric. (It's safe to assume the words went through Lowell's personal rewrite grinder several times before he showed them to me.) We got together and ironed out some minor details in the tune and the lyric, and the song was completed. We're still looking for a home for it. I include it here because I think it is a wonderful demonstration of several points of craftsmanship in writing.

Let's start with the obvious challenge that Lowell faced: the music was fairly well set, and he had to write words to fit. This is a classic approach to songwriting, but it doesn't suit every writer. All the amazing songs Richard Rodgers wrote with Lorenz Hart were written music first, lyrics second. However, the equally amazing songs Rodgers later wrote with Oscar Hammerstein were the reverse: lyrics first, music second. Writing words to an existing melody is a particular creative challenge for the lyricist. The music sets the shape of the song, the mood, the stress points, and sometimes even suggests where the rhymes happen. The lyricist must allow the melody to lead the creative process—in a way "discovering" the lyrics that are hiding inside the music. Some lyricists feel that this approach is too restricting. Others delight in allowing the music to set the pace. In this situation, it is certainly to Lowell's advantage that he is an excellent musician as well as a terrific lyricist. He can absorb the music both intellectually and emotionally, which has got to make it easier for him to scale the lyric wall.

Now let's examine the form. The music is an AABA song form that is altered and somewhat unusual. (Far be it from me to make Lowell's task easier.) The A sections are ten measures long, not the typical eight. Each A is made up of two four-bar phrases and a two-bar extension. The B section is seven measures long, made from a three-bar phrase and a four-bar phrase. And the song has a tag, or coda. The tag was not part of my original tune. Lowell wrote four additional brief lines to cap off his lyrics, and together we wrote the music for those lines.

The words are awash in imagery, beginning with the title and opening line, which evokes a picture of someone looking out at life through a cold pane of glass. (It's December, after all.) Because this is an AABA form, Lowell plants the title firmly in the first line of each A section, then brings it back in the last two lines, as a sort of summation of the stanza. The first two A sections begin with a picturesque simile, which Lowell supports in the following lines. Examine how he uses action words ("falls," "gathers," "brushed," "appear," "wake," "stirs," "sweeps," "warm," "melt") combined with descriptive words ("winter work of art," "dust from stars," "purple shadows," "pines of green," "frosted," "silver," "sapphire") to paint his word pictures. Given that the lyrics are relatively brief, there is no shortage of adjectives and simile.

Because the song has an AABA form, the lyrics must have a single fluid thought. The final words of the song must be a satisfactory conclusion to the opening lines. Lowell accomplishes this masterfully. Note the progression of thought in the lyrics. The singer's heart is melted. The singer's "child" is awakened. The singer longs for a "clearer view" (of winter? of life?). The singer's memory is stirred. And in a touch of irony, the cold month of December "warms the cold." Finally, the tag tells us this is a familiar and welcome cycle in the singer's life.

A1: December through my window / *Always seems to melt my heart*

A2: December through my window / *Seems to wake the child in me*

 B: To gain a clearer view

A3: December through my window / *Stirs memories of a time not long ago*

A3: December through my window / *Comes each year to warm the cold*

Tag: Every newborn winter when again it starts

As for the rhyme scheme: even though I didn't write the words to this song, I will take some of the credit for the rhyme scheme, because it is outlined by the melody. Being the craftsman that he is, Lowell couldn't ignore the rhyme scheme that was imbedded in the tune. Notice how he was careful to see that each A section matches. Lowell hints at a double rhyme in the first and third lines, but just enough to make it feel good without forcing a hard, and perhaps obvious, rhyme. The second, fourth, and sixth lines all are single rhymes. The B section uses a simple single rhyme.

The music for "December Through My Window" was the original creative force for the song. Because of that, I would hope the melody is memorable. (Most AABA songs are melody-driven to begin with.) It was no small compliment that Lowell liked the tune well enough to write lyrics without really altering it at all, other than to help create the tag. The melody is in the style of the American standards of the '40s and '50s. The work tape I created for Lowell was a piano track that had the melody played on top with a bit of a pop-bossa rhythm underneath. Once we married the somewhat melancholy words to the melody, we discarded that rhythm in favor of a classic piano ballad approach. The range of the basic melody is not excessive: an octave and a step. However, the melody is not simple. It is actually challenging to sing because of some of the leaps in the tune. The song is also somewhat complex harmonically, which is in keeping with the style of American standards.

You can find a simple piano-vocal demo of "December Through My Window" posted on my Website.

DECEMBER THROUGH MY WINDOW
Words and music by Lowell Alexander and Robert Sterling

A1	RHYME SCHEME
December through my window (hook)	a
Is framed just *like a winter work of art. (simile)*	b
The snow falls 'cross the meadow	a (soft)
And gathers 'round there *like the dust from stars. (simile)*	b
December through my window (hook)	a
Always seems to melt my heart.	b

RHYME SCHEME
MATCHES VERSE 1

A2

December through my window (hook)

Is *like a Christmas canvas brushed with dreams.* (*simile*)

The shape of purple shadows

Appear *as castles midst the pines of green* (*simile*)

December through my window (hook)

Seems to wake the child in me

B

I stop to rub the frosted panes

To gain a clearer view

    (Implies a view of more than just the landscape)

When *skies of drifting silver gray*

    (*synecdoche*: reduces clouds to a single aspect)

Turn to *sapphire* blue

    (*sapphire*: nice use of an not-so-ordinary word)

RHYME SCHEME
MATCHES PREVIOUS
A SECTIONS

A3

December through my window (hook)

Stirs memories of a time not long ago

    (Wonderful description of the singer's emotions)

Seems footprints left in childhood

Somehow still sweep across the fields of snow

December through my window (hook)

Comes each year to warm the cold

    (Ironic picture: December and "warms the cold")

TAG

Every newborn winter when again it starts

December through my window (hook)

Always seems to melt my heart

    (More irony: December "melts my heart")

SONG 3: "ALIVE AND WELL"

"Alive and Well" was written in the early 1990s in direct response to a hit song recorded by Bette Midler that offered the philosophy that God keeps an eye on his flock "from a distance." I didn't buy that idea, and so I wrote "Alive and Well" as a response. The ultimate point of the song became more than a rebuttal to another songwriter's philosophy, but that was its genesis. The song has been recorded at least twice: first by Luke Garrett, and then by Steve Gatlin (the middle brother in the Gatlin Brothers Band). Both are my friends, and both did a fine job.

"Alive and Well" has a standard verse/chorus form with a bridge. The title is a familiar phrase, with the twist being that it applies to God in a time when some say God is dead. The opening line starts with the words "Some people say," but the song soon makes it clear there is also a view other than what "some people say." Verse 1 speaks about God. Verse 2 shifts to Jesus, which gives the chorus a fresh perspective on the repeat. The chorus states the point of the song with the additional imperative: "Gotta go and tell somebody." (It seems I am never very far from my evangelical roots.) Finally, the bridge reminds the listener that there is an unchanging Truth to cling to, and then swoops back into the chorus.

The verses employ repeated phrases (see "Anaphora," in chapter 3) to strengthen the imagery and make the lyrics memorable. In verse 1 it is "Some people say" and "Some people feel." In verse 2 I used "Some people planned" and "Some people tried." Those four actions occur in what I believe to be the best logical order. To strengthen those same lines further, they each contain an internal rhyme:

- Some people *say* God's an arm's length a*way*
- Some people *feel* He's not even *real*
- Some people *planned* to do away with the *man*
- Some people *tried* when Christ was cruci*fied*

The rhyme scheme of the verses uses alternating single rhyme and double rhyme. Both verses are followed by the same channel, which sets up the chorus. The first line of the channel contains a subtle internal rhyme: "I know that it's been *said* that He is *dead* and gone." If you carefully examine the verses, you'll find they match each other in terms of form and rhyme scheme.

Musically, I played it safe and by the book on "Alive and Well." It's well constructed, but I didn't break any new ground. (You don't have to re-invent the wheel every time you write a new song.) The musical energy increases as the song shifts from the verse into the channel. It lifts even more at the chorus. The process repeats. The bridge maintains the energy between the final two choruses but goes someplace new harmonically. The bridge also reaches a new high point in the melody. I used the chord changes from the first four bars of the verse as a musical hook in the intro, again in the turnaround between the first chorus and second verse, and finally in the last bars of the song.

"Alive and Well" has been recorded by Steve Gatlin on his CD *Love Can Carry* (Cheyenne Records, 1993), and by Luke Garrett on his project titled *Here and Now* (New Vision Records, 1994). Steve's version is posted on my Website, with many thanks to Steve for his permission to do so.

ALIVE AND WELL
  Words and music by Robert Sterling

VERSE 1   RHYME SCHEME
Some people *say* God's an arm's length a*way.*
  (*internal rhyme*)   a
He keeps an eye on his flock, but from a *distance.*
  (*double rhyme*)   b
Some people *feel* He's not even *real* (*internal rhyme*)   c
There's no way to prove His *existence.* (*double rhyme*)   d

CHANNEL
I know that it's been *said* that He is *dead* and *gone,*
  (*internal rhyme*)
But they're *wrong* (Oh they're wrong) (*single rhyme*)

CHORUS
He is **alive and well, (hook)**
Alive and well. (hook)
God is still *Almighty.*
He is still *Emmanuel.* (two contrasting names for God)
He is **alive and well (hook)**
Gotta go and tell somebody
Jesus is **alive and well (hook)**

                                                      RHYME SCHEME
                                                      MATCHES VERSE 1

VERSE 2
Some people planned to do away with the man
  (*anaphora*; also in verse 1)
And the crazy ideas He was teaching.
Some people tried, when Christ was crucified (*anaphora*)
To put an end to a love so far reaching.

REPEAT CHANNEL
REPEAT CHORUS

(BRIDGE)
Don't be fooled by *worldly* lies (*POV addresses the listener*)
That seek the *wayward* soul (*alliteration: worldly and wayward*)
The Truth won't change. It never dies.
God is in control.

REPEAT CHORUS

SONG 4: "TAKE ME DOWN"

I remember once hearing a particular piece of music in a movie score that moved me. The scene was the aftermath of a horrible battle. Death was everywhere. The music was mostly a low drone with a Celtic-type vocal singing a haunting minor melody above it. There was very little harmonic motion, and the melody didn't range beyond an octave. It was an exercise in simplicity and emotion. Not long after that, I was writing songs for an Easter project, and I thought to use that sound for a song about the crucifixion and burial of Jesus. That was the birth of "Take Me Down."

I chose to use "Take Me Down" in this book primarily because of its form. The song has an AAA form, one I rarely use. The challenges of the form are daunting, and there is not a lot of commercial demand for AAA songs. As you recall from chapter 3, the AAA song form requires the lyrics to tell a complete story, repeating the title/hook in each A section only. There is no repeated chorus, nor is there a B section to break the music up.

"Take Me Down" has three A sections, or stanzas, all musically identical. The title is placed in the first line of each stanza, which is typical. (The other standard placement of the title is in the last line of the A section.) Each stanza in "Take Me Down" paints its own picture that, when joined with the others, tells a complete story of a Believer who wants to understand the pain and sacrifice of Jesus at Calvary. The first stanza puts the singer in Jesus' footsteps on the way to the cross. The second places the singer at the foot of the cross and then at the grave. The third reveals the singer grieving through the night, but somehow remaining confident that death cannot defeat the love of Jesus. Originally, I wrote a fourth stanza that dealt with the singer's death and coming to face with the risen Jesus in heaven. It was not needed for the Easter project, and so I dropped it from the song.

Each A section is made up of eight lines with a simple a-b-a-b-c-d-c-d rhyme scheme. The rhymes are all single rhymes. Interestingly, each stanza in "Take Me Down" is its own little eight-line AABA song. Each pair of lines constitutes a section of the mini-AABA. Musically, the A lines are all based on the same melody, with the B lines being a release from the tune of the A lines. You can only detect this by listening to the song. The lyric page alone will not make this little hidden AABA evident.

The tone of the lyrics in "Take Me Down" is fairly elevated—almost liturgical. This was deliberate. I wanted it to sound like a song that could have been written in an earlier century. As a result, I wasn't concerned by using contractions like "e'er" and "'neath." The use of phrases like "Plumb the depths of tragedy" or "In vain conceal my precious Lord" would be a no-no in most contemporary songs, but my goal was not to sound contemporary.

In contrast to the lyrics, the music of "Take Me Down" is plain and simple. It attempts to capture the pain of the words without drawing too much attention to the melody. The tune is built on a pure minor scale and, like many old American hymns, has a limited range of just an octave, plus a half step. The limited range allowed me to do a full-step modulation in the choral arrangement without stretching the soloist too far. The harmonies are mostly simple diatonic chords built up over a fairly static bass line.

Even though "Take Me Down" has limited applications and will never be a big song, it was a joy to write. I have a feeling that it is a song I'll be proud of many years from now. I've tagged the deleted fourth verse onto the lyric page, so you can see what was cut from the song. Who knows—maybe years from now they'll dig it out and sing it at my funeral.

"Take Me Down" was first used in the Word Music choral recording of *The Resurrection and the Life* (wordmusic.com). I have also posted the original demo on my Website. This demo includes the final (unused) fourth verse.

TAKE ME DOWN
    Words and music by Robert Sterling

NOTE MINI-AABA
FORM OF EACH
STANZA

A1

Take me down the rugged road **(hook/title)**   A

Where Jesus stumbled weak and worn

'*Neath* the dark and heavy load   A

    (use of hymnlike contraction)

Of every sin my heart has born.

Place my feet inside His steps   B

All the way to Calvary's tree.

Let me follow Him in death,   A

Just as He gave His life for me.

NOTE RHYME SCHEME
OF EACH STANZA

A2

Take me down beneath the cross **(hook/title)**   a

And let its shadow cover me.   b

Let me suffer heaven's loss   a

And plumb the depths of tragedy.   b

Let me see where rock and stone   c

In vain conceal my precious Lord.   d

Let me show the love He's shown   c

With all the tears I can afford.   d

RHYME SCHEMES OF
ALL STANZAS MATCH

A3

Take me down to heaven's shore **(hook/title)**

And let me face the stormy night.

For I'll feel this pain no more

When comes the dawn of morning's light.

Yet even though He bled and died

On the cross so blamelessly,

There's no grave that *e'er* could hide

    (another hymnlike contraction)

All my Savior's love for me.

THIS VERSE IS
THE MOST HYMLIKE
OF THE SONG

A4 (CUT FROM THE SONG)

Take me down. The time has come **(hook/title)**
That I shall leave this mortal place.
There! My Savior bids me home
To finally greet him face to face.
Weep no more, though I have died,
For I have traveled fast and sure,
Safely to the other side,
Where the love of God endures.

SONG 5: "THE COST OF THINGS"

I'm pretty sure there is a Nashville city ordinance requiring every songwriter living within a 50-mile radius of Music Row to write at least one country song a year. And it applies even to those of us who are not in the country-music business. If you don't comply, you have to leave town. Okay, maybe not. But that's the excuse I use when I occasionally write a country song.

I know for a fact I am more likely to win the lottery than to land a single on a country recording (and I've never bought a lottery ticket, mind you). The country song business is pretty tightly sewn up by very talented writers who spend long days, year after year, writing dozens upon dozens of really solid songs in hopes of getting one big artist cut. Although I write songs for a living, in the country-music world I am little more than a dilettante. I could maybe, just maybe, get very lucky one day. But the odds are stacked against me, mostly because I don't spend my every creative moment writing country songs. Still, that doesn't keep me (and every other Christian and pop songwriter in town) from writing country songs every now and again. It's lots of fun, and hey—it could happen, right?

"The Cost of Things" is one of my more recent country song attempts. It tackles the theme that everything in life has a price. And the currency we use for the important things is love. It has a pretty straightforward verse/chorus song form. The title/hook is placed prominently at the end of every verse and the end of the chorus. (With that many repetitions, the listener should remember the title by the time the song is through.) The song form is notable in one respect: it has four verses.

For the record, it is unusual to see even three verses in a country or pop song anymore. Four verses are almost unheard of. Perhaps this is a weakness in my song. I'll let you decide that for yourself. My rationale for writing them was this:

1. The verses are brief. (Even with four verses, the lyrics fits easily on a single typewritten page.)

2. The song has no bridge.

3. The song needs the verses to complete the story.

About the story: there are actually two stories in the lyric. Both unfold as the years progress in the singer's life. One story is about the loss of a childhood friend. The other is about the value of a loving wife and family. I laid the groundwork for both stories in verses 1 and 2 before ever going to the chorus. Then, by placing the seemingly insignificant conjunction "but" in front of the first chorus, its meaning serves as a warning for things yet to come: "*But* everything in this life / Takes its toll or has a price."

The third verse explains the loss of the friend. The chorus that follows is prefaced with "for" instead of "but," telling us the singer has learned the lesson of the chorus: "*For* everything in this life / Takes its toll or has a price." The final verse resolves the "what happened to the girl?" question and shows how the singer is now concerned with teaching the lesson of the chorus to his own children. Once again, the conjunction preceding the chorus is changed to allow for the singer's growing perspective: "*'Cause* everything in this life / Takes its toll or has a price." If nothing else, let these lyrics serve as a demonstration of the significance even the smallest words can have in your lyrics.

The passage of time is central to the lyrics' message. The opening lines introduce the singer at age 13. The second verse takes place four years later. The third verse is two years later still. In the final verse, the singer is now an adult, married with kids of his own. And with each new verse, we see the singer grow in his understanding of what is really important and what "the cost of things" really is. Note the progression in the phrases that precede the hook line at the end of each verse:

Verse 1: *And I had yet to learn* the cost of things.

Verse 2: *But I sure thought I knew* the cost of things.

Verse 3: *And I began to see* the cost of things.

Verse 4: *And teach my kids to know* the cost of things.

The tone of the lyrics is conversational but descriptive, providing insights into the singer and his world. The singer's friend is named specifically, because I think we always remember our close childhood friends by their first names. The girl is simply known as "the brown-eyed girl," telling us the one physical trait the singer found most striking about the girl he loved. Verse 1 suggests a carefree childhood. Verse 2 demonstrates that the singer was willing to work hard to get what he wanted—a car to impress the brown-eyed girl. Verse 3 tells us something of the friend's values—why he went off to war. Can we assume that the singer felt the same way? Or did he feel differently? He doesn't say. But verse 4 clearly shows who the singer has become as an adult. He is now a family man who is married to and still loves his childhood sweetheart. He is a man of some faith and conviction, evidenced by the fact that he prays, thanks God, and cares about the values he is imparting to his children. Without ever saying, "I am happily married. I believe in God, and I want my kids to know what's important," we know that's how the singer feels by his actions. *(Show, don't tell.)*

This song really went through the rewrite grinder. I have five "finished" drafts of it on my computer. And that doesn't count the several drafts that never made it past the legal-pad stage. Significantly, in the original version the chorus was considerably more melancholy. What's worse, in the fourth verse the singer cheated on his wife and lost her. When my wife read those lyrics (and she is a tough critic who loves country music), she made it clear that the original ending was a real downer, and strongly encouraged me to change it. I did, and the song has a stronger payoff as a result.

The music for "The Cost of Things" is middle-of-the-road country, with a laid-back, acoustic feel. The demo musicians wisely knew to not overpower the lyrics with an aggressive track. Realizing that I was probably pushing the listener's patience by the end of the second chorus, I chose to modulate up a step for the fourth verse. Even with the modulation, the range of the melody barely exceeds one octave. The demo of this song can be heard at my Website.

THE COST OF THINGS
Words and music by Robert Sterling

VERSE 1
Back when bread was fifty cents and candy cost a dime,
Billy and me did nothing much 'cause all we had was time. (a carefree childhood)
I didn't need much money then when I was just *thirteen* (time reference)
And I had yet to learn the **cost of things**. **(hook)**

VERSE 2
I worked three years in the Texas sun to pay for my first car (willing to work hard)
So I could take a brown-eyed girl to park beneath the stars.
I didn't have a nickel left when I was *seventeen*. (time moves on)
But I sure thought I knew **the cost of things**. But … **(hook)**

CHORUS (Chorus is brief. Every line focuses on the point of the song.)
Everything in this life
Takes its toll or has a price
Sometimes we pay too little. Sometimes we pay too much.
But if it's worth it all—**the cost of things** is love. **(hook)**
(Note how the verse tells you that Bill was a soldier who fought and died, without actually
    using the words "Bill was a soldier who fought and died.")

VERSE 3
In a year or two, my buddy Bill, he sailed across the sea.
He stood up for his country, for what he did believe.
Then he came home wrapped in a flag. He would have been *nineteen* (The element of
    time continues)
And I began to see **the cost of things**. For **(hook)**

REPEAT CHORUS

VERSE 4
Now I wake up every morning and thank the Lord to see (Time is now. The singer is
    adult.)

The brown-eyed girl who said, "I do," lying next to me. (The singer's wife)
And I pray that I can be the man that I was meant to be
And teach my kids to know **the cost of things.** 'Cause … **(hook)**

REPEAT CHORUS

SONG 6: "LONG TIME AFTER THE RAIN"

Writing from one's own personal experiences can be an invaluable tool for any writer. (As chapter 1 stresses, "Write about what you know.") The process can even be cathartic, offering the writer the opportunity to pour out unexpressed feelings on the page. However, if the writer is completely honest, writing from personal experience can also be a painful thing. The fresher and more painful the personal experience, the more likely the writer's emotions will be raw and unfiltered. That can be a good thing—a very good thing, even. But sometimes a little distance is needed to gain a more objective perspective.

I wrote "Long Time After the Rain" nearly a decade after my mother's death, and some 20 years after my parent's divorce. It was not an easy song to write, but I don't think I could have written this song any sooner than that. It wasn't until then that enough time had passed and I could approach the subject with some objectivity, compassion, and tenderness. The lyrics are essentially a memoir of the aftermath of my parent's divorce. I tried to make it specific enough so that it rang true, but general enough so that it could be experienced more universally.

My mother's inability to move on with her emotional life after her divorce from my father was proof to me that the old adage Time Heals All Wounds was simply not true. Sadly, sometimes we hold on to an awful hurt because dealing with a familiar difficulty is less frightening than facing an uncertain future. So in "Long Time After the Rain" I employed a metaphor of rising water as an unrelenting pain throughout the lyric. The metaphor is never stated directly. It is couched in the ironic question, "Why's the water rising such a long time after the rain?" It is not until the final A section that an answer or resolution to the question is offered.

The song grew from the central theme of the hook/title. The lyrics were written first, and rewritten as the music evolved. I instinctively chose an AABA song form. (Note the placement of the hook in the last line of each A section.) The AABA form best suited the continuous action of the song's story line, which I've outlined here:

A1　　The parents had a good relationship on the surface. ("Mom and dad seemed to get along. I never saw 'em fight.")
　　　The singer never saw the splitup coming. ("I guess the clouds came quietly. Must've slipped in through the night.")
　　　The divorce is in the past. ("The damage is done now, and the storm has rolled away.")

The pain of the divorce has grown worse with time, and the singer wants to know "why." ("Why's the water rising such a long time after the rain?")

A2 The mother is still mired in the pain of the divorce. ("All the tears my mother shed could have sailed a ship or two.")

The singer struggled unsuccessfully to ease his mother's pain. ("I could sometimes stop her crying, but I could never stop her pain.")

The singer still doesn't understand why the situation isn't getting any better with time. ("Tell me, why's the water rising...")

B The song's bridge expresses the singer's own philosophy that there comes a time to put the past behind you. But when? ("There comes a time to start over...")

A3 We all have our ways of dealing with life. ("Everybody's holding something fast.")

The mother held on to the past until the very last moment of her life. (She held on to memories 'til this morning's early light.")

- Death was the one thing that could stop her pain. ("A quiet stream of mercy came and carried her away / And stopped the water rising...")
- The lyrics hint (but do not hammer) at the idea that God is in the business of mercy, not the business of death, when He calls his children home. There is no grand conclusion, but merely the singer's observations.

In addition to the rising-water metaphor, I used the metaphor of clouds and a storm for the difficulties of the parent's relationship, and of a quiet stream of mercy for death. You'll find hyperbole in the second line of A2: "All the tears my mother shed could've sailed a ship or two." The bridge contains a simple simile: "Yesterday's rain like yesterday's pain is gonna pass." Finally, in A3 I employ another water metaphor to portray us all as doing whatever it takes to emotionally survive: "Everybody's holding something fast to stay above the tide." Notice that all the imagery is connected by a common theme: water (storms, clouds, rising water, rain, tide, stream).

The rhyme scheme is simple and consistent. Notice that by rhyming the hook line in the AABA form, I forced myself to come up with three different rhymes for the line. Fortunately, it was a simple, single rhyme. But let this be a heads-up for whenever you're creating a rhyme scheme that requires multiple rhymes of the same word. If you're not careful in those situations, you can rhyme yourself into a corner (the result often being stilted and forced rhymes). Also, one could make the argument in the B section that "pass" and "past" are awfully close in sound (almost homonyms, but not quite), and thus create a weak rhyme. I wouldn't necessarily disagree.

The music is melancholy. There is tension in the harmonies—a steady back and forth between chords and suspended chords. This hints at the tension in the relationship. It is also fairly fluid, to be consistent with the water metaphor in the lyric. The only "big" music moment is the bridge, which quickly subsides back to the melancholy feel. I hope the music conveys the sense that the singer has found some greater understanding about life, even if he is still affected by the pain of his parents' actions.

Scott Kryppayne sang the demo recording, which is posted on my Website.

LONG TIME AFTER THE RAIN
Words and music by Robert Sterling

A1   RHYME SCHEME

Mom and Dad seemed to get along. I never saw 'em fight.   a

I guess the clouds came quietly. Must've slipped in through the night.   a

The damage is done now, and the *storm has rolled away*.   b

    (*metaphor:* storm/clouds = conflict in relationship)

So why's the *water rising* such a long time after the rain?   b

    (*metaphor:* rising water = unrelenting pain)

A2

There's a story 'bout a mighty flood, and I believe it's true.   a

'Cause all the tears my mother shed could've *sailed a ship or two*.   a

    (*hyperbole*: a flood of tears that would sail a ship)

I could sometimes stop her crying, but I could never stop her pain.   b

Tell me, why's the water rising such a long time after the rain?   b

    (*Tell me* adds emphasis to the hook.)

B

Yesterday's *pain, like yesterday's rain,* is gonna pass.

    (*pain/rain: internal rhyme; simile*)

There comes a time to start over, a time to let go of the past.

    (Singer draws his own conclusion about how to deal with the past.)

A3

Everybody's holding something fast to stay above the tide.   a

    (*metaphor*: We're all doing the best we can.)

And she held on to memories 'til this morning's early light,   a

When a quiet *stream of mercy* came and carried her away,   b

    (*metaphor*: stream of mercy = death)

And stopped the water rising such a long time after the rain.   b

TAG

Mercy stopped the water rising such a long time after the rain.

SONG 7: "BIGGER THAN THAT"

I met Warren Sellers in the late 1990s, when I was judging songs for a regional GMA competition and Warren was a competitor. (He won the competition.) Fast-forward a decade or so, and Warren is now on the other side of the table, evaluating songs for others studying the craft of writing. It was no surprise to me to watch him get signed to a country songwriting deal. Warren has a natural gift for writing a good hook—an invaluable ability, especially in the world of country songwriting. He and I have collaborated on a handful of songs over the years, and every one of them began as a hook from Warren.

Warren lives in Los Angeles, but our collaborations aren't long-distance ones, because he makes semiregular journeys to Nashville to work with various country writers. So we occasionally get together and hammer on a Christian song. "Bigger Than That" was another of Warren's hooks, and it happened faster than most of our collaborations. (Confession time—Warren and I are a painfully slow writing team. One song took us over three years to complete. No exaggeration.) Warren's idea for "Bigger Than That" was simple and singular: God is bigger than we are. Bigger than our problems. Bigger than our politics. Bigger than our petty differences. The words and music evolved simultaneously. I sat at the piano and came up with an R&B shuffle groove and the simplest of chord changes, and we wrote the words together. The melody worked itself out between the two of us taking stabs at it. One thing that pleases me most about "Bigger Than That" is that there is a deeper meaning to this song with the deceptively simple title. Hidden in the clever words is the message that, try as we might, we cannot capture the enormity of God.

The words are very casual in their tone, matching the R&B style of the music. The first verse opens with an attention-getting simile: "God don't live in a bottle like some genie in a lamp." The chorus follows with the simplest of responses that answers the "why" of each statement—because God is "bigger than that." The second verse rifles through six more ways we try to make God small and explainable. They are followed by the same direct explanation of the chorus. Both verses take the approach of saying what God is not. The bridge turns that around and lists some things that God is bigger than: our problems, our pain, our questions, and our politics. Notice the deliberate increasing significance of each line of the bridge.

The rhyme scheme for the verses is a simple a-a-b-b. The chorus is just a single line, repeated. The bridge shares the same rhyme scheme as the verses (a weakness, perhaps?) but has a different rhythmic and musical feel. You will see a smattering of simile and creative wordplay throughout the lyrics. I've marked those instances in the lyrics below.

The music for "Bigger Than That," like the lyrics, is simple and to the point. Only two chords hold the entire song together. The melody range is just one octave, and most of the song falls within a minor sixth. The end of the second verse takes some impromptu liberties away from the melody established in the first verse, but that's really nothing more than a natural building of the intensity leading back into the chorus. Warren and I created an intro riff, which we used later as an interlude or turnaround. In the hands of a great hip-hop producer, the song could take on a whole new sound and still remain true to the basic music of the original.

I've posted a streaming version of Warren's demo on my Website.

BIGGER THAN THAT
Words and music by Warren Sellers and Robert Sterling

VERSE 1   RHYME SCHEME

God don't live in a bottle *like some genie in a lamp.* (*simile*)   a

He don't grant my every wish, or jump at my command.   a

He's no slave to my desires, or whatever I believe.   b

I don't tell Him when to come and go. He don't answer to me,   b

'Cause …

CHORUS

God is bigger, bigger,

He's bigger than that

Yeah, God is bigger, bigger,

He's bigger than that.

RHYME SCHEME
MATCHES VERSE 1

VERSE 2

Can't keep Him in a *building. Can't* hide Him in a *box*,

    (*alliteration: building/box*)

Imprison Him behind *four walls with theological locks.*

    (*metaphor = church*)

Can't put Him down on paper. *Can't* capture Him in rhyme.

    (*anaphora: Can't*)

Can't squeeze Him 'til He's just the size to fit my space and time,

'Cause …

REPEAT CHORUS

BRIDGE (Note the progression of the ideas in the bridge lyrics.)

He's *bigger than* my problems, *bigger than* my pain,

Bigger than the *questions bouncing 'round inside my brain,*

    (interesting word picture)

Bigger than the President and all the Heads of State,

Bigger than the walls that all our differences create.

    (*anaphora:* repeating *bigger than*)

REPEAT CHORUS

SONG 8: "PRAY FOR ME"

In chapter 1, I discussed the importance of point of view. I stressed that though there are three different points of view from which to write, a good song generally sticks to one POV from start to finish. Like all the rules of songwriting, the single-point-of-view rule can be broken if you do it carefully and purposefully. "Pray for Me" breaks this rule—big-time. It employs all three points of view, in one form or another. And yet, it still works. (Feel free to disagree.) I've included it here so that you can see what is involved in changing point of view in the body of a song. Decide for yourself if it's worth the effort.

The idea for the song came from my co-writer, Chris Machen. His concept was to show the disenfranchised people we pass every day that covet our prayers. But these societal outsiders don't ask us to pray for them directly, because we don't know them and, worse still, we ignore them. He wanted the chorus to center on the line, "Will somebody pray for me?" We believed that if the song was to make its point, we needed to tell multiple stories in the verses, but it felt clumsy to tell so many stories in the first person. So, we realized we would have to shift POV as we moved into the chorus. But how?

Take a look at the verses. The first verse begins plainly in third person. The vocalist is singing about a homeless man (the "dusty man"), a starving girl (the "hungry child"), and a runaway boy (the "troubled boy"). The second verse is also in the third person, and the vocalist is singing about an abandoned elderly man (the "ancient man") and a lonely foreigner ("she's from another land"). These people are representations of others like them, reduced to a single line with a quick picture.

The same channel follows both verses: two brief lines that express a shared emotion of each of these people ("There's an emptiness inside"), along with a common desire ("There's a question in their eyes"). From that point on, Chris and I were free to shift the chorus into the first-person POV simply by revealing what the "question in their eyes" is: "Will somebody pray for me?" The chorus continues in the new POV, and the listener hears the inner thoughts of the people described in the verses.

The POV shifts abruptly back at the beginning of the second verse. The listener should be able to detect the change because the lyrics parallel the form of the first verse, describing more individuals who are at the fringe of society. Once again the channel begins to change gears and the chorus moves back to the first person.

The bridge makes yet another shift in POV—this time to the second person, also called direct address. The vocalist is now singing to the audience while including himself, referring to "we." The bridge is the point of the song, the moral of the story. Essentially, it says, "If not us, then who?" It ends with its own version of the channel that facilitates the return to the first person: "Gonna take some trying / When we hear them crying." But what are they crying? Once again, the chorus answers the question, asking, "Will somebody pray for me?"

Note that all the shifts in POV happen at the beginning of a new section of the music. Verse: third person. Channel: shift. Chorus: first person. Bridge: second person. This was no accident. By placing the POV changes on top of the changes in the music, the listener should be better able to hear and understand the shift in POV.

A quick examination of the lyrics for poetic imagery shows a healthy dose of anaphora, or repeated phrases. Alongside the anaphora, I've noted metaphor, hyperbole, and synecdoche. There's even an internal double rhyme in the last line of the bridge. The rhyme scheme is obvious, but not predictable.

The music for "Pray for Me" is mellow pop, based on two familiar chord progressions: I, iii7, ii7, iv6 (verse) and I, vi7, ii7, iv/V (chorus). We used a subtle 16th-rhythm groove throughout, lifting the chorus a bit melodically. As you listen to the demo (at robertsterlingmusic.com), notice throughout the verses and chorus that all the IV chords are minor (spelled with lowercase letters—iv). Then at the top of the bridge, we land squarely on a IV maj7 chord, one of the brightest-sounding chords available. That change sets the bridge apart as a new musical idea. This is important, because the bridge contains a new POV and a distinct lyric thought.

A word about my co-writer: Chris Machen was my first ongoing professional collaborator. Together we wrote about 30 songs from 1984 to 1994, landing songs both on artist recordings and in choral print music. Most notable of our songs is "I Have Seen the Light," which has sold more than 200,000 copies in print and has been recorded by a half-dozen artists, including the Gatlin Brothers. Chris is to this day one of my dearest friends. He's a terrific singer (something I've always envied) and a handsome guy.

PRAY FOR ME
   Words and music by Chris Machen and Robert Sterling

VERSE 1
(third-person POV)
He is the dusty man whose home is in the street. (*dusty*: interesting adjective)
She is the hungry child who cries herself to sleep.
He is the troubled boy who can't go home again. (*anaphora*: *He is/She is/He is*)

CHANNEL
(making the shift in POV)
There's emptiness inside. (more *anaphora*)
There's a question in their eyes …

CHORUS
(first-person POV)
Will somebody **pray for me? (hook)**
Will somebody hold my hand?
Will somebody touch my life (more *anaphora*: *Will somebody* …)
And just try to understand
That I'm all alone out here,
Lost on *a stormy sea*. (*metaphor*: stormy sea = difficult life)
All that I'm asking you,
Will somebody **pray for me? (hook)**

VERSE 2
(third-person POV)
He is the *ancient* man, forgotten and alone. (*hyperbole*: *ancient* rather than merely "old")
She's from another land so very far from home.
They are the million souls lost without a hope.

CHANNEL

(making the shift in POV)

There's emptiness inside.

There's a question in their eyes ...

REPEAT CHORUS

(first-person POV)

BRIDGE

(second-person POV/direct address)

Every day these are the *faces* that we meet. (*synecdoche*: people reduced to "faces")

We just might be the only Jesus that they see.

It sounds so simple, but it's up to you and me.

Gonna take some *trying* when we hear them *crying* ... (shift in POV; *internal double rhyme*: *trying/crying*)

REPEAT CHORUS

(first-person POV)

SONG 9: "SO LONG, SMALL TOWN"

Over the years, I've been privileged to write several musical theater works for the church. *The Christmas Post, Two From Galilee, One Voice,* and *For Unto Y'all* are examples of my theatrical musicals that are available commercially through Word Music. But way back around 1992, I was invited to write songs for an original musical being produced by a large church in Florida. *The Bell Ringer,* by Claire Cloninger and Angela Hunt, was a lighthearted Christmas work, set at the turn of the 20th century. The music had to sound modern enough to appeal to contemporary audiences, but needed to have touches of an earlier time so that it was compatible with the story's setting. It was a fun challenge that produced a half-dozen original songs that I wrote with Claire.

The primary challenge of writing for the musical theater is to write songs that present a character's viewpoint—not the songwriter's. The lyrics must spring authentically from the characters' mouths, or the audience won't believe them when they sing. As always, the songs must show who the characters are, not tell about them. Consider the best songs from your favorite Broadway musicals. (I'm assuming you are a fan of Broadway musicals.) Chances are those songs were successful because they were memorable, well written, and believable when their respective characters sang them.

Because more and more churches are launching drama ministries and the major church print-music companies are mostly ignoring this market, churches sometimes create their own musicals. And for the savvy church music/drama director, that means writing original songs to fit their original script. I've included "So Long, Small Town" as an example of writing for that very need. You will see from the lyrics and the demo recording (at robertsterlingmusic.com) that writing a character song isn't so different from writing any other sort of song. But the song must ring true for the character.

This sort of opportunity offers a refreshing chance to write outside the typical box we have built for church music. Songs for musicals can be funny, lighthearted, and even outrageous. One thing they must not be is preachy. The drama must *show*, and so must the songs. If the story is compelling and the songs are well written, the audience will come to the conclusion that the authors guide them to without being hit over the head with a heavy, preachy message.

"So Long, Small Town" is a fairly typical character song for a musical. Character songs are often used to tell the audience what is going on inside a character's head. The lyrics will sometimes voice things that the character would never say aloud to anyone. "So Long, Small Town" expresses the inner thoughts of Leslie Van Horton, a self-involved ingénue, just as she leaves town (and her poor fiancé, Franklin) for greener pastures. Ms. Van Horton is hilariously snooty—a perfectly awful person, who is guaranteed to be fun to portray. As she sings the song, she stands at the station awaiting the morning train that promises to whisk her away to a place better than the small berg where she has been stuck her whole life. The lyrics display her true personality with delicious snobbery.

In the staging of the song, Leslie mocks the town and its citizens. She then quickly composes an insincere and syrupy-sweet "Dear John" letter to poor Franklin. She does this out loud, of course, so the audience can hear just how awful she really is. She writes the letter after singing through the song once. Music continues under her as she composes the letter aloud. She repeats the AABC portion of the lyrics as she hands the letter off to be delivered to the unsuspecting Franklin. As the songs ends, she steps aboard the train and departs. If you listen to the demo while you study the lyrics, you will hear the contents of the letter. I haven't included it below, because it's not part of the song itself, but rather is part of the script.

I chose "So Long, Small Town" for an additional purpose. It employs a little-used form (AABC) that works well for musical theater. Claire Cloninger began the lyrics with an introductory "verse"—a popular device for allowing the character to ease into the main thought of the song. For the body of the song, Claire used the AABC form (as a variation of the AABA.) The body of the song is so brief that it might be difficult to see the AABC, but it's there. The music is a waltz, and so each line of the lyrics is 4 bars long, forming a classic 32-bar form. The final 8-bar section is related musically to the A sections, but is different enough to be called a C section rather than another A section.

Claire used a lot of sophisticated rhyme in the lyrics, hinting that Leslie Van Horton is a bit of an intellectual (or at least thinks she is). The introductory verse includes two instances of internal rhyme, placed to match in the first and third lines. Claire used a soft but artful triple rhyme in the body of the song ("potential"/"provincial"). Triple rhymes always shine a powerful spotlight on the rhyming words, so it's important to notice that Claire wisely chose words that reveal something about Ms. Van Horton's true character. The next line contains another clever internal rhyme, again landing on significant, picturesque words: "One-horse avenue / One-track point of view."

The lyrics were complete when I received them and (miracle of miracles!) I don't think I changed a word. One of Claire's greatest gifts as a lyricist is that she writes to well-organized forms that are generally easy to see on the page. The natural rhythms of these words are obvious.

Read them aloud with normal stresses, and the built-in waltz feel should be evident. I simply had to find the right waltz melody to fit the attitude of the lyrics. My tune features a lot of angular motion and chromatic surprises that are reminiscent of the melodies from that time period, as well as befitting Ms. Van Horton's high opinion of herself.

A word of caution: There was no time or money to hire an actress to perform the demo. So, when listening to the demo recording (at robertsterlingmusic.com), you will hear *me* singing the song in character as best I could. This may provide a higher degree of comic relief than intended, but let it be a lesson to you that as long as the demo sells the song to its intended audience (in this case, the show's producer), that's all that really matters.

SO LONG, SMALL TOWN
Words by Claire Cloninger; music by Robert Sterling

INTRO – "VERSE"   RHYME SCHEME

At ten *fifteen* on December *nineteen* (internal rhyme)   a

I'll be checking out of here *forever* (double rhyme)   b

When the train pulls *in,* I'll be boarding and *then*   c
(internal rhyme)

I'll be taking off for something *better* (double rhyme)   b

AABC (EACH SECTION IS EIGHT BARS)

A1

So long, small town   a

Leaving for a scene with more *potential*   b

A2

So long, small town   a

Somewhere glamorous and less *provincial* (triple rhyme)   b

B

One-horse *avenue,* one-track *point of view* (internal rhyme)   c

I'll be seeing you around   a

C

So long, so long, small town.   a

(REPEAT MUSIC UNDER CHARACTER MONOLOGUE)
(REPEAT AABC)

SONG 10: "CASUAL OBSERVER"

Every professional songwriter has songs he or she considers to be their best work but that have never been recorded. "Casual Observer" is one of those songs for me. It's a character study of a sad, unlikable person, unaware of the fact that life is passing him by every single day. (Suffice it to say, this is not the sort of song that record companies are looking for these days.) The song says something significant. The music is solidly married to the lyrics. "Casual Observer" is "right" in so many ways, and yet it will likely never be recorded beyond a demo.

However, for the purposes of this book, "Casual Observer" is a great teaching tool. If nothing else, I hope you will learn from it that the recorded status of your songs is not the ultimate measure of their quality. Beyond that, it has much to demonstrate to student writers regarding characterization and imagery, not to mention rewriting a song over a long period of time.

Let me start with the rewriting. I first wrote "Casual Observer" in 1989. It took me about a day to write. The lyrics, though much like this version, had a completely different point of view. (The song was originally written in the first person.) The original melody was essentially the same, but the music bed had a driving Latin groove. There was also a third verse, which was edited out and later lost forever. (There's a lesson for you right there. Always keep your unused/discarded lyrics in a file somewhere. You never know when you might need them.)

After the song languished in my catalog (and Word Music's catalog) for more than a decade, I pulled it out and spent another day rewriting. I changed the POV to third person, making it much easier for a singer to perform. (What singer wants to sing about a sad loser in the first person?) I changed the music into a ballad, altering the chorus melody more than a bit. And I reharmonized the tune using more-complex harmonies, giving it a bit of a jazz feel. I made a simple piano-vocal demo, playing and singing it myself. (I loved the song, but I wasn't about to spend any money making a demo for a song that nobody wanted to record.) If anybody ever asks me how long it took me to write "Casual Observer," my honest answer would be "Two days—and ten years." I needed to live with the song for a decade before I was ready to rewrite it. And even as recently as a couple of months ago, I spotted a single word change that helped to improve it. So, I guess I'm still rewriting it.

What makes "Casual Observer" a favorite of mine is the vividness of its title character. (The title is a well-known phrase that adds its own depth of meaning to the song.) Every line of the lyrics spools out another small insight into this pitiful man's head and heart. Here are a few things we learn about him from the first verse and the chorus:

1. He has an unchanging and uninteresting daily routine.

2. He is content to watch life pass by, never even speaking.

3. He is distant and uncaring.

4. He is completely unaware of his shortcomings.

In addition to the title character, there is the bag lady in verse 1 and the unhappy neighbors in verse 2. The bag lady carries her life's possessions about in a shopping bag, wandering through the park babbling nonsensically. All we know for certain about the neighbors is that they are unhappy. Their arguments seep through the paper-thin apartment walls and "sound remarkably like tears."

I employed a metonym in the opening line, referring to breakfast specifically as "toast and eggs." That gives a better mental picture than does the word "breakfast." There is also some subtle alliteration in verse 1. The second verse opens with a quirky personification of the sofa: the main character "shares the TV with the sofa," as if the sofa is a companion to share in the TV viewing. Later in that verse is this simile: "Faceless words that sound remarkably like tears." In addition to these specific poetic devices, you'll discover that the lyrics use ordinary words in less-than-ordinary ways. Finally, the entire set of lyrics is infused with a melancholy sense of understatement that is most obvious in the final lines of the chorus: "He'd participate if there was only time / But there's never enough hours in a day." Here is a man with nothing but time on his hands, but he tells himself he is too busy to join in with the world around him.

"Casual Observer" is a verse/chorus song. The tune starts to repeat halfway through the each verse, making them feel like double verses. The music captures the melancholy of the lyrics. It is not a rangy melody nor is it difficult to sing (as evidenced by the fact that I can sing it). The harmonies are somewhat complex. They certainly go way beyond the world of the basic I, IV, and V chords. The demo is available for listening on my Website. You get to hear me sing. Lucky you.

CASUAL OBSERVER
Words and music by Robert Sterling

VERSE 1
Every morning after *toast and eggs* he takes his place (*metonym*)
On the park bench that is just outside his door.
As the *daily d*rama passes, he *s*its *s*ilently— (*alliteration*)
The **casual observer**, nothing more. **(hook)**
A nameless *w*oman *w*anders by him aimlessly (*alliteration*)
The sum of her existence in a shopping bag from Sears.
She recites to him her well-worn lines of tragedy.
He nods to her and tries to look sincere.

CHORUS
Oh … he's a **casual observer** of mankind. **(hook)**
He watches every day.
He'd participate if there was only time (*irony*)
But there's never enough hours in a day.

VERSE 2
Every evening he goes home to a *one-room flat* (implies a small life)
And *shares the TV with the sofa* in the dark. (*personification*)
The *picture shows a vague similarity* (*ironic*: Real life and TV look the same to him.)

To his casual observations in the park.

And voices sometimes carry through the *hollow walls* (He lives in a cheap place.)

Faceless words that sound remarkably *like tears* (*simile*)

It's probably *those people* just across the hall (He doesn't know his neighbors)

But the TV makes it difficult to hear. (*ironic*: He drowns out real life with the TV.)

REPEAT CHORUS

He'd participate if there was only time,

But there's never enough hours in a day.

SONG 11: "THE BALLAD OF LUPÉ (THE CHIHUAHUA WHO DANCED THE BALLET)"

Back in chapter 2, we covered the question "Where do song ideas come from?" "The Ballad of Lupé" is an example of a song that came from a casual conversation colliding with an actual need for a song. My wonderful wife, Cindy, is, among other things, a children's entertainer. At the time this song was written, she worked as a performing artist for the Nashville Public Library's downtown children's theater. Along with two other performers, she acted, sang, read books to kids, and performed puppet shows daily. (It's a very big library.) In addition, she cohosted the Nashville Ballet's occasional visits to the library, where the ballet company would teach the children classical dance. (Like I said, it's a *very* big library.)

In the course of working with the ballet dancers, Cindy became friends with the company's educational director, Sharyn Wood. That's how Cindy came to meet Guadalupe Louisa Maria Josefina Esperanza Wood, Sharyn's pet Chihuahua—a dog that believed she could dance. Lupé, as her friends and family knew her, had her own little doggy dance outfits and was something of a diva. Cindy told me about Lupé while the two of us were working on an independent children's record for Cindy's alter ego, Aunt Cindy Rose. I thought the story was hilarious, and perfect for Cindy's record.

I wrote the song in a single day, much of it coming very quickly. The first two lines came out right away, and they set the stage for the entire story and the tone of the music. (Unlike a lot of writers, I frequently begin without a hook if my opening line is engaging enough.) The lyrics spilled out in a natural 3/4 time signature. The challenge was to tell a complete story that would come to a satisfying conclusion that children would enjoy. Kids are much smarter than we give them credit for being, and so I didn't dumb down the lyrics or the music for them.

I believe that the song works because it tells the story of someone who persevered and followed her dream until she achieved it. Even if young children can't express that concept yet, they can understand that simple theme. "The Ballad of Lupé" is always on the list of favorites from Aunt Cindy Rose's record. A couple of years ago, I sang the song in Estes Park, Colorado, for a roomful of amateur Christian songwriters and artists. Judging from the positive response, they too appreciated the story. After all, everyone has a dream.

Just as the title says, "Lupé" is a ballad, or a story song, written in a verse/chorus form. A good story song should unfold quickly and efficiently, and so "The Ballad of Lupé" wastes no time telling the listener who Lupé is and what she wants in life. In four brief lines we learn that Lupé desires to be not simply an ordinary ballet dancer, but a *star*. Of course, what makes the whole story preposterous (and hopefully funny) is that Lupé is a dog—better yet, a Chihuahua. The song plot blazes along, and before the first verse is through, Lupé has packed her bags and headed off to chase her dream.

Verse 2 is filled with action. (Action is good. It shows rather than tells.) We learn that Lupé is not only an accomplished dancer, but that she is determined and clever, as well. She does what it takes to get an audition by sneaking into the theater and "pretending to be someone's pet." The brief channel that segues from the verse into the chorus prepares Lupé (and the listener) for Lupé's rejection by the arrogant maestro. (Note: In the song, I don't bother to explain that a "maestro" is a musical conductor. The kids will figure it out, or their parents will explain it to them, and they will have learned a new word. The same goes for "bravo" and all the French ballet terms in the song.)

The chorus voices the obvious question: "Whoever heard of a dancing Chihuahua?" And the even more melodramatic question follows: Would Lupé ever hear the crowds cheer for her on stage? To find out, you must listen on.

Verse 3 shows us that Lupé is not a quitter. Every day she persistently practices to achieve her goal. Again and again, the maestro brushes her aside—not because she can't dance, but because (can you believe it???) she's a Chihuahua! The chorus repeats Lupé's painful rejection.

In the fourth verse, the plot thickens. (And the music melodramatically changes to a minor key.) A bee sting has felled a dancer named Tina. Who could possibly step in and take her place? Why, Lupé, of course! The final channel shows that Lupé is prepared to meet her glorious moment of opportunity.

The last chorus is an altered parallel to the original chorus, changed in order to complete the story: "Now everyone's heard of the dancing Chihuahua." We also learn Lupé's dance debut was a smashing success: "Her marvelous moves saved the day." And best of all, not only did Lupé hear the crowds cheer for her, but the whole world heard the cheers. A star is born!

The universal theme of the song is "follow your dream." But it also teaches that one should be persistent in the face of obstacles and be prepared when opportunity strikes. It doesn't matter if you are 5 years old or 55, those lessons remain true. What is great about the song is that it allowed me to show the message to be true without ever preaching. Beginning Christian songwriters can learn a lot from this simple example. Showing really is better than telling.

The primary poetic device used in "Lupé" is the obvious use of rhyme. This is a fairly involved story song with four verses, a channel, and two different choruses. Rhyme is an effective way to keep the listener on track through all those words. Careful examination of the lyrics also reveals a healthy dose of alliteration. Any song with a sense of humor benefits from clever words that trip off the tongue. Below are some of the alliterations in the lyrics. As you listen to the song, notice how most of them fall on strong beats in the music.

- "Her only *d*ream was to *d*ance"
- "She packed up her *t*ights and her *t*utu"

- "A *p*erfectly *p*ure *p*irouette"
- "Seeking her *f*ortune and *f*ame"
- "The maestro, he *t*ore off his *t*oupee"
- "Her *m*arvelous *m*oves saved the day"

The music for "The Ballad of Lupé" is what I affectionately call *faux mariachi*. During my years as a jingle writer, I composed music for several Mexican food restaurant chains. I became fond of mariachi music and its infectious, joyful attitude. This song borrows heavily from that style of music to emphasize the Mexican heritage of Chihuahua dogs. It also creates a naturally bright and rhythmic framework to hang the lyrics on. The verses are built over an *ostinato* (repeating) bass line. The channel uses chromatic harmonies over a dominant pedal tone. The chorus then sails into a "three to the bar" walking bass line that outlines the simple I- and V-chord harmonies. The intro is built on the music from the channel. I also borrowed the common use of the "two against three" syncopations in mariachi music for the chorus rhythms. Notice that the handclaps in the chorus are "two to the bar" against the bass line's "three to the bar."

The range of the melody is only one octave. The words scan very naturally. I deliberately extended the second line of the chorus ("He shooed poor Lupé away") for two reasons: first, it is in keeping with mariachi music to "milk" a line like that, and second, it allows the humor of the first line of the chorus time to sink in with the listener. The change from major to minor at the top of the fourth verse also has two purposes: first, it supports the humorous melodrama of the lyrics, and second, it provides a nice harmonic surprise near the end of the song. It isn't necessary to stay in the minor key, and so the music shifts back to major halfway through the verse.

I believe that "The Ballad of Lupé" does a whole lot of things right. It has an intriguing opening line. The story is compelling (at least to preschoolers), and it comes to a satisfying conclusion. It has a universal human theme, and the music fits the words well. It will surely never be a hit on the radio, but Aunt Cindy Rose's fans don't care about that. And neither do I. It was worth it to me just for the chance to rhyme the word "toupee" in a song.

The recording of Aunt Cindy Rose singing "The Ballad of Lupé" is posted on my Website.

THE BALLAD OF LUPÉ
(THE CHIHUAHUA WHO DANCED THE BALLET)
Words and music by Robert Sterling

VERSE 1
There was a Chihuahua named Lupé (pronounced "LOO-pay")
And her only *d*ream was to *d*ance. (*alliteration*)
She'd be a big star in the ballet
If someone would give her the chance.
So she packed up her *t*ights and her *t*utu (*alliteration*)
Her toe shoes and best leotard. (toe shoes for a dog?)
She *d*id what a smart *d*oggie should do (*alliteration*)
She followed the call of her heart. (As opposed to the "call of the wild"?)

VERSE 2 (lots of insight into Lupé in verse 2)
Lupé sneaked in backstage at the ballet,
Pretending to be someone's pet.
She then demonstrated her plié (use of French ballet terms)
And a *perfectly pure pirouette.* (more *alliteration*)
The fait accompli was her jeté,
Oozing with fire and romance.
"I'm here to *be* in the *b*allet" (more *alliteration*)
Lupé said, "Won't you please let me dance?"

CHANNEL
"Not bad," said the maestro. "I admit, I'm impressed,
For I've never seen such a fine arabesque. But … (more foreign words)

CHORUS
Whoever heard of a dancing Chihuahua?"
He shooed poor Lupé away. (music stretches for emphasis)
Would she ever hear the audience cheer,
"Bravo!" for little Lupé,
The Chihuahua who danced the ballet (hook)

VERSE 3 (action in verse shows Lupé's character)
But Lupé kept right on believing
That one day she'd get her big break. (Lupé is a true believer.)
She practiced all morning and evening
Until her little paws ached. (Lupé is diligent.)
And each day she went to the ballet,
Seeking her *f*ortune and *f*ame. (Lupé is persistent.)
She begged, "Give a chance to poor Lupé."
But the answer was always the same.

CHANNEL (ALT.)
"That's good. Very good," the maestro would say. (Lupé is talented.)
"There's no doubt about it. A world-class plié. But. . .

REPEAT CHORUS

VERSE 4 (Music shifts to minor key; melodrama)
Then one day a dancer named Tina
Was stung on the toe by a bee,
And the *b*allet had no *b*allerina (more *alliteration*)
To whirl and to twirl in Act Three.
The maestro, he tore off his toupee (back to major key)

The moment that he heard the news.

And then every eye turned to Lupé,

As she calmly laced up her shoes. (Lupé is confident.)

CHANNEL (ALT.)

"I'll do it," said Lupé. "I'll finish the show. (Lupé is prepared.)

I'm ready. I'm willing. I'm raring to go."

ALTERED CHORUSES

Now, everyone's heard of the dancing Chihuahua.

Her *marvelous moves* saved the day. (more *alliteration*; Lupé succeeds.)

The whole world could hear the audience cheer,

"Bravo!" for little Lupé,

The Chihuahua who danced the ballet. **(hook)**

Yes, everyone's heard of the dancing Chihuahua.

Her *marvelous moves* saved the day.

The whole world could hear the audience cheer,

"Bravo!" for little Lupé,

The Chihuahua who danced the ballet. **(hook)**

SONG 12: "I CHOOSE JESUS"

"I Choose Jesus" has had an interesting journey. It began as a song I wrote in 1988 for my home church's Easter musical. It was the climactic moment near the end of the show, as the centurion who crucified Jesus made his ultimate decision to follow the risen Lord. A few months later, Luke Garrett recorded the song on his *Fine Joy* project (Home Sweet Home Records, 1989). Not long after that, Word Music released the song in print as a choir anthem. Then, a year or two later, I wrote my first dramatic musical, *The Choice* (Word Music, 1992), and used "I Choose Jesus" once again as the conversion moment for the centurion whose life was changed by Jesus. Then, as is often the case, it fell out of favor for newer and hipper songs. It was sung in churches occasionally, but was largely forgotten. That is until just a couple of years ago when Mike Speck, a prominent Southern Gospel artist, chose to use it in a Christmas project. The Christmas project was a big success, and that prompted Word to release a new arrangement of the song for solo, choir, and orchestra. So "I Choose Jesus" is enjoying a bit of a rebirth in the church.

"I Choose Jesus" is a big, inspirational ballad, with the simplest of messages. It captures the moment when a person chooses to either follow Jesus or go another way. There aren't many major artists recording songs like this these days. Still, I believe that there will always be a home, however small, for well-written inspirational songs. And the pendulum of musical style is always moving, and may swing back this way again someday. But more importantly, "I Choose Jesus" will always be special to me for the simple reason that it is my own confession of faith in song.

"I Choose Jesus" is a straightforward verse/chorus song with two verses and a single repeated chorus. The hook is planted squarely in the first, second, and last lines of the chorus. It states the entire point of the song. Since the chorus makes the point so plainly, it was important for the second verse to delve into more-personal ground than the first verse, to keep the song moving forward. The two verses match each other structurally. The song needs no bridge or channel, because the verses are eight lines long and that allowed me to say all I needed to say.

The verses break down into four couplets rhyming every other line: a-b-c-b-d-e-f-e. The rhymes are all single rhymes. The next to last line in both verses (the *f* line in the rhyme scheme) contains an internal rhyme. Another way to analyze the verses is by the music. If you do that, each verse breaks down into four sections (two lines to each section) like this: ABAC. The music in the first and second lines is repeated exactly in the fifth and sixth lines. The last two lines (the C section) build toward the chorus and, as a result, feel a little like a channel. But because the rhyme scheme of the verse isn't complete without the last two lines, those lines are the completion of the verse.

There is a sprinkling of poetic imagery in the lyrics. You will find occasional subtle alliteration: "some say," "live and learn," "sailed the sea," "live life." I used repeated phrases (anaphora) in the back half of the chorus: "Not for miracles, but for loving me / Not for Bethlehem, but for Calvary / Not for a day, but for eternity." Note that those three lines also rhyme, which focuses more attention on them. You'll find metaphor in verse 1, where life is a "crossroad." The second verse is built on a sailing metaphor.

The repetition in the chorus of "not for" and "but for" focuses on the singer's reasons for choosing to follow Jesus. Each statement is a balanced reason within itself, and each statement leads logically to the next, finishing with "eternity." To be enamored of Jesus' miracles, to think only of his birth, or to follow him for only a day—these things aren't enough. Instead, the singer chooses Jesus for his love, his sacrificial death, and for eternity.

The music for "I Choose Jesus" is pure inspirational ballad. There is a built-in modulation going into the chorus that automatically lifts the melody to a higher range, setting it apart from the verse. Because the tempo is slow, there is room for harmonic complexity. A chord change occurs every two beats in most measures of the song. There is a healthy dose of added tones and suspended fourth, major seventh, dominant seventh, and minor sixth chords throughout. Don't let all those extra notes confuse you, though. The primary motion of the harmonies in this song is a basic cycle of fifths—dominant chords resolving to their tonics. The musical stretch in this song happens in the large range of its melody. (I wrote the song for a big dramatic moment, and I was confident the singer could handle it.) "I Choose Jesus" is a demanding feature solo, not intended for an average vocalist or for congregational singing. By the time the final modulation comes around, the written range is an octave and a fifth. When Luke Garrett recorded it, he sang the optional high D-flat on the end, making the range a full two octaves. Keep in mind that Luke is not a normal singer. He is a freak of nature.

You can find "I Choose Jesus" on several choral recordings (wordmusic.com), as well as on Luke Garrett's CD *Fine Joy* (Home Sweet Home Records, 1989).

I CHOOSE JESUS
    Words and music by Robert Sterling

VERSE 1

Some say life is just a series of decisions.
We make choices. We live and learn.
Now I'm standing at a crossroad
And I must choose which way to turn.
Down the one road is all the world can offer (*metaphor*)
All its power, its wealth and fame.
Down the other, just a *man* with nail scars in his *hands*.
   (*internal rhyme*)
But there's mercy in his eyes and power in his name.

CHORUS

I choose Jesus. I choose Jesus. (hook)
Without a solitary doubt **I choose Jesus. (hook)**
Not for miracles, *but for* loving me (*anaphora*)
Not for Bethlehem, *but for* Calvary,
Not for a day, *but for* eternity
I choose Jesus. (hook)

VERSE 2

All my life *I sailed the sea of reason.* (*metaphor*)
I was captain of my soul.
There was no need for a Savior.
I could live life on my own.
Then I heard him speak a language of compassion,
Words of healing for broken lives.
When they nailed him to a *tree* his love included *me.*
   (*internal rhyme*)
Now he's calling me to follow, to leave the past behind.

REPEAT CHORUS

VERSE STRUCTURE

A

B

A

C

VERSE RHYME SCHEME

a
b
c
b
d
e
f

e

Building a Demo (Is It Live, or Is It Memorex?)

Capturing Your Song for Posterity

If you happen to be one of those rare songwriters who sings their own songs only in a live setting and has no desire to pitch their songs to anybody else, and you have a cultlike conviction that your songs should never be recorded unless they go straight to a finished mass-marketed CD, then you can skip this chapter—because you have no need to demo your songs. But if you're like most writers, you desperately want to play your songs for anybody who will listen. Every day you cling to the magical hope that maybe, just maybe, somebody will record your latest musical masterpiece on a smash hit album, making you rich and famous. (Admit it—you've already got your Grammy acceptance speech prepared. Be sure to thank your mom.) If you do suffer from this very common delusion (I do), you need to know how to make a good demonstration recording *(demo)* of your songs so that you can get them out there in the world to be noticed.

And even if you are levelheaded enough to have no desire to chase the fantasy of full-time professional songwriting, you didn't go to all that trouble of writing your songs so they could sit mute in a three-ring binder left over from your senior year English class. You've told all your friends and family that you write songs. Wouldn't it be nice to hand them a recording of your latest creations? You want them to hear your songs, not just hear you talk about your songs. All other reasons aside, one day you will be old and gray and will want a reminder of the all the hours you shared being creative with the Creator. Quality recordings will be the best archive you can ever have, better than lyric sheets, lead sheets, or even typeset music pages. Printed forms of music are great. I'm a big believer in printed music—trust me on that. But music exists first to be heard, so a recording is always a superior archive.

So whether it's to pitch your songs to big-time record producers, to show them off to your buddies, or to preserve them for your grandkids, the time is going to come when you will need a recorded prototype of your songs. Sooner or later, every songwriter needs to know how to make a decent demo.

Focus on the Song

As I said above, a demo can serve more than one purpose. It can be a professional pitch to a record company or a casual recording to show your friends. It can be a sales tool for your writing career or a simple archive of your latest creative effort. But every demo shares one primary purpose, one main goal, and that is to be a clear representation of the song. This is true regardless of whom the target audience may be: record producers, artists, your church congregation, or your mom and dad. A good demo captures the words, melody, harmonies, and rhythms of your song in the way you intend them to sound. While that may seem painfully obvious and simple enough to do, the fact is lots of song demos don't turn out the way the writer expected. If you're not careful, the focus of your demo can shift to become a showcase for something other than your song. A showcase for what, you ask? Here's an incomplete list of what your precious song demo is *not*:

1. Your demo is *not* a chance for the session guitarist to demonstrate how many notes he can play in a 16-bar break.

2. Your song demo is *not* a launching pad for a session singer looking for a record deal.

3. Your song demo is *not* an opportunity for a recording engineer to experiment with all his latest computer plug-ins. (Not unless your engineer is working for free.)

4. Your song demo is *not* the place for a music programmer to test his theory that every song sounds better with a few hip-hop drum loops wailing in the background.

I repeat: the primary purpose of a song demo is to be a clear representation of your song. To accomplish that, it is important for you to know what your song should sound like before you begin the demo process. The more clearly you can hear your song in your head, the better you will be able to communicate with those who work on the demo.

Further, it's imperative that everyone involved in the production of the demo stay focused on the song. A song can change significantly in a recording session—sometimes for the better, sometimes for the worse. In any session, the musicians, vocalists, engineers, and arrangers all put their own unique touches on the song. This can be a wonderful thing, especially if these talented folks are intent on serving the song. However, if you're not careful, your song may morph into something completely different from what you imagined. If the song's groove or mood is drastically altered, or if the melody disappears inside the singer's vocal stylings, your demo could turn out to be worthless to you as a writer. Worse still, you probably paid good money for it!

Preparing for the Demo

CONVENTIONAL WISDOM

One of the first and most important decisions regarding making a demo is how elaborate it will be. Should you hire a rhythm section, or will a simple piano or guitar track be sufficient to demo your song? Will a single voice get the point across, or do you need to add harmony vocals, or even a choir? Most songwriters have limited resources to produce demos, so I recommend you spend only what you can afford—nothing more. Keep in mind that demo recordings are demonstrations, not final recorded masters.

If you are fortunate enough to have a publisher footing the bill, the publisher will not want to spend any more money than is necessary—I assure you of that. Further, it's likely that you, the signed writer, will have to recoup some of your demo production costs from future royalties. In that case, you should also try not to spend any more money than necessary. In my 16-plus years as a signed writer, I was very fortunate that none of my demo costs were ever recouped from my royalties. That is increasingly rare in the music business. Most writers with publishing deals have to recoup part, or sometimes all of the cost of demos from future royalties. If you are an independent songwriter paying for your demos out of your own pocket, don't spend more than you can afford, and don't waste money funding other people's recording ambitions.

But what is necessary? Ask yourself this: What elements *must* the song have in order to be presented well? If all that's needed is a simple piano/vocal demo, then that's all you should do. Don't waste your time and money building an elaborate track with lots of backing vocals if something simple will do the trick. However, there certainly are those songs that demand a more involved treatment in order to show what the song is all about. Up-tempo songs, rhythm-heavy songs, groove-oriented songs—these often require a full rhythm section or a complex programmed rhythm track to showcase the song. Songs being pitched to vocal groups might call for multiple vocal parts. In those cases, go for it. But always stay focused on the song.

In Their Own Words

> *I am old school. Most of my songs work with just me at the piano.*
> —PAUL SMITH

> *If your song isn't effective with a simple piano-vocal or guitar-vocal recording, all the production in the world won't make it a better song.*
> —KYLE MATTHEWS

AN OPPOSING VIEW

There is another view regarding demos that is diametrically opposed to the "Keep It Simple" conventional wisdom above. The opposing view, born from the world of creating artist demos, says to make the demo sound like a finished record because music executives are tone deaf and have no imagination.

Which view is correct? It depends on whom you're pitching to. If you are pitching pop songs to major record labels, the standards for song demos has risen along with the standards for artist demos. The competition for these coveted opportunities has upped the proverbial ante for creative submissions. Today, artist demos sound like finished masters. As a result, song demos, which were historically simpler, have become more and more polished, often approaching the sophistication level of an artist demo. According to Molly-Ann Leiken, "Publishers expect the demo to sound produced and slick by the time they hear the song" (*How to Write a Hit Song*, p. 81). I read in an interview a couple of years ago that a famous pop songwriter produces every song demo as though it were a finished record. Since she has had more than 20 No. 1 pop hits, she can certainly afford to do that. But most of us are not playing in that league.

A Christian-record executive recently told me that, in his opinion, very few decision makers at Christian-record labels have what it takes to listen to a simple piano-vocal demo and imagine the finished recording. As a result, Christian song demos are getting more elaborate as well. The dirty little secret that goes unsaid is this: For those of us working in the Christian trenches, the monetary rewards often won't support the production of lavish demos. So, at least until you are getting some songs cut by independent artists, I recommend you stick to conventional wisdom and don't spend more than you can afford on your demos. Make as good a demo as you can while sticking to a reasonable budget. A quality piano-vocal demo is better than an overproduced synthesized demo. Focus on the song and let it shine through. And never forget: it's a demo.

Lyric Sheets, Lead Sheets, and Chord Charts

No matter how simple or elaborate a production you choose for your demo, it is almost certain that somewhere in the process you will need either a lead sheet, or a simple chord chart, or a lyric sheet. Whether you are going to be working with a room full of musicians, a single vocalist, or all by yourself, a properly prepared lyric sheet, lead sheet, or chord chart will make your demo production easier. They are the simplest forms of jotting down pop-styled music on paper, so that musicians and vocalists can read the song. Let's examine each one separately, starting with the most basic—the lyric sheet.

THE LYRIC SHEET

A lyric sheet is nothing more than the lyrics of a song typed out on a sheet of paper. No notes, no rhythms, no chords—just words on the page. It is the minimum standard requirement for any recording session. If you walk into the studio with nothing else, make sure you have accurate lyric sheets and enough copies for everyone working on the song. Some session singers don't read music all that well, and they prefer a lyric sheet to a lead sheet. The notes on the page only serve to slow them down. They learn faster by ear. Even those vocalists who read music well are generally quick studies and are comfortable working from a lyric sheet.

The key to a good lyric sheet for the recording studio is this: make the lyrics easy to read. Use a comfortably large font—say, 14 point, or even 16 point. Some writers put the lyrics in all caps (as I've done below) to make the words appear larger still. Double-space the lines. This leaves room between the lyric lines for singers to scribble their own personal hieroglyphics that they alone understand to help them remember what to sing. It also leaves room on the engineer's copy of the lyrics (the engineer should always get a copy of the lyrics) to make mix notes, add auto-locate numbers, and scribble vocal "comp" notes.

Don't confuse this studio lyric sheet with the lyric sheet you would attach to a demo when submitting the song to an artist or a publisher. A demo lyric sheet will be single-spaced, and will have a copyright notice, a contact phone number, and writer's credits on it. The studio lyric sheet doesn't need all that information. The point of the studio lyric sheet is to put the words on the page so that the singer can read them easily. Because of the larger font size and the double-spacing, the lyrics may fill two pages. That's fine. When you submit your lyric sheet to a publisher, you will go back to a normal font size and single-spacing, which should fit the lyrics onto one page.

See Example 1 for a sample of a studio lyric sheet for a recent song of mine, titled "So Worthy." Note that I deliberately indented the fifth and sixth lines of the verses. Those lines are the channel. The indentation serves as a subtle visual signal to the singer that the music is shifting at that point in the song. I have posted the original programmed demo of "So Worthy" on my Website (at robertsterlingmusic.com), in case you want to hear what you're looking at as you study the lyric sheet, the lead sheet, and the chord chart that all follow.

EXAMPLE 1: STUDIO LYRIC SHEET

SO WORTHY
  Words and music by Robert Sterling

VERSE 1
SING TO GOD AND PRAISE HIS NAME
WE WILL DECLARE HIS NAME TO THE PEOPLE
HE IS LORD AND WE PROCLAIM
HIS POWER AND MAJESTY OVER ISRAEL
  GREAT IS THE LORD AND MIGHTY IN POWER
  WE PLACE OUR HOPE IN HIS UNFAILING LOVE

CHORUS
SO WORTHY, SO WORTHY
TO RECEIVE HONOR AND POWER AND PRAISE
SO WORTHY, SO WORTHY
WE GIVE HIM GLORY FOR ALL OF OUR DAYS
FOR THERE IS BUT ONE SO WORTHY, SO WORTHY

VERSE 2

GOD IS GREAT AND GOD ALONE

DELIVERS HIS PEOPLE TO SALVATION

HE IS LIFE—THE CORNERSTONE

TELL YOUR CHILDREN, TELL EVERY NATION

    GREAT IS THE LORD AND MIGHTY IN POWER

     WE PLACE OUR HOPE IN HIS UNFAILING LOVE

REPEAT CHORUS

BRIDGE

MERCY AND GRACE AND GOODNESS HE GIVES

OUR LIPS WILL PRAISE HIM FOR AS LONG AS WE LIVE.

REPEAT CHORUS

THE LEAD SHEET

Creating a lead sheet is the simplest way to capture all the essential elements of a song on paper. It has a single melody line. Below the melody line are the lyrics. Above the melody line are the chord changes. (Because it contains all the essential parts of a song, lead sheets are an ideal way to copyright a song that hasn't yet been recorded.) A lead sheet can be sketched out on manuscript paper, or it can be printed from a computer program such as Finale or Sibelius. Like the lyric sheet, it's important the lead sheet is easy to read.

Good session players and vocalists are comfortable working from a lead sheet. If you go into a demo date with good lead sheets, you will probably save yourself time and money because the session will move more smoothly. The recording engineer can also work from a lead sheet, making his necessary notations on it.

To create a lead sheet you must know how to properly notate music and interpret chord changes. If you don't have those skills, you may want to consider paying someone to create a lead sheet for you from a rough piano-vocal recording. There are differing opinions as to how detailed a lead sheet needs to be, especially concerning the rhythm of the melody. Some writers feel that it's important to capture all the syncopations and rhythmic "pushes" in the melody line. When it comes to very syncopated melody lines, I sometimes simplify the rhythms on the lead sheet a bit, which makes it easier to read. Once I am in the studio, I can coach the singer if I want more complex rhythms.

Example 2 is the lead sheet for "So Worthy."

EXAMPLE 2: LEAD SHEET

So Worthy

ROBERT STERLING

So Worthy - Page 2

THE CHORD CHART

A chord chart is a simple piece of music that shows all the measures in a song, and the chords that go in those measures. Occasionally, in a more sophisticated chart, the writer will include specific licks or figures the band is to play. For the most part, however, a chord chart is a rudimentary road map, giving the rhythm players just enough information to stay together from the downbeat to the end of the song. Even the most rhythmic songs with complicated grooves look simple in a chord chart, because the music measures are generally filled with quarter note forward slashes (known as virgules), unless there is a specific pushed or syncopated rhythm somewhere in the bar.

Example 3 is the chord chart for the song "So Worthy." Notice that I did include some specific figures for the band to play in a couple of spots. I also placed a tempo marking at the top of the chart and a phrase indicating the "feel" of the song. These notations answer questions that are certain to arise in the session, again helping to save time (and money).

EXAMPLE 3: CHORD CHART

So Worthy

ROBERT STERLING

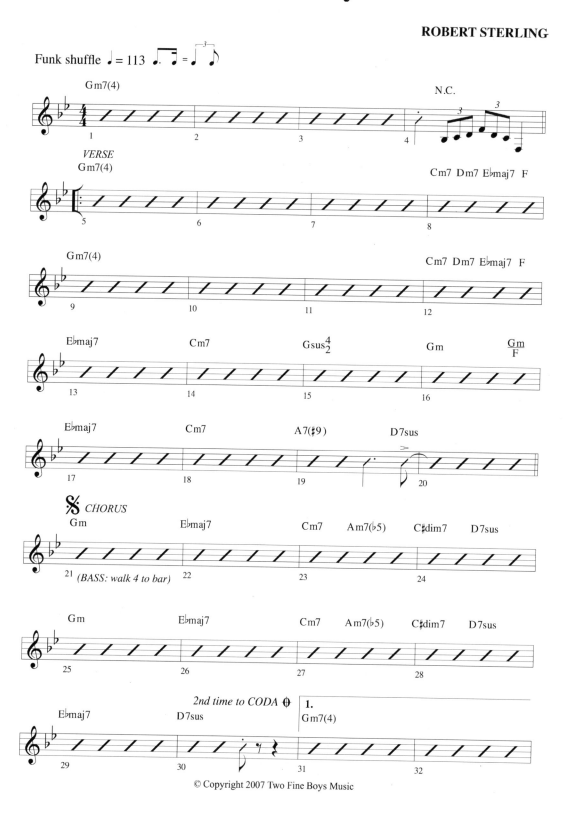

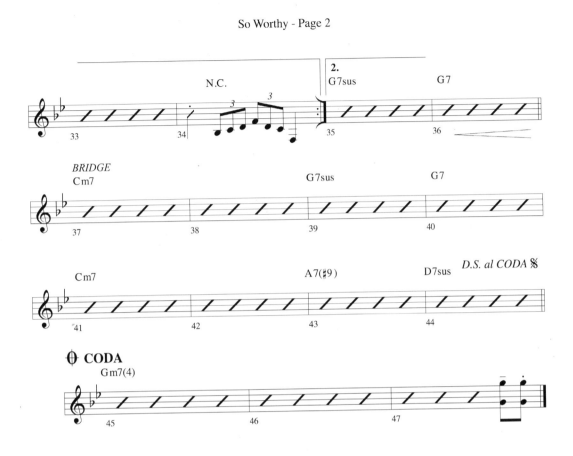

So Worthy - Page 2

THE NASHVILLE NUMBER SYSTEM

In the Nashville country music scene, there is a form of chord chart known as the "number chart." Chords are represented numerically by their diatonic scale position. Thus, in the key of C, a C chord is called the 1 chord. An F chord is called the 4 chord. An Em7 chord would be simply the 3 chord. (Because the number system is based on the diatonic scale, the assumption is that all "3" chords are minor seventh chords.) Number charts are often scribbled on plain paper. Bar lines are used only if a measure has more than one chord in it. So, two measures of C chords, followed by a measure of Am7, and a measure of G7 would look like this: 1 1 6 5. Very simple, right? An entire chart can be sketched out on a paper napkin if need be.

The biggest advantage of the number system is that players can quickly change the key of the song if the vocalist wants a higher or lower key. The chart never changes, because the numbers are relative to the key of the song. The system works especially well for guitarists and bass players, but many keyboardists and singers also are adept at reading number charts. The method is quick and easy, which is ideal when working within the time pressures of a recording environment. The major disadvantage of the number system is that it works well only with truly simple music. If the harmonies of a song include chords that have multiple extensions (ex: F♯13♭5), inverted chords (ex: A7/C♯), or nondiatonic chords (ex: E♭9—in the key of F), the number system begins to falter. Complex harmonies, when converted into the number system, begin to look like an algebra equation. If you are going to learn the art of chart writing for a rhythm section, I recommend using the traditional chord chart. It is more specific and more complete. However, if you want to know more about the Nashville Number System, Chas Williams, Nashville session musician, has written a book, appropriately titled *The Nashville Number System*, which explains it thoroughly.

Choices, Choices, Choices

When I exited college back in the Dark Ages (the late 1970s) and began my songwriting career (such as it was), I never had to ask: Should I use live musicians, or should I program a track? That's because the only way to record anything back then was with live musicians. The first affordable synthesizers were just hitting the store shelves, but this was pre-MIDI, and they had to be played in real time like any other instrument. The first drum machine was still in Roger Linn's laboratory. The first computer-sequencing software was another five years away. When the Synclavier and Fairlight samplers finally arrived in the early 1980s, they cost tens of thousands of dollars and played only eight notes at a time.

Similarly, there were few choices as to where to record. Aside from a few amateurish demos recorded live in the church fellowship hall with my college buddies, all my early song demos were cut in professional recording studios. We recorded on 2-inch analog tape and were thrilled to have 16 tracks. Mix automation was a brand-new thing, and lots of studios didn't yet have it. Oh, and did I mention that these studios were expensive to rent for a starving young songwriter with a wife and two kids? The first affordable home-studio equipment didn't show up until the mid 1980s. As soon as I could, I took out a loan to purchase a small 8-track recorder with a mixing board, a single microphone, a cheap reverb unit, a DX-7 synthesizer, and a drum machine. I thought I was set for life.

Every year since, technology has continued to change the recording landscape. Today there are dozens of software sequencers and digital recorders on the market. Synthesizers come straight out the box with thousands of built-in sounds at a fraction of the cost of those old dinosaurs. You can buy digitally recorded sample libraries of every imaginable instrument. Sophisticated digital recording software with unlimited tracks costs less than $500. Any songwriter can record professional-sounding tracks using nothing more than a laptop computer and a few software synths. But is this always the way to go?

In the Studio with Live Musicians

Despite the fact that I have a fairly complete home studio in the room next to where I am writing this book, I am still a big fan of using live musicians in a real studio environment. There is nothing like the excitement that four or five great musicians can bring to a song. The energy they generate is unmatched by any computer program. For certain styles of music, there is no suitable substitute. Here in Nashville, live musicians still play on virtually all country song demos. Country music is still about real players playing real instruments. Similarly, jazz-styled songs almost always sound better when played by live musicians (computers can't swing). Genuine rock music and a lot of the more innovative pop music coming out these days sounds best when played by real musicians, too.

If you've got the right musicians, their instantaneous ideas and collective creativity can elevate a song to a wonderful new place. Smart studio players know their job is to make your song sound good. Because they are experts on their instruments, session musicians will almost always have ways of improving your basic ideas. I have never met a studio bass player that couldn't improve my bass lines, and I come up with pretty good lines to begin with. A session keyboardist who is comfortable on piano, B-3, electric piano, and synthesizers can find just the right sound for any track. A great studio drummer can play grooves that even the most sophisticated drum program cannot match—and it will feel human, not machinelike. A guitarist who can read a chart and is current with what's hot on the radio is worth whatever union scale may come to be.

What's more, real professionals are fast. Very fast. A good rhythm section, working in a comfortable studio environment (where the equipment all works) can produce a finished demo track every 30 to 45 minutes. (I can't even power up my home-studio gear in that little time.) In a typical three-hour Nashville demo session, an experienced rhythm section will complete five or six songs. It helps tremendously if you arrive at the session prepared, with work tapes for them to hear and lead sheets or chord charts for them to read. (Bring enough copies for everyone. Don't assume the studio's photocopier is working.) If you do not bring a chart of some sort, the band will make charts for themselves, which slows things down a bit. Good session players have remarkable ears. They can hear a song once or twice and write it down with amazing accuracy.

Similarly, a well-equipped professional demo studio will improve the quality of your song demos. Trained staff will see to it that your session runs smoothly so you get more accomplished in less time. An experienced recording engineer oversees dozens of details regarding the sound of the music, freeing you and the musicians to concentrate on your songs. The engineer can also be an invaluable objective listener whose frame of reference comes from recording hundreds of songs. A good demo studio will have a wide variety of quality recording equipment.

Of course, all this expertise comes at a price. My most recent demo sessions cost me roughly $2,000 to complete three songs, from tracking a six-piece band to vocals to mixing. As I write this in the spring of 2008, session musicians make about $65 an hour for demos on a union session. Generally, one of the players is paid double scale to be leader of the session. The minimum session is usually three hours. So, very few writers or publishers schedule a live demo session until they have at least five or six songs ready to record. Otherwise, it isn't cost-effective. If you have only two or three songs ready to demo, try to find another writer who would be willing to split a session with you. (This is how I did my three-song demos.) You would also split the fixed costs, like cartage (see below).

Next, you must factor in the expense of the studio, which varies greatly from facility to facility. Here in Nashville, studios that specialize in demo recordings cost from $40 to $60 an hour, including the engineer. Other studios charge a day rate that is typically based on a 12-hour block of time. Day rates begin as low as $300 per day.

In larger cities, musicians often employ cartage services to bring their instruments to the studios. For a full rhythm section, and depending on the city where you are recording, the total cartage bill can approach $1,000. This bill is the responsibility of the client. That's you, the writer. Some studios maintain a drum kit and perhaps a Hammond organ or a Wurlitzer electric piano. This eliminates the need for some of the cartage, and helps the cost-conscious writer. Ask about these instruments and cartage costs when you are booking a studio for your demo dates.

CHOOSING MUSICIANS FOR YOUR SESSION

Most session musicians are versatile, capable of playing most every style of music. However, individual players often play certain styles of music better than other styles. If your songs fall into one particular genre of music, try to book players that feel comfortable in that genre. For example, musicians that play a lot of Southern Gospel sessions may not feel at home in the world of rock music, and vice versa. When you are booking the players, let them know what kind of music you write and ask if they are comfortable with that style. If you have any special instrument requirements (five-string banjo, Hammond B-3, or the electric zither), let them know ahead of time, so they can be sure to bring the instrument to the studio.

If you don't know any session musicians, ask the studio manager or engineer for suggestions. Chances are they have worked with dozens of players and will know whom to recommend. Once you hire the first player, he or she will be happy to give you names and numbers of other players. Typically, one player is paid extra to lead the session. Often that person is the keyboard player or the lead guitarist. The leader is also responsible for making chord charts if you don't have them at the date.

PLANNING A DEMO SESSION WITH LIVE MUSICIANS

Whether I am producing song demos or master tracks for a major label artist, I have found that preparation and planning always saves time and effort in the studio. Nowhere is the saying "time is money" more true than in the recording studio. Every hour you save is money in your pocket. Below is a sample schedule for recording and mixing five new songs using a professional studio, four live musicians, and a couple of studio singers. The schedule requires two full days in the studio to record and mix the demos. Use the sample as a guide for planning your next demo sessions. Notice I left time between the rhythm session and the first vocal session. The engineer will need a break for lunch and a few minutes to change the microphone setup. I also left an hour between the two vocal sessions. This allows a little breathing room in case a problem arises. Also, the engineer may need this time to create a single lead vocal take from several vocal takes. (This process is known as making a "comp" vocal track, or "comping" the vocal.)

SAMPLE SCHEDULE FOR CREATING A DEMO

PREPRODUCTION:

1. Create chord charts and/or lead sheets and lyric sheets for the sessions. Make sufficient copies for players, singers, the engineer, and yourself. (Don't scrimp on copies. Copies are cheap.)

2. Book a studio and an engineer for two days.

3. Book musicians for one three-hour session.

4. Book singers for two hours each.

DAY 1 IN THE STUDIO:

10 a.m.–1 p.m.	Three-hour session with band; shoot for recording five song tracks and any overdubs.
2 p.m.–4 p.m.	Vocal session with singer number 1; record lead vocals on three songs; add harmony on one song.
4 p.m.–5 p.m.	Engineer comps for lead vocals, if needed.
5 p.m.–7 p.m.	Vocal session with singer number 2; record lead vocals on two songs; add harmony on both.
7 p.m.–8 p.m.	Engineer comps for lead vocals, if needed.

DAY 2 IN THE STUDIO:

Mix: All day.

Five song mixes will take the entire day, upward of 10 to 12 hours. Don't scrimp and assume that the songs can all be mixed in an hour or two. Mixing, even if only for demos, is an art, and you should devote as much time to the mix as you did to the recording process.

A SUGGESTION FROM THE VOICE OF EXPERIENCE

Allow the engineer to begin the mix without you. He doesn't need your help to get the kick drum EQ. You may not need to arrive until the afternoon to listen to the mixes and make changes. Unless you are a seasoned studio pro, heed the mix advice of the engineer. His ears will be more objective than yours.

Cutting demo tracks in a professional studio with live musicians isn't always the right option for every writer or every song. Money is almost always an issue for beginning writers, and cutting live musicians is an expensive proposition. In addition, good session musicians, talented recording engineers, and quality studios are found mostly in larger urban areas. So if you live in a small town, they may not be readily available to you. Also, there are times when a programmed track is the better choice for musical reasons, as well as financial reasons.

Programmed Tracks: The One-Man Band

Never before has so much technology been available for the making of music. If you don't believe me, pick up a copy of *Mix* magazine, *EM* (formerly *Electronic Musician*), *Keyboard* magazine, or any of a host of similar publications dedicated to the world of professional audio and recording. Their pages are filled with advertisements and reviews for the latest digital recorder-sampler-mixer gadget guaranteed to make you a better songwriter-producer-singer. These products are amazingly affordable tools that, if used properly, can aid you in making a quality recording right at home. These tools will not, however, automatically make you a great songwriter, despite what their advertisements may suggest. Still, any serious songwriter would be well advised to at least consider building a modest home-recording studio, or to find someone in town who owns one.

The advantages of building your own demo tracks in a home-studio environment are obvious: affordability and flexibility. You can work as long as you like and whenever you like, and there are no studio bills or session musicians to pay. You can toil away into the wee hours of the morning dressed in your PJs and nobody's going to demand overtime pay. You can work in fits and starts, if that's what your schedule demands. And you can do all this for less than the cost of a couple of sessions with live musicians. That is why there are no less than a thousand home studios in and around Nashville. (Seriously. I'm not kidding.)

What does it take to get started? For less than $1,000, you can buy a small digital recorder, an inexpensive but decent-sounding microphone, and a compressor, and be on your way to a world of recording fun. For less than $5,000, you can buy a computer loaded with sophisticated MIDI sequencing and digital recording software, a couple of software synthesizers, and some nice computer plug-ins to make your recording sound truly professional. If you want to keep things simple, all the new Apple Macintosh computers come loaded with GarageBand, an amazing self-contained piece of digital audio/sequencing software for the beginner. There are literally hundreds of options to consider, based on your budget. You would be wise to do some smart research shopping before you buy. But the technology you need to record your demos at home is out there, and it is affordable.

Of course, you still have to learn how to use all this gear. That will be a daunting task for some, a piece of cake for others. If you still listen to music on cassette tape and never learned how to program a VCR, this new technology may be more than you care to handle. If, however, you grew up with sophisticated technology (in other words, you are less than 30 years old), it may come quite easily to you. If you own a synthesizer, chances are that it has sequencing software built in, so you may already be familiar with the basics. If you play electric guitar or if you are interested in home electronics, the new recording technology won't scare you too badly. If you're interested in learning about digital audio and music programming in depth, many community colleges offer classes in music technology. And there are scores of books and magazines dedicated to the subject.

Two Alternatives

THE BLENDED APPROACH

There is one giant creative drawback to the one-man-band method of programmed tracks: You are relying solely on your own creativity, with no input from anyone else. Personally, I enjoy having another musician add his or her ideas to the creative soup. That's why whenever I can afford it, I hire a guitarist to come in and play on my programmed demo tracks. I find that by adding even one live musician, my demo tracks feel much more spontaneous and less computer generated. Guitar is one of the few instruments that synthesizers and samplers cannot readily emulate. A good guitarist can add a world of color and energy to a programmed track. And you get the added benefit of another musician's creative input.

HIRE A PROGRAMMER

If the thought of building a home studio and programming your own tracks makes you want to give up songwriting, and the cost of hiring session musicians and a professional studio is prohibitive, there is another solution: hire someone who has already invested in a home studio and programming gear. Let him build your tracks for you. Every town has a music geek or two who have bought all the latest recording and programming gear on credit and need a way to pay for it. Often these folks are talented, enthusiastic, and in debt. They will gladly hire out to program songs on a per song basis. The current going rate here in Nashville for such work is $400 to $500 per song. This fee often includes the time spent recording vocals and mixing the demo, as well. Ask around at your local music store about somebody with a nice home studio. When you find the person, listen to samples of his work. Be prepared to negotiate price. Cash talks.

Working with Singers

LEAD VOCALS

The single most important element of a song demo is the lead vocal. If the singer is out of tune or mumbles the lyrics, it won't matter how cool the track sounds. This is especially true in Christian music, where the words are what define the song as being Christian. You certainly don't want people to wonder, "What was that lyric?" when they listen to your demo. So, make every effort to get the best singer possible for your song. The lead vocal session is not the time to save money by hiring your cousin who sings on the weekends at the local country club. Nor is it the time to make points with your girlfriend or boyfriend by asking them to sing your latest tune—unless, like me, you happened to marry a studio singer. I highly recommend you hire a confident, experienced professional for the job—one who can deliver a solid, in-tune "radio-sounding" performance in less than an hour.

Some singers charge by the song. (The going rate for a seasoned studio singer in Nashville is currently from $100 to $150 per song.) Others charge by the hour. (Figure from $75 to

$100 per hour.) If you don't know whom to hire, ask your fellow songwriters and musicians for recommendations. Most professional studio singers have a demo reel for you to hear examples of their work. Just be sure that they sound right for your song and its target market. If you are aiming for pop/CCM radio, hire a singer that sounds like she belongs on a pop radio station, and not on a Broadway stage.

If the words to your song are not gender specific, then you have to decide whether to hire a male or a female vocalist to sing your song. If you are aiming the demo toward a specific artist, then choose gender on that basis. If the song will work for either gender, consider recording both a male and a female vocal. This may require two separate cuts of the song in different keys to accommodate both singers, but it could be worth the added expense to broaden the number of potential pitches for the song. Keep in mind that if your tracks are programmed, printing the track in a different key is as easy as hitting the transpose key on the computer. If you recorded studio musicians, once they have learned a song they are adept at quickly playing it again in a different key.

Here is another little secret: If your budget limits you to only one vocal performance and the song is not gender specific, I recommend using a male singer. Why? Because female artists have little difficulty listening to male vocal demos, but male artists often cannot get past a female vocal demo. You will get more pitches out of a demo with a male lead vocal.

BACKGROUND VOCALS

Background vocals, also known as BGVs, can dress up a demo and make it sound more like a finished record. And most studio singers are adept at quickly adding harmony vocals to their leads, generally for little or no extra cost. So, slap some BGVs on every demo, right? Not so fast. Background vocals can also limit the imagination of the listener. Three-part BGVs might make your song sound less "cool" to an artist who rarely uses backing vocals. Even a single harmony line can sometimes get in the way of the lead vocal. When considering the use of BGVs, let the song help you decide. Does it cry out for an extra vocal part or two? Will BGVs help sell the song to that certain vocal group you are hoping to pitch to? If so, go for it. If not, remember—it's a demo.

Presenting Your Demo

I have purposely avoided writing about the business of songwriting in this book, focusing instead on the craft. There are plenty of well-written books on the music business, and I didn't need to duplicate that information here. However, I am going address the very first step into the music biz, and that's presenting (or "pitching") a demo. After all we've been through together in these pages, I want you to be armed with some good basic information before you take that first step.

WHO WANTS TO HEAR MY SONGS?

There are lots of people on the lookout for truly good songs. That's because there is money to be made from them. So, assuming you now have a handful of truly good songs to pitch, who are these people and where can you find them?

1. **Artists.** There are recording artists of every size and shape in every city in America cutting songs of every style and tempo. At the top of the heap are the Big Deal artists. Big Deal artists are very hard to reach. They are shielded by their managers and record companies. And most of them write their own songs. Unless you know them personally, it's unlikely you will crack their defenses. But there are local and regional artists in the heap, too. Thanks to the Internet and home-based recording studios, more and more independent artists are popping up every day—even in your own town, maybe in your own church. One of them may be the next Big Deal.

    I remember meeting four pretty college girls in Estes Park, Colorado, who called themselves Say So. They went on to become Point of Grace, and made a big impact on my professional life. I also remember meeting Mark Hall and Casting Crowns in south Florida when they were just another group singing in coffeehouses and local churches. Independent artists are much more approachable, and may even be looking for people to write for or with them.

2. **Record producers.** Much like their Big Deal artist counterparts, top-notch record producers swim in a fairly exclusive creative pool—and their pool boys are all pitching them demos. However, there are local producers in most towns working with local artists. Pitch to one producer, and you effectively reach all the artists the producer works with. Even if he passes on your songs, you may begin a relationship that will lead to opportunities in the future. The music business, like any business, is a relationship business.

3. **Record executives.** These folks listen to music every day for a living, and they tend to be overworked and a bit jaded. The bigger the record label, the more jaded they are. But, if you can get your foot in the door of an independent label, your chances of success are greater. Just be sure that when you get your chance, you've got good songs to pitch. Otherwise, you may never get a second chance.

4. **Music publishers.** Music publishers are always searching for fresh talent. But they rarely take unsolicited material any more. (The threat of a lawsuit is too great.) However, you can meet publishers and music professionals at music seminars like The Gospel Music Association's summer seminar, Immerse (gospelmusic.org). There, you can submit songs for an informal critique. If your song is good, it may open doors to music publishers. A good relationship with an ethical music publisher is the Holy Grail for most songwriters.

HOW DO I PRESENT MY SONGS?

You may get only one chance to pitch your songs to any particular artist or producer or publisher, so the presentation should look professional. The good news is that's easy to do. Here are a few simple rules to follow.

1. **Put your songs on a plainly labeled CD.** Make sure that your name and a contact number is on the CD and the jewel case insert. When listening to your demo CD, if someone has an interest, they will want to see your information while it's playing, especially if they are listening to a stack of demo CDs in one setting. If you haven't put your information on the jewel case insert, the listener is forced to either take the CD out of the tray before it finishes playing or wait until it's finished.

2. **Put no more than four songs on the CD.** Three is better still. The only exception to this rule is if you know the person you are pitching to personally, and you know the names of her kids and her husband's birthday. Choose your very best, most appropriate material for the pitch. Better that the person like your songs and ask for more than to shut off the CD on song No. 3 and never hear song No. 7.

3. **Include a typed lyric sheet for each song on the CD.** There are no exceptions to this rule. The lyric sheet must be typed. Every sheet should have your name and contact number on it, as well as a simple copyright notice at the bottom of the page like this: © 2009 by Your Name Here.

Another method for presenting your songs is over the Internet. Many writers now send song demos via e-mail as MP3 files. (Due to the size of most MP3 song files, you can typically send only one song and its lyrics at a time.) Some writers upload their songs to a server so that potential users can listen online and download them. There is a catch, though: to send a song via e-mail, you must still first make a personal contact with that person and obtain their e-mail address and their consent to submit songs. Do not submit unsolicited songs to anyone online. You want to avoid annoying someone who is not in the market for material, and you want to protect yourself from any sort of copyright infringement.

Coda

Building a song demo can be one of the most rewarding parts of the songwriting journey. It is exhilarating to hear your songs come to life. Over time, you may discover a particular demo process that suits you best. And with the constant changes in technology, I wouldn't be surprised if there are entirely new ways available to record demos and send them to listeners by the time this book is in print. Regardless which recording method or methods you choose, always focus on the song. The technology will take care of itself.

Before you even start the demo process, be sure your songs are as good as you can make them. Quality songs are what matter to a dedicated songwriter. A weak demo won't keep a great song from being noticed, and the world's greatest demo won't get a bad song recorded. Spend more time writing well-crafted songs, and don't spend money you don't have making fancy demos. After all—it's a demo.

Give It Your Best
(Some Parting Thoughts)

Jesus' Chairs, Jesus' Chairs, Jesus' Chairs

I'm guessing you've figured out by now that I'm pretty big on the importance of craft in songwriting. And so it saddens me just how few Christian songwriters today pay attention to the importance of song form, poetic imagery, good melody writing, and interesting harmonic structure. It's no secret American culture has been dumbing down for decades now. But do we Christian songwriters really want to be a part of that process? Shouldn't we instead be a force in the opposite direction? I am a true believer that the best songwriters in the world should be and could still be Christian songwriters. But that can happen only if we forsake "God gave it to me" as an excuse for a poorly written song. We must accept that inspiration is only part of the writing process, and learn that rewriting is essential to the discipline of creating a well-written song.

I believe we worship God best when we give Him our best. What's more, I think our best should always be improving, bit by bit. We should not remain content with our skills at their present stage. We should work to hone them to a finer degree so our next song is our "best song ever." I've used the metaphor of "Jesus' chairs" throughout this book as a gentle reminder to pursue the craft of songwriting using the highest standards as your guide. None of us will ever achieve perfection, but with every song we write, we should strive to improve. I hope this book is of some help to you in that regard. I trust there is worthwhile information in these pages that will aid you in becoming a better writer. And I pray the songs you write, be they explicitly or implicitly Christian songs, will be a blessing to the Kingdom of God.

In Their Own Words: Any words of advice for a beginning christian writer?

Listen, listen, listen.
—KURT KAISER

Being a good songwriter will require you to work harder than you can imagine. Do it only if you are truly passionate about the process.
—SUE SMITH

> *Never assume you can't do a better job on your next song.*
> —CHARLES F. BROWN
>
> *Write every day—even if it is for only 15 minutes.*   —PAUL SMITH
>
> *Study the songs of great writers whose songs are still being recorded decades later. There's a reason for that!*   —TONY WOOD
>
> *Keep growing and improving at your skill. Have fun with it. And don't lose the wonder of the fact that you're called to make music for the Kingdom.*   —CLAIRE CLONINGER
>
> *Take your work seriously, and don't take yourself seriously.*
> —J. PAUL WILLIAMS
>
> *Prepare and persist.*   —LOWELL ALEXANDER

An Absolutely True Story

I am sometimes commissioned to write a song for a specific occasion. In the summer of 1983, my own church in Texas asked me to write a piece for the adult choir to sing to celebrate the arrival of a new pastor. I wrote a song called "Sing to the Lord." I arranged it for choir and piano, and everything went fine. My friends and family thought I was brilliant. I was the hero of the day. Later, I submitted the music to Shawnee Press for publication. Shawnee accepted it, and "Sing to the Lord" was on its way to becoming a choral anthem.

About that same time, our church began a major pledge drive to raise funds to build a new church. The new pastor challenged us all one Sunday to give our best to God and let God do the rest. "Sing to the Lord" was my best anthem ever, I thought. It would certainly generate $2,000 in royalty income for me, maybe more, in its first three years. And so I committed the next three years of royalties from that song to my church's building fund. I was filled with secret self-importance at my magnanimous act of generosity. But the plot thickens.

Even though "Sing to the Lord" was originally written for a choir, I always believed the song had potential for an artist to record it. I did a demo recording of the song, with a Dallas-area rhythm section backing up my wife, Cindy, singing the lead. At Christmastime, I played the demo for a good friend and old college buddy, Dennis Worley. Dennis worked in the Christian music business in Nashville, and he was back home in Texas for the holidays. He liked the song and offered to show it around Nashville for me. The holidays passed, Dennis went back to Nashville, and I went on with my life as a Dallas jingle writer.

A few months later Dennis called with an amazing story. He had pitched my song to Greg Nelson, the megaproducer of Christian music. Then a few weeks after that, Dennis happened to run into Greg in the recording studio where Greg was working with Sandi Patti. Over the phone, Dennis told me this: "Sandi saw me and said, 'Hey Dennis, come in here! We're cutting your song!' 'What song?' I asked. 'You know,' she said, 'the song you showed us—"Sing to the Lord."'"

Needless to say, I was more than a little excited. At that time, Sandi Patti was the most successful Christian recording artist ever. If she recorded a song, it became a standard. I began composing my Song of the Year acceptance speech in my head. But Dennis cautioned me. "We have a saying in Nashville," he said. "It's not final 'til it's vinyl. Not every song an artist records makes the final record." So I waited patiently for the record to be finished to see if I made the cut or not.

Sandi's album, *Songs from the Heart*, was released in 1984, and "Sing to the Lord" was on side one, cut No. 2. But the bigger news was that my little church anthem was the first single from the album. It quickly climbed to No. 1 on the Christian radio charts. The record went gold, and at least a dozen print publishers put "Sing to the Lord" in every songbook and choral collection they released that year. By the time the church building campaign had run its course, the song I thought would generate $2,000 or $3,000 had contributed more than $30,000 to my church.

Instead of feeling pride, I was stricken with humility. It was as though God was saying to me, "Do you see what I can do when you give me your best? When you don't hold back? When you give me your all?" I will treasure that experience for the rest of my life. For the first time, I knew what it was like to be a co-worker with the Creator. He took my best efforts, feeble as they may have been, and made something more of them—something much more. For all of us who toil in the creative trenches, hoping to write something that will benefit the Kingdom, let me offer this: God can do with you what He did with me. Just give him your best. Work diligently and hold nothing back. God will do the rest.

Jesus' chairs.

Songwriting Exercises

NOTE: Many of these exercises require lyric sheets. You can download lyric sheets for most songs at any of the dozens of online lyric sites on the Internet. Or you can create your own lyric sheets by typing them up yourself. Make sure the lyrics are laid out on the page properly, line by line (see the lyric sheets in chapters 7 and 9 for reference). This will make it easier for you to complete the analysis work in the exercises properly.

Some of the exercises require commercial lead sheets or sheet music. Buy the music. Don't photocopy it. Every song suggested in these exercises is a song that any self-respecting songwriter would be proud to own.

CHAPTER 2
Getting Started

EXERCISE 1
Read the front page of your local newspaper—every word if need be. Create at least two separate song ideas from this one source. Your song idea can be on a general topic, or you might find a specific line that intrigues you for a title or a concept.

To make this exercise more interesting, find two song ideas using either the front page of the Sports or the Living section of your newspaper or the covers of magazines.

EXERCISE 2
Find at least three good song ideas from the book (or books) you are currently reading (No, not *this* book), or from the books you have read in past 30 days. This includes fiction, nonfiction, even books of poetry. Your song ideas can be serious or silly.

EXERCISE 3
This weekend go to the movies, go to church, go to the park, and eavesdrop on friends and family—all with the express purpose of picking up good song ideas. Write down

anything that remotely resembles a song idea. (In two days, time you should have several ideas to choose from.) Pick the best and write a good hook/title for it.

EXERCISE 4

Reflect on your most recent creative endeavor (hopefully, a song) and recall as many specific details as you can about the process you experienced. Use Henri Poincare's four stages of creativity as an outline, listing all that was involved in each stage. (Make sure that when you examine the verification stage that you actually did rewrite!)

Now ask yourself which stages were easy for you? Which were difficult? Did the specific creative process work well for you? What changes in your creative process might improve your next creative outing?

EXERCISE 5

Rewrite a hymn text in your own words following the thought progression and theology of the original hymn. You may borrow lines from the hymn, but 50 percent of the words must be your own. If the hymn has no repeated refrain or chorus, write one. This is an excellent way to write a new worship song and stay on solid theological ground.

EXERCISE 6

Change all the radio station presets in your car. Listen to different radio stations for a full month.

CHAPTER 3
The Shape of a Song

EXERCISE 1

Analyze three of your own existing songs using the five questions in the chapter under the section "Think Before You Write." For each song, ask yourself the following questions:

1. What is the song's point of view?

2. What one emotion do you want to convey in the song?

3. What is the specific setting of the song?

4. What is the song's universal human theme?

5. How will the song (or the story within the song) unfold?

Ask yourself how might these songs be different today if you had asked these questions *before* you wrote the songs.

EXERCISE 2

Pick two songs from each of the three song form lists in the chapter (AAA, AABA, and Verse/Chorus). Either download or type out an accurate lyric sheet for all six songs. Analyze the song form of each of the songs:

1. Underline the hook/title each time it occurs.

2. Check for placement of the hook/title. Is it placed well in the song?

3. Identify each section of the song (AABA, verse, chorus, bridge, and so on).

4. Check to see if the verses (A sections) match in length and shape.

5. How many measures of music are in each section?

EXERCISE 3

Analyze the same three of your own songs from Exercise 1, using the steps in Exercise 2.

CHAPTER 4
Lyrical Odds and Ends

EXERCISE 1

Examine the opening lines of three songs other than your own (the songs listed under "Opening Lines" in the chapter are all good choices). Follow the progression of the opening line through the chorus, and then ask yourself the following questions:

1. Does the opening line grab your attention? How?

2. What did the writer do to get from the opening line to the chorus?

3. Is there a discernible progression of thought from verse to chorus?

4. Is the listener propelled toward the hook from the opening line? How?

EXERCISE 2

Using the same three songs from Exercise 1, identify the lyric hook of each song, and then do the following:

1. Underline every occurrence of the hook.

2. Highlight every word and line in the lyrics that relate directly to the hook.

3. Notice the focus (or lack thereof) of the verses.

4. Do the verses lead to the chorus? How?

5. Does the chorus support the hook? How?

EXERCISE 3
Brutally examine three of your own songs (recent ones are best), searching diligently for the use of clichés, church words, and weak scansion. Mark every problem spot. Fix them.

EXERCISE 4
Play the game "Guess the Title." This is a good way to determine if your song has a strong (or even the proper) title. Play your song for several friends, with absolutely no setup or explanations about the song, and no lyric sheets. Ask each friend to guess the title of your song. If they all guess wrong, then your title may be weak or you have given your song the wrong title. (Or you have dim friends.)

CHAPTER 5
Poetic Devices

EXERCISE 1
Analyze the rhyme scheme of three of your favorite songs. Write the rhyme scheme at the end of each line of lyrics. Make a specific note for all uses of internal rhyme, contiguous rhyme, double rhyme, and triple rhyme.

How many of the rhymes are perfect (as opposed to imperfect) rhymes?

EXERCISE 2
Analyze the rhyme schemes of three of your own sets of lyrics using the guidelines from Exercise 1. Be critically aware of the following:

1. Did you rhyme "the important stuff"?

2. Did you settle for imperfect rhyme, when you could have found a more perfect rhyme?

3. Do the three songs' rhyme schemes demonstrate genuine variety? Is there more than just single rhyme? Do the rhyme schemes resemble each other too much?

EXERCISE 3
Using the three songs from Exercise 1, analyze each set of lyrics using the "How Colorful Are Your Lyrics?" test from chapter 5. Use a different color to mark each type of poetic device. Search for metaphor, simile, characterization, and all the other devices mentioned in the chapter.

EXERCISE 4

Now do the "How Colorful Are Your Lyrics?" test on your own three songs. Are your lyrics colorful enough?

EXERCISE 5

This exercise shows you how to create metaphors and similes:

Brainstorm on a single word, writing down every characteristic of that word you can think of, along with words and phrases that associate well with the word. Choose any of the individual characteristics and think of other things that share that characteristic. Create a metaphor or simile using your original word and the new word that shares the characteristic(s) you chose. This is the verbal equivalent of the algebra equation: If A = B and B = C, then A = C.

Here's an example using the noun "journey":

Characteristics of a journey: long, tedious, life changing, exciting, are we there yet?, adventurous, ups and downs, on the road, new beginnings, melancholy endings, lonesome, roaming, exploring, off the beaten path, planning, new worlds, new faces, new places, exotic, destination.

I chose to use "life changing." My list of words for "life changing" is: love, college education, salvation, having a child, marriage, heart attack, cancer, winning the Masters, a No. 1 hit single.

Here are a few metaphors/word pictures that sprang from those two lists of words: "coasting down College Avenue," "there's another world in my baby's eyes," "the roller coaster we call wedded bliss," "finding redemption on the less-traveled road."

Now you do the exercise. Choose from this list to begin: harmony, fury, moon, cross, soldier, betrayal, disease, virtuoso, liar, prophet. Create your own lists or, better yet, choose words from your own lyrics to create metaphors or similes.

CHAPTER 6
Musical Beginnings

EXERCISE 1

Study the melody of "Over the Rainbow" (E. Y. Harburg and Harold Arlen). In a 2001 poll conducted by the National Endowment for the Arts and the RIAA, "Over the Rainbow" was voted the best song of the 20th century, so it's definitely worth your time and effort to learn it. Search for large melodic leaps (more than a fifth) and notice which way the melody moves after the leap. Look for phrases that move in a step-wise motion. Look for instances in which the melody supports the pictures in the lyrics. What is the range of the melody? How does the coda that follows the final A section cap off the song melodically?

EXERCISE 2

Do a similar study of the melodies of the following songs. In addition to analyzing the melodic shape of the song, determine its musical song form. Mark each section of the song and count the measures of music in each section. Of those songs that are verse/chorus forms, pay special attention to what changes occur in the music at the beginning of the chorus. (Does it get busier? Simpler? Higher in range? Lower in range?) Look for places where the lyrics might not scan well.

"Awesome God" (Rich Mullins)

"Because He Lives" (Bill Gaither and Gloria Gaither)

"Come Harvest Time" (Lowell Alexander)

"God of Wonders" (Steve Hindalong and Marc Byrd)

"Moon River" (Johnny Mercer and Henry Mancini)

"The Great Divide" (Grant Cunningham and Matt Huesmann)

"White Christmas" (Irving Berlin)

"Wind Beneath My Wings" (Larry Henley and Jeff Silbar)

"Yesterday" (John Lennon and Paul McCartney)

EXERCISE 3

Do all of the above analysis on three of your own songs.

EXERCISE 4

1. Write an eight-bar melody in a minor key that has a range of no more than an octave. Teach the melody to a friend.

2. Write an eight-bar melody in a major key that has a range of no more than a major sixth. Teach the tune to a friend.

EXERCISE 5

1. Noodle around at the piano or on the guitar until you happen upon a motif or a riff you like. Develop the motif into an eight-bar phrase with interesting chord changes. Add a singable melody on top, using nonsense syllables.

2. Extra credit: Write it all down.

EXERCISE 6
Reharmonize "Amazing Grace." Shoot for three distinct and different sets of chord changes (very challenging).

CHAPTER 7
Writing Is Rewriting

EXERCISE 1
Examine three of your own songs using the ten questions in chapter 7 under the heading "The First Draft."

Rewrite any weak spots you discover in your songs after answering the ten questions.

Look for unnecessary verbiage and try to get rid of it. Tighten up your lyrics without losing meaning.

CHAPTER 9
Critical Thinking

EXERCISE 1
Examine these three songs using the questions listed below:

1. "By the Time I Get to Phoenix" (Jimmy Webb)
2. "The Living Years" (Mike Rutherford and B. A. Robertson)
3. "The Great Divide" (Grant Cunningham and Matt Huesmann)

THE QUESTIONS:

1. What is the universal theme of the lyrics?
2. What is the song form? Is it traditional? Does it break any rules?
3. Where are the word pictures?
4. Are the characters and emotions in the song believable and honest? Why or why not?
5. Is the title intriguing? Why or why not?
6. How does the opening line catch the listener's attention?

7. How does the song build to a solid payoff?

8. How do the music and lyrics complement each other?

EXERCISE 2

Put three of your own songs through the same test as in Exercise 1. If you are really bold and have a friend who is a writer, exchange songs and critique each other's songs using the questions from Exercise 1.

CHAPTER 10
Building a Demo

EXERCISE 1

Prepare a studio lyric sheet for three of your songs.

EXERCISE 2

Prepare a chord chart for three of your songs.

EXERCISE 3

Prepare a lead sheet for three of your songs.

EXERCISE 4

Put the chord charts and lead sheets in front of a keyboard player, guitarist, or rhythm section and see if the songs sound the way you thought they would.

References

Each book in this bibliography is a part of my personal library and would be an excellent resource for any beginning songwriter. These publications provided me with quotes, specific information, and background for this book. I have also included a handful of Website and magazine interviews, each of which was used as a resource or reference.

Arvin, Reed, ed. *Tools for Ministry and Career*. Nashville: The Gospel Music Association, 1999.

This book is part of the Academy of Gospel Music Arts Music Curriculum. It contains six chapters written by authors including Reed Arvin, Harold Best, and Charlie Peacock that focus on general creative philosophies for the Christian artist and Christian songwriter. It also contains four chapters written by Steve Green, Dan Posthuma, and others that address specific issues for the Christian performing artist. The book concludes with four chapters dedicated to the craft of songwriting, written by Margaret Becker, Joel Lindsay, Don Cason, and myself.

This book is worth obtaining even if only for two chapters: "The Role of Music in Worship," by Harold Best, and "The Creative Christian Life," by Reed Arvin. These men will challenge your thinking.

Basden, Paul. *Exploring the Worship Spectrum: Six Views*. Grand Rapids: Zondervan, 2004.

Paul Basden assembled six of the preeminent thinkers on worship styles and had each offer a thoughtful defense of a particular style of worship, including liturgical, emerging, contemporary, charismatic, blended, and hymn based. The authors then had the opportunity to respond to each other's assertions. I was struck by the passion with which all the authors wrote, and with their thoughtful and sincere responses to one another. The authors are Harold Best, Joe Horness, Sally Morgenthaler, Robert Webber, Don Willimas, and Paul Zahl. Any reader who is interested in the subject of worship will find this to be an engaging book.

Brabec, Jeffrey and Todd Brabec. *Music Money and Success: The Insider's Guide to Making Money in the Music Industry.* **6th ed. New York: Schirmer Trade Books, 2006.**

The Brabec brothers are both heavy-hitting music professionals. Todd is a vice president with ASCAP, and Jeffrey is a vice president for the Chrysalis Music Group. Both are music attorneys and adjunct professors at USC. This is the textbook used in music-publishing classes at Belmont University. It is thorough and complete. As the title suggests, it "follows the money" in the music business, whether in songwriting, music publishing, motion pictures, television, or public performances.

The book is revised frequently. Be sure to get the latest edition if you buy it.

Bernstein, Leonard. *The Unanswered Question: Six Talks at Harvard.* **Boston: Harvard University Press, 2002.**

Leonard Bernstein requires no introduction. His legacy as a composer, conductor, and educator speaks for itself. This book is a compilation of six talks Bernstein delivered at Harvard in 1976, on musical topics ranging from folk music to symphonies, from Mozart to Copland, and from tonal music to atonal music. *The Unanswered Question* is not about songwriting, but it is an interesting treatise on aesthetics, musical metaphor, and the universal language central to all artistic expression.

Braheny, John. *The Craft and Business of Songwriting.* **Cincinnati: Writer's Digest Books, 1988.**

My copy of this book is now out of print. But I noticed in my last visit to Borders Books that there is a second edition of this very helpful book available. As the title suggests, Braheny divides the book into two sections, covering both the craft and the business of songwriting. In the section on craft, his topics include creativity, subject matter, lyric-writing basics, music-writing basics, collaboration, and song construction. The section on the business of songwriting provides helpful and accurate information on copyright, making a demo, self-publishing, and even getting a record deal.

The book is well organized and easy to read. While it focuses primarily on writing secular pop songs, any beginning Christian songwriter will find it a useful tool for improving his craft.

Briner, Bob. *Roaring Lambs.* **Grand Rapids: Zondervan, 1993.**

The simple premise of this book struck such a strong chord with me when I read it some 13 years ago that I wrote the author, the late Bob Briner, and we shared a brief correspondence. Briner, an Emmy Award–winning television executive, believed the Church had abdicated its role in shaping culture, and had become content to borrow from culture in order to "preach to the choir." The book serves as a wake-up call for all creative Christians to be salt and light in the "real world."

Carnella, Craig. "A Conversation with Stephen Sondheim." *Playback,* **vol. 14, issue 3 (Summer 2007), pp. 44–47.**

This is an edited transcript of an interview with the legendary Broadway composer, Stephen Sondheim. It was first printed in the May/June 2007 issue of *The Dramatist,* the journal of the Dramatists Guild. *Playback* is the member magazine of ASCAP. The interview was reprinted from *The Dramatist,* which holds the copyright on the interview.

Davis, Sheila. *The Craft of Lyric Writing.* **Cincinnati: Writer's Digest Books, 1985.**

This is the single most complete book on the subject of writing lyrics that I have ever found. It should be on the bookshelf of every songwriter, from the rank beginner to the accomplished professional. Davis goes into great depth on every aspect of writing lyrics, and demonstrates her points with hundreds of song examples from every genre of music. Her chapter on rewriting is alone worth the price of the book.

Engel, Lehman. *Words with Music: Creating the Broadway Musical Libretto.* **New York: Applause Books, 2006.**

The late Lehman Engel was the dean of Broadway musical directors and the founder of the BMI Musical Theater Workshops. This book examines how the three main parts of a musical—the libretto, the lyrics, and the music—all work together to create a successful Broadway show. Howard Kissel, theater critic for the *New York Daily News,* updated *Words with Music* to include shows written since the book's original publication in 1972.

Gillette, Steve. "Songwriting and the Creative Process." Sing Out! Corporation, 1995.

This book owes its beginnings to the "Counting the Muse" columns of *Sing Out!* magazine. Gillette writes from the premise that songwriting can indeed be taught, and he breaks down each of the book's 16 chapters into several easy-to-read minichapters. The book focuses on the creative side of songwriting, but there is one full chapter on the music business and another on showcases and workshops. He includes short essays from other writers, including a foreword by none other than Judy Collins.

Krasilovsky, William, and Sidney Shemel. *This Business of Music.* **7th ed. New York: Billboard Books, 1995.**

I currently own the seventh edition of this most venerable music-business text, replacing the copy I purchased in college some 30 years ago. (The tenth edition is being released as I write this.) This book is, quite simply, the bible of the music business, covering music publishing, copyright, record companies, music production, recording artists, labor agreements, agents, and much more. Its appendixes contain virtually every copyright form and basic legal agreement one will ever encounter in a lifetime in the music business. The book contains so much valuable information that it is a must-have for any serious songwriter. Be prepared: *This Business of Music* is not a chatty guide to the music biz. It is a quality reference book.

Leiken, Molly-Ann. *How to Write a Hit Song.* **4th ed. Milwaukee: Hal Leonard Corp., 2000.**

Leiken is a respected songwriter with a long list of credits, including Platinum-selling songs and popular TV theme songs. She is also a successful writing consultant and songwriting teacher. This brief tome (only 119 pages) is about writing hit songs and getting them played on the radio. In a breezy, conversational style it covers lyric writing, melody, collaborating, and some of the basics of the music business. Leiken also includes useful writing exercises, designed to jump-start the beginning writer. Chapter 8, called Overcoming Writing Blocks, is an interesting combination of music business insight and pop psychology. The latest edition of her book adds a chapter on marketing your song over the Internet. This book is further evidence that the principles of good songwriting don't change with the years, even if the music business and technology do.

L'Engle, Madeleine. *Walking on Water: Reflections on Faith and Art.* **Wheaton, Ill.: Harold Shaw Publishers, 1980.**

My paperback copy of this book is showing the wear and tear of a book that has been read many times over. L'Engle is the author of dozens of books, her best known probably being *A Wrinkle in Time.* She is also a deep Christian thinker. In *Walking on Water,* she shares her honest, humble, and humorous reflections on her life as a Christian and as an artist, or as she puts it, a "cocreator with God." Christians who dare to explore the world of art and creativity will find this book inspiring.

Maisel, Eric. *Fearless Creating.* **New York: Jeremy P. Tarcher/Putnam, 1995.**

Maisel is a therapist who works primarily with writers, artists, and performers. *Fearless Creating* is a workbook designed to get the creative person past the point of inertia and fear and back to creating. I refer to Maisel's "stages of creativity" in chapter 2 of this book.

Matthews, Kyle. "Songwriting 101" and "The Life of the Songwriter." www.kylematthews.com.

Kyle Matthews is a talented singer-songwriter, storyteller, and teacher. He has had more than 60 songs recorded by a broad array of Christian artists. Perhaps his most notable hit was "We Fall Down," recorded by Donnie McClurkin. He authored this booklet containing two helpful essays, available online at www.kylematthews.com. The first essay, "Songwriting 101," is cleverly subtitled "Everything I Wish I'd Known Before Moving to Nashville and Making a Fool of Myself." It was written in response to the many requests Kyle receives from young Christian songwriters seeking basic information about the business of songwriting. It is coupled with a second essay, "The Life of the Songwriter," which delves into the motivations, attitudes, and goals of a Christian songwriter progressing from amateur to professional status.

Pattison, Pat. *Writing Better Lyrics.* **Cincinnati: Writer's Digest Books, 1995.**

Pat Pattison is a professor of songwriting at Berklee College of Music in Boston. He is the author of two other books on songwriting and is a contributor to *Home and Studio Recording* magazine. This book is for the more advanced lyricist. It assumes the reader already knows the basics of songwriting and examines a higher level of creativity. Chapters cover subjects such as finding unexpected rhymes, avoiding clichés, creating better imagery, and generating fresh ideas for your lyrics. Every chapter contains clear examples and lots of specific exercises for the reader to work through.

Peterik, Jim, Dave Austin, and Mary Ellen Bickford. *Songwriting for Dummies.* **New York: Wiley Publishing, Inc., 2002.**

Songwriting has become so popular that the folks who created the *Dummies* series had to offer us a book. Like the countless other books in the *Dummies* lineup, this book is clever and easy to read. It contains loads of tips and anecdotes. Most of the references are from current pop, rock, and country songs, but the authors do offer a nod to the world of Christian music. It gives equal time to lyrics and music. It offers some basics on the music business, including building a demo and networking for songwriters. The book closes with three Top Ten lists: Ten Songwriters You Should Know, Ten Songwriting Teams You Should Know, and Ten Songs You Should Know. (In my opinion they got the songwriter lists mostly right, but they blew it on a couple of the songs.)

Prestwood, Hugh. "MTV, Adolescents, the Church of Hollywood, and the Collapse of Grace." www.hughprestwood.com (accessed April 22, 2007).

This "no holds barred" essay on Prestwood's Website takes dead aim at what he believes to be the causes of the downward spiral of American pop music. It is one of two such sermons posted on the Website at the time of this writing. Prestwood's writing credentials speak for themselves. Among the many major artists that have recorded his songs are Judy Collins ("Hard Times for Lovers"), Trisha Yearwood ("The Song Remembers When"), and Randy Travis ("Hard Rock Bottom of Your Heart"). Prestwood has been showered with songwriting awards. He teaches advanced songwriting at the New School in Manhattan and leads workshops for the NSAI.

Webb, Jimmy. *Tunesmith: Inside the Art of Songwriting.* **New York: Hyperion, 1998.**

Jimmy Webb is one of America's greatest songwriters, of any generation. I enjoyed reading his book if for nothing but the anecdotes and personal references he sprinkles in along the way. The book has plenty of examples and diagrams to support Webb's approach to writing. He is an accomplished lyricist and musician, so he writes with authority on both halves of the songwriting equation. This is a book of powerful insights written by a man who is every bit as much a philosopher as an artist.

Williams, Chas: *The Nashville Number System.* 7th ed. Nashville: Chas Williams, 2005.

Williams is an experienced Nashville musician (guitar and dobro) who has used the famed Nashville number system for years in his work with Wynonna Judd, Nanci Griffith, Maura O'Connell, and others. In this brief but helpful book, Williams explains everything a writer needs to know about how to read and write a number chart. *The Nashville Number System* is used as a textbook at Berklee College of Music, Belmont University, and Middle Tennessee State University to prepare students for a career in music in Nashville. The book can be purchased online at www.nashvillenumbersystem.com.

Index

About the Author

Robert Sterling is a Christian songwriter and Dove Award–winning record producer and arranger. His songs have been recorded by a variety of Christian artists, including Point of Grace, Gold City, and Sandi Patti. His tunes have worked their way to the top of the Christian pop, Southern Gospel, and inspirational-radio charts. Among Sterling's record-producing credits are the certified Gold albums *Point of Grace, The Whole Truth,* and *24,* by Point of Grace, and the Grammy-nominated *Love Will,* by the Talleys.

His extensive body of choral compositions and arrangements can be found in the catalogs of Word Music, Alfred Music, Shawnee Press, Lorenz Music, and LifeWay Music. Robert is a five-time winner of the Gospel Music Association's Dove Award. For five years he headed the songwriting faculty for the Academy of Gospel Music Arts.

In 1997, Sterling served as the chairman of the Coalition for the Protection of America's Gospel Music Heritage, lobbying and testifying before Congress on behalf of Christian songwriters. In addition to his work as a writer, arranger, and orchestrator, he has also served as an adjunct professor of Music Publishing at Belmont University in Nashville and on the advisory board of Baylor University's Center for Christian Music Studies.

A 1977 cum laude graduate of Baylor University's School of Music, Sterling currently resides in Brentwood, Tennessee, with his wife, Cindy. They have two sons, Matthew and Aaron, who have grown up and moved far away from home. Matthew lives in New York City, working as a video and film editor. Aaron is a much-in-demand studio drummer working in Los Angeles.